THE WALLED GARDEN

The Walled Garden

The Saga of Jewish Family Life and Tradition

Chaim Bermant

Macmillan Publishing Co., Inc.
New York

Macmillan Publishing Co., Inc.
866 Third Avenue, New York, N. Y. 10022
Collier-Macmillan Canada Ltd.

First American Edition 1975

Printed in Israel

Contents

Photo Credits

The author and publishers wish to thank the following individuals and institutions for their kind co-operation and permission to reproduce the photographs in this book: Israel Museum, Jerusalem, jacket, endpaper, ii, 17, 18, 28, 34, 43, 53, 54, 55, 63, 89, 100, 110, 119, 120, 121, 130–1, 146, 147, 152, 160, 163, 167, 171, 175, 185, 219, 230, 241, 244; David Harris, ii, 18, 20, 63, 71, 110, 128, 130, 131, 150, 152, 163, 164, 175, 183, 185, 189, 202, 209, 210 (left), 219, 250, 269; Benny Hadar, 154; Rijksmuseum, Amsterdam, 8; Werner Braun, 11–12, 36, 41, 62, 103, 105, 201, 257, 268; Walters Art Gallery, Baltimore, 12; Rosenfeld Collection, Tel Aviv, 13, 135, 207, 213; Menucha Brafman, 13; David Rubinger, 17, 194, 220; I.P.P.A., Tel Aviv, 22, 40, 45 (top), 46, 49, 94, 172, 178; Einhorn Collection, Tel Aviv, 24, 25, 35, 77, 80, 109, 144, 145, 181, 190–1, 192; Photo Hadani, 24, 25, 35, 109, 135, 145, 190–1, 192, 207, 213; Museum of Ethnology and Folklore, Ha'aretz Museum, Tel Aviv, 27; Ya'on Lithography and Photocolour, 27; Weizmann Archives, Rehovot, 30; Israel Government Coins and Medals Corporation, 37; J. S. Lewinski, 38, 45 (bottom), 143, 177; Alfred Rubens Collection, London, 50, 51, 228; Austrian National Library, Vienna, 52; Ze'ev Radovan, 56, 230, 255, 261; Micha Bar-Am, 14, 58, 136, 173, 200, 242; United Press International, 59, 95; London Illustrated News, 64; Israel Museum Reproduction Archive, 66; American Jewish Historical Society, 73, 156–7, 158; Tel Aviv Museum, 78–9, 97, 106–7, 138, 204; Jewish Museum, London, 83, 132–3, 184; Inbal Dance Theatre, 90; Ida Kimche Art Gallery, Tel Aviv, 98; I. Zafrir, 106–7; British Museum, London, 113; Schocken Library, Jerusalem, 71; Moshe Raviv, 115, 142, 214, 239; Jewish National Fund Archive, Jerusalem, 117, 199, 254, 256; Jean Besancenot, 119, 212; Sir Isaac and Lady Wolfson Collection, Hechal Shlomo, Jerusalem, 112, 128, 202; Universitaats Library, Hamburg, 124; Royal Library, Copenhagen, 127; Alex Berlyne, 168–9; Jüdisches Museum der Schweiz, Basle (no. 107), 176; Mirlin-Yaron, 187; Pappenheim Collection, Jerusalem, 175; American Jewish Archives of the Hebrew Union College, Jewish Institute of Religion, 196, 227; Musée de Cluny, 198; Rolf Kneller, endpaper, 211, 249, 252, 262–3, 264, 267; The Jewish Chronicle, 215, 216; Embassy of Israel, Washington, 218; Pierpont Morgan Library, N.Y. (m. 638, f. 18), 222; Yitzhak Goren, 233; Jan Lukas, 236; Haganah Archives, Tel Aviv, 258; Jewish Agency Photo Archive, Jerusalem, 259; Alinari, 112.

To the memory of
Feige Tzirl Bat Chloine—
an Eshet Chayil

1 The Walled Garden

Traditionally, the family has been a walled garden within which the young flourished and the old declined; now the wall seems to be crumbling, and the question has been raised: is the family finished?

The question has been of particular moment to the Jew, for the family has been the basic unit of the Congregation of Israel, and an end to the family would mean an end to Judaism, as we know it. Judaism is almost an emanation of family life, and family life an expression of Judaism. No faith is so sustained by the family and none so sustains it, and it reverberates through generations that have long ceased to believe, affecting their outlook, their habits, their conduct – their whole way of life.

The Jewish home, as conceived by the Rabbis, is a temple, the father a priest, the children acolytes, and so simple an occasion as a meal can assume the nature of a holy communion. Almost every Jewish ritual revolves round the family, and almost every family occasion has its own ritual.

Abraham, the 'Patriarch's patriarch', who according to tradition observed God's laws some seven centuries before they were revealed on Mount Sinai, established a pattern of family life that later generations sought to emulate, though not perhaps in every respect. Sarah, Abraham's first wife, was also his half-sister, and although Judaism tolerates – in some ways even encourages – marriage within the family, such encouragement stops well short of incest. And while Jewish married life has turned out to be decidedly monogamous, Abraham took a second wife, Hagar, during Sarah's lifetime – albeit at Sarah's behest and for the worthiest reason. The first of the many commandments ordained by Jewish law is *p'ru ur'vu*: 'thou shalt be fruitful and multiply' (Genesis 9:1). Everything in marriage and almost everything in life is secondary to that, and thus when Sarah, after many years of married life –

Rembrandt's portrayal of Abraham entertaining the angels as Sarah lingers behind the door. The low-profile status of the Jewish woman was maintained by custom for centuries

The cohesiveness of young and old in modern family life usually finds expression around the dinner table during the Sabbath and holiday celebrations. Here an American family celebrates a modest *kiddush* and discusses the weekly Torah reading

forty-five, according to tradition – was still childless, she said to Abraham: 'See, the Lord has kept me from bearing. Consort with my maid; perhaps I shall have a son through her' (Genesis 16:2). And she did. Sarah, of course, later had a son of her own, and through Isaac and his sons there was established the patriarchate from which many of the basic Jewish traditions flowed.

First among these was the patriarchal principle itself. The father was lord and master over his entire household: he found wives for his sons and husbands for his daughters; he divided his property among them and allotted roles and functions to them all. While the formal authority of a father was often more than tempered by the wiles of his wife or the insubordination of his children – for every dutiful Jacob there was a rebellious Esau – the underlying right to rule was never seriously questioned, for the source of parental authority was divine authority. 'Honour thy father and thy mother' comes early in the Ten Commandments. To love and fear God was to love and fear one's father. And beyond divine authority lay simple affection. Love persisted even when authority weakened, so that even the rebellious Esau craved for his father's blessing.

The further fact that the family, in its early stages, was a military encampment, and the patriarchy a high command, left little room for individuals or individualism. The mutual need for protection forced the concourse of generations under one roof, or within one compound. A common ancestry and faith, common experiences and dangers insured the cohesiveness of young and old. All these forces, in one way or another, have also helped to sustain Jewish family life right up to our own times.

It was from Abraham, too, that Judaism derived its most ancient, and perhaps its most fundamental, rite: *brit mila*, the circumcision performed by Abraham on himself, his sons and his male servants and until today the initiation rite of every Jewish male into the Congregation of Israel. Other guidelines derived from the lives of the Patriarchs include the care taken by the father to find the right wives from the right stock for his sons; the insistence on sons and sons' sons, as procreation was the nearest man could come to creation; the concern of a man for his wife, perhaps to the point of uxoriousness; and the devotion of parents to their children.

Another element basic to Jewish family life not touched on directly in Genesis, but dwelt on at length by exegesists and com-

mentators, is instruction. The Jewish creed begins: 'Hear O Israel, the Lord is our God, the Lord is One,' and continues:

> ... And these words which I command thee this day shall be upon thine heart: and thou shalt teach them diligently unto thy children, and shalt talk of them when thou sittest in thine house, and when thou walkest by the way, when thou liest down and when thou risest up (Deuteronomy 6:6–7).

This encompassing obligation enabled the father – in so far as external forces allowed him – to transmit his world to his son intact. One might be driven by hunger to Egypt, or by persecution out of Egypt, or hounded like a pariah over the face of Europe, but

opposite During patriarchal times, obedience to the Lord came before even familial love and obligations. This depiction of the impending sacrifice of Isaac is from a 15th-century French Book of Hours

right The exhaustion and despair of a Russian-Jewish family after a wave of pogroms passed through their town, by the Polish painter Maurice Minkowski

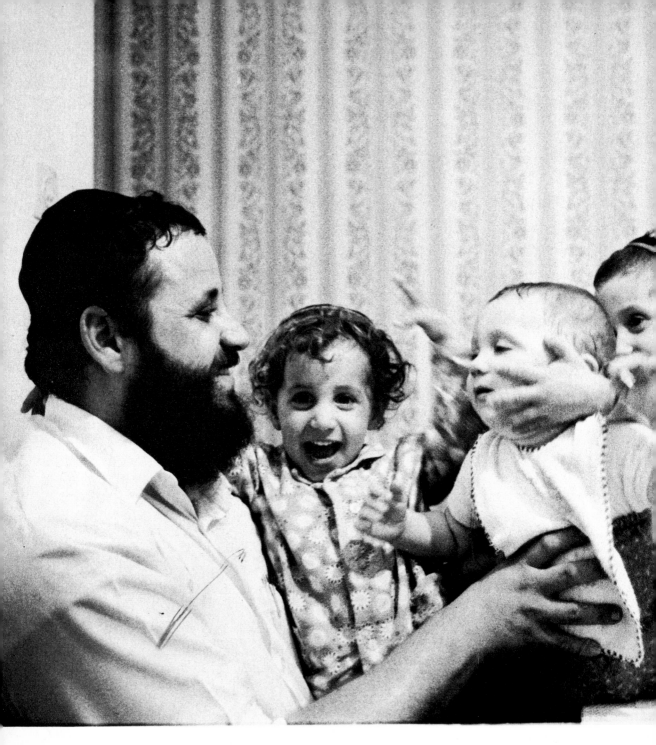

the inheritance was preserved, for it formed a portable *milieu*. What's more, the obligation to teach established a tradition of literacy centuries before it was regarded as essential elsewhere.

In Jewish teaching there is a constant hark back to precedent enjoined by Isaiah: 'Look unto the rock whence you were hewn, and the hole and the pit whence you were digged. Look unto

'Look unto the rock whence you were hewn . . .'

Abraham your father and unto Sarah that bore you' (51:1–2). That which has been shall continue to be. Thus instructed, the Jew felt he was not only part of a lateral family of contemporaries – brothers, sisters, uncles, cousins – but of a vertical family stretching back into history and forward into time. He became part of an organic unit that was essentially immortal (though he had to make his own contribution to immortality with a sufficient quota of children). One finds something of this idea in T. S. Eliot's *Notes Towards the Definition of Culture:*

. . . when I speak of the family I have in mind a bond which embraces . . . a piety towards the dead, however obscure, and a solicitude for the unborn, however remote. Unless this reverence for the past and future is cultivated in the home, it can never be more than a formal convention in the community.

To be part of a Jewish family is thus to be hemmed in, to a greater or lesser degree, by history, by antecedent and precedent, by the attitudes of past generations and responsibilities to future ones. There are, indeed, families whose reverence for the past and the future is so complete that they are almost bypassed by the present. It would seem almost as if one had no life of one's own and even where one was not consciously conforming to precedent, one became conditioned by it.

Ours, more than any other, is the age of the individualist. Each man does, or at least would like to do, according to that which is right in his own eyes. The necessary restraints of family life are resented and there has been a fairly widespread rebellion against the very loyalties on which family life is based, for it is felt that the sense of duty to kin that it inculcates can mean a deficient sense of duty to society, that the family that stays together 'preys' together.

External forces are also threatening the continuity of family life: the erosion of faith; a decline in all forms of authority (perhaps a by-product of the first); greater mobility, which makes it easier for scattered members of a family to maintain contact, but at the same time tends to scatter them; and above all, the pace of change. One is born in one world, matures in another and dies in a third. The present generation is not at all sure where it has been or where it is going, let alone confident to direct the next. Can the family withstand such pressures? We hope to answer this question in the course of the following chapters.

2 Sons of the Covenant

Some Jewish customs are more widely observed than others. There are Jews who do not keep the Sabbath, never attend synagogue, do not fast on the Day of Atonement, do not celebrate Passover, cheerfully eat pork and, indeed, may have married out of the faith, but who will nevertheless take care to initiate their sons into the Covenant of Abraham. They may have the circumcision done clinically rather than religiously, by a surgeon, without the benefit of clergy or the customs usual to the rite, but their purpose is nearly always the same: to follow, however falteringly, in the ways of their fathers. It is almost as if the disposition to have one's sons circumcised has, through the centuries, become an acquired trait.

The practice of circumcision was fairly widespread in the ancient world. Herodotus mentions that the Egyptians circumcised their sons 'for the sake of cleanliness, considering it better to be clean than comely' and suggests that others borrowed the custom from them. Most of the tribes to the east of Egypt were circumcised – except for the Philistines, who were described as *arelim*, the uncircumcised ones. The word passed into the Hebrew language as an expression of reproach, and the foreskin itself somehow came to symbolize coarseness. It represented an unfinished area in man, and circumcision came to complete an act of creation begun by God.

The original function of the operation may have been mainly hygienic, but it is difficult to disentangle religion from medicine at this stage in history. It also was not free of the sacrificial element: the yielding up of a part in order to save the whole, a prophylactic against the human sacrifices demanded by Moloch. To the Jew, however, the act was purely religious, as explicitly directed by God to Abraham:

Silver instruments used in the ritual circumcision ceremony

Every male among you shall be circumcised. And you shall be circum-

cised in the flesh of your foreskin, and it shall be the token of a covenant betwixt Me and you. And he that is eight days old shall be circumcised among you, every male throughout the generations (Genesis 17:10–12).

Abraham was ninety-nine years old, and his son Ishmael thirteen, when they, and all the males of the household, were circumcised. Isaac was the first to have his *brit*, as it came to be called, at the age of eight days. The rite was firmly established by the time of Jacob, and when the King of Shechem sought to unite his son in marriage with Jacob's daughter, Dina, he and all his people were required to circumcise themselves.

Some authorities believed that circumcision may have lapsed during the long sojourn in Egypt, for the Jews wanted to distinguish themselves from the Egyptians. Moses, brought up in Pharaoh's household, may have been circumcised, but his son was left uncircumcised and, if not for the presence of mind of his Midianite wife, Zipporah, Moses might have perished as a result:

And it came to pass on the way to the lodging-place, that the Lord met him and sought to kill him. Then Zipporah took a flint and cut off the foreskin of her son, and cast it at his feet, and said, Surely a bridegroom of blood art thou to me (Exodus 4:24–5).

The incident occurred after Moses left Midian to return to Egypt as leader of the Israelites, and it is one of the most mysterious and cryptic passages in the Bible. Its very obscurity has added somehow to the gravity of the rite and the significance attached to it by later generations.

In the wilderness, Joshua circumcised all the male Israelites with flint-stones, at what came to be known as 'the hill of foreskins'. Many centuries later, when the Greeks dominated Judea, and the whole Mediterranean basin had succumbed to Greek influence, the human body was venerated almost as an object of worship, and the more Hellenized Jews tended to regard circumcision as a form of disfigurement; it was no longer thought to complete the act of creation, but to mar it. Some Jews underwent painful operations to de-circumcise themselves. During this period, there was an attempt by a Greek viceroy, Antiochus, to suppress the practice of Judaism altogether, and anyone who sought to initiate his son into the Covenant of Abraham did so at the risk of his life. There is, perhaps, nothing like proscription and martyrdom to sanctify a rite, and thereafter circumcision was established for all time.

The Prophets ascribed particular symbolic significance to the

A depiction of a *brit mila* from a 15th-century Hebrew illuminated manuscript of the Rothschild Miscellany

rite as an act of dedication that made Israel more amenable to divine influence. If the foreskin came to mean coarseness and a state of incompletion, the lack of it came to symbolize rectitude, purity and refinement.

Jews have been criticized by St Paul, among others, for placing excessive stress on externals; to which the traditional Jew would answer that inner feelings are indeed more important than outer signs, but that outer signs are an aid to the attainment of inner grace.

The twelfth-century philosopher Maimonides, considered to be the Aristotle of Jewish thought, saw a unifying force in the rite: 'It gives all members of the same faith, that is, to all believers in the Unity of God, a common bodily sign.' He also suggested a secondary purpose:

As regards circumcision, I think that one of its objects is to limit the pleasures of sexual intercourse, and to weaken the organ of generation as far as possible, and thus cause man to be moderate.

Circumcision simply counteracts excessive lust, for there is no doubt that circumcision weakens the power of sexual excitement, and sometimes lessens mutual enjoyment: the organ necessarily becomes weak when it loses blood and is deprived of its covering from the beginning. Our sages say distinctly: 'It is hard for a woman with whom an uncircumcised man had sexual intercourse to separate herself from him.'

Maimonides, apart from being a scholar and thinker, was one of the foremost physicians of his day, but these observations have not been supported by orthodox medical opinion.

The operation is generally performed by a *mohel* (circumciser) who has been trained in the elementary principles of surgery and antisepsis, and who has received Rabbinical recognition as an Orthodox Jew. In many cases the *mohel* is also a qualified physician, but the occupation is more frequently combined with that of rabbi, cantor or ritual slaughterer (*shochet*). In fact there is nothing to prevent a cobbler, tailor or blacksmith from becoming a *mohel*, and not a few have done so. Orthodox Jews tend to feel that the doctor-*mohel*, no matter how devout, is inclined to treat the rite as but another minor operation. With his white coat, rubber gloves and glittering instruments, he could almost be performing a tonsillectomy, rather than initiating their sons into the Covenant of Abraham. There is no flourish to his art: he mumbles his prayers and is clinical and peremptory about the whole affair. They want pomp and ceremony and a sense of the past and will generally opt for the non-medical *mohel*. Some fathers even take pains to initiate

The circumcision of Isaac from the 14th-century Birds' Head Hagadah (southern Germany)

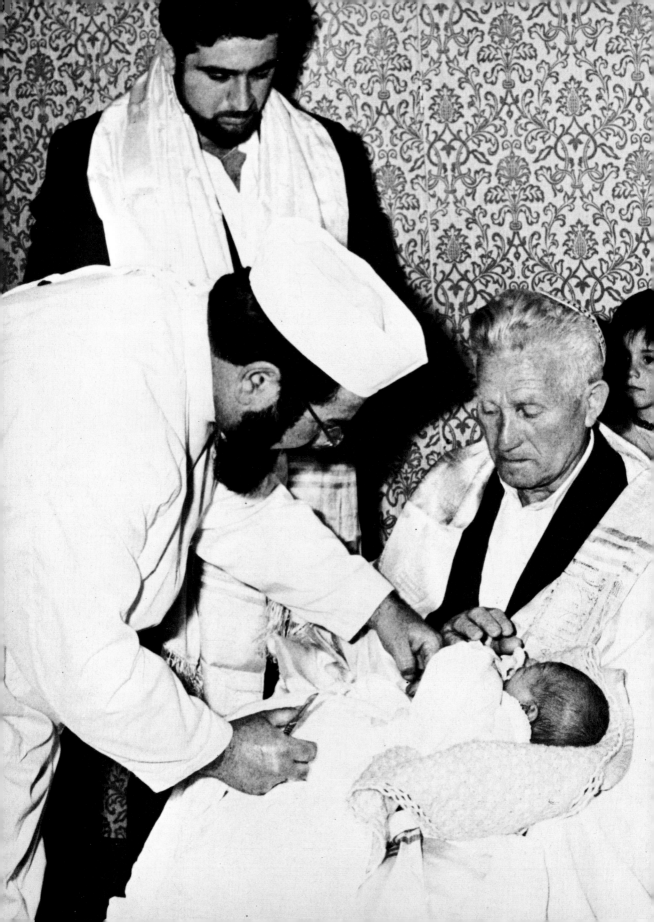

their sons at the hands of the same *mohel* who initiated them: his hands may be shaky, but he somehow strengthens the bond between father and son.

The training for a *mohel* is not particularly prolonged. After having studied the laws of circumcision in detail, the apprentice accompanies a qualified colleague to perhaps a score of ceremonies before being entrusted with a knife on his own. As he performs this operation exclusively, he quickly becomes an expert. Occasional mishaps are not unknown, although when they happen, they do not – for understandable reasons – receive wide publicity. In 1970 one London *mohel* so deformed a child that the aggrieved parents took him to court and received a large sum in compensation! Such incidents do not generally occur to young practitioners, but to old ones with failing eyesight or palsied hands who have reached retirement and do not know it.

The ceremony should be performed when the boy is eight days old, but it can be delayed in case of sickness, and in the case of a child whose brother died as a result of the *brit* – an extremely rare occurrence – it need not be performed at all. The *mohel* generally visits the child a day or two before the ceremony to make sure that he is ready for it.

In many Jewish homes, the birth of a boy is celebrated on the Friday night (Sabbath eve) before the *brit* with a ceremony known as the *shalom zakhar*. Women can attend, but generally it is a jovial, informal, men-only affair, a sort of sacred stag-party. The *Shema* ('Hear O Israel . . .') is read, psalms are recited, hymns are sung, an occasional drink is drunk and, for no convincing reason, chick-peas are eaten.

Among oriental Jews, the *shalom zakhar* is celebrated on the eve of the circumcision. The fare is somewhat more exotic, and the mood of elation is, if anything, even greater. There are extensive readings from Jewish legends in honour of the prophet Elijah, who occurs and recurs in Jewish lore as guardian of the family, and in particular of small boys.

The term *shalom zakhar* means 'peace unto the male child' and is derived from a verse in the Talmud: 'If a boy is born, peace comes to the world.' No such assurance is offered on the birth of a daughter, and that is probably why no such ceremony exists for that occasion.

Until comparatively recent times, the new-born child and its mother were thought to be particularly susceptible to the intrusion of dark spirits. In many homes, a special *vaknacht* ('night watch')

The performance of a ritual circumcision

was kept on them during the mother's confinement, but especially
on the eve of the *brit*, when both were thought to be at their most
vulnerable. Some spirits were more sinister and fearful than others,
and the most fearful of all was Lilith. The very whisper of her name
could reduce a company to silence for she was said to regard every
new birth as an affront to her powers, and where she could, she
would strangle infants in their cribs. The Talmud describes her as a
winged creature with a woman's face and long flowing hair.
Infants were her main prey, but she was also said to invade the beds
of solitary men. It was commonly believed that if an infant laughed
in his sleep, she was molesting him, and startled parents would
promptly tap the baby on the nose in order to exorcise her. Some
legends identified her with the Queen of Sheba who, according to
Arab myths, was a jinnee – half woman, half demon and wholly
terrifying.

Ashkenazim (western Jews) and Sephardim (oriental Jews) differ
widely in background and tradition, and their dissimilar experience
has given rise to largely distinct bodies of folklore. But Lilith
troubled the sleep of both, and the bedrooms of women in labour
were crowded with all sorts of spiritual netting to keep her at bay.
The walls were inscribed with the names of angels, archangels and
incantations; psalms were read; the blessed name of Elijah – from
which Lilith was said to recoil – was invoked with every breath;
and at night all the windows were closed and the shutters barred.
Among Moroccan and Caucasian Jews it was common to draw a
chalk circle as a *cordon sanitaire* around the bed and to inscribe within
the circle the names of three angels: Snwy, Snsnwy and Smnglf.
These precautions began when the child was born, continued
nightly after his birth and reached a climax on the eve of the *brit*,
when the whole house blazed with candles and friends and acquaintances assembled to eat, drink, study and pray well beyond midnight, intent on disturbing the evil spirits with the clamour and fervour of their devotions. Before departing, they formed a circle round
the mother's bed, and in an atmosphere heavy with smouldering
wax, they chanted the *Shema* in unison at the top of their voices.

There was a brisk trade in amulets throughout the Jewish world
until well into the eighteenth century (in Eastern Europe they
circulated for much longer), and theological disputes about the
efficacy and use of these amulets accompanied them all the way.
Amulets generally took the form of ornaments inscribed with different permutations of the names of God and His host: one was
for fertility, another to guard against miscarriages, yet another to

opposite and below Two
Persian bronze amulets to
protect the household
against the evil spirit
Lilith. The names of the
patriarchs and their wives
are inscribed for good
measure, as are a number of
quotations from the Bible

וידבר ה' אל משה לאמר דבר אל אהרן ואל
בניו
לאמר כה תב
את בני ישראל אמור לה
סנוי סנסנוי
סמנגלף
ואני
אברכם
אדם
אברהם
יצחק
יעקב
וחוה
ושרה
ורבקה
ולאה

ease labour pains. They were generally considered useful to have about the house and on one's person, for there was no knowing what dark forces might be batting their wings in the depth of the night. They were to the medieval Jewish household what a bottle of antiseptic might be to ours. In fact these amulets have never fallen totally out of use. Here and there, in one family or another, one may find some mysterious metal disc with faded inscriptions that has been handed down from mother to daughter and is cherished as a precious family heirloom. In a sense, they exist in a modern form as well, only they are not called amulets, but *mazels* (good-luck charms). They too are worn as an ornament and are usually made of precious metal. One finds them in the form of a *mezuzah*, a Star of David, as the word *Shadai* (one of the names of God) or *chai* ('life'), but it is doubtful that anyone wears them to deal with barrenness, miscarriages or to guard against Lilith.

The *vaknacht* ritual has fallen into disuse, and the *shalom zakhar* is commonly celebrated only among Orthodox Jews. The *brit*, however, is still performed now as it has been throughout the ages. The mother herself is usually absent from the ceremony and the infant is generally brought in by the grandmother. As he appears, all rise and chant *baruch haba*, 'blessed be he that cometh'. The infant is handed to the *sandek* (godfather), who in turn passes him to the father, waiting on the side with a *tallit* over his shoulder. The father carries the obligation to perform the *brit* (the *mohel* is merely his agent), and he intones the following prayer:

> I am ready to perform the commandment to circumcise my son, even as the Creator, blessed be He, hath commanded us, as it is written in the Law: 'And he that is eight days old shall be circumcised among you, every male through the generations.'

The ceremony was commonly performed in the synagogue, and a special chair – upholstered, ornate, almost a throne – was reserved for the unseen guest of honour, Elijah. There is hardly a Jewish ceremony at which he is not accorded some place of honour, but at the *brit* he reigns supreme; he has traditionally been regarded as a special messenger, as God's own representative, to bless, to protect and to grace. Today, the *brit* is usually performed in the hospital or at home, and any available chair can be used for Elijah. The *mohel* takes the child from the father and rests him on Elijah's chair for a moment; then he is returned to the *sandek*, who places him on a pillow on his knees.

Now comes the moment that may be more traumatic for the

A 19th-century Turkish cover for the Elijah's chair used at the *brit mila*, with the blessing used during the ceremony inscribed by hand on the silk

father than the infant. The *sandek* holds the wriggling infant firmly in his grasp, pulls his legs apart and holds them still; the *mohel*, intoning a special prayer, fixes a small shield over the penis to protect the glans from injury and, grasping the foreskin firmly in one hand, removes it with one sweep of his knife. The baby may let out a scream that echoes through the building (sometimes as far as the bedroom of the anxious mother) and tries to wriggle free, but the operation is not yet over. The *mohel* takes the mucous membrane, which now stands exposed, and tears it down the centre as far as the corona. Finally, in the part of the ceremony known as *mezizah*, he draws the blood from the wound with a swab or pipette. Until comparatively recent times – and in some cases even today – the *mohel* performed *mezizah* by applying his mouth to the wound. The purpose was to cleanse the wound, but it sometimes led to infection. In the nineteenth century, after a number of infants in Vienna died of syphilis, presumably contracted through the *mohel*, oral *mezizah* was abandoned in most communities.

With the circumcision over, the father steps forward to make the blessing:

Blessed art thou, O Lord our God, King of the universe, who has sanctified us by thy commandments, and has commanded us to make our sons enter into the Covenant of Abraham our father.

To which the gathering responds:

Even as the child has entered into the Covenant, so may he enter into the Law, the nuptial canopy, and into good deeds.

A 19th-century silver cup from Russia for the wine used in the *brit mila* ceremony

The Law refers to the Law of Moses; in other words, may he grow up to be an observant Jew. The nuptial canopy refers to the *chupah* under which Jewish marriages are solemnized: one cannot become a good, observant or complete Jew until one marries. In some communities it was customary to plant a cedar on the birth of a boy and a pine on the birth of a girl. These were cut down on the eve of their wedding and used for the frame of the *chupah*.

After the father has recited his blessing, the *mohel* makes a prayer over the wine, another in thanksgiving for the Covenant and a third for the welfare of the child. Then comes the announcement that everyone waits for – a matter which has been kept secret until this very moment – the baby's name. Finally, the infant is given a few drops of wine – usually on the finger of the *mohel* – which somewhat eases his discomfort, and he champs his lips hungrily for more.

But his part in the affair is over, and he is passed back without further ceremony to his mother while the company adjourns for a festive meal.

Beyond the actual circumcision, the main event of the ceremony is the name giving. What's in a name? A headache. A name transmitted is a name preserved, and every Jew is anxious for a touch of immortality. And if he is not anxious for himself, his next of kin most certainly will be anxious for him after he is gone. Thus it naturally will be assumed that one of the grandsons will bear the name of his deceased grandfather, and a grand-daughter that of her grandmother. But in every family there is a childless widow, anxious to perpetuate the name of her dead husband, who will waylay her niece the moment she conceives with the plea that her dear departed should not be lost to eternity. In that way, most Jewish children are living memorials to grandparents, great-grandparents, uncles and aunts. It is unusual – indeed it is considered unlucky – to name a child after a living relative. (In some Jewish circles it is also considered unlucky for one's wife to have the same name as one's mother, and many a budding romance has been quashed by an apprehensive mother just for that reason.) But these superstitions seem to be confined to Ashkenazim.

In biblical times, a name often described the circumstances attending the birth: 'And Leah conceived and bore a son and called him *Reuben*', 'behold, a son' (Genesis 29:32). 'She bore him a son and Moses called him *Gershom*', 'a stranger was I there' (Exodus 2:22). It was only in later times that one began to name children after an ancestor or relative. During the Greek period it became common, especially among Hellenized Jews, to give a child two names: one in Hebrew and its equivalent in Greek. The practice continued over the centuries in Germany and Poland, right up to modern times, and the results include such combinations as Tsvi Hirsch, Dov Ber, Zeev Wolf and Arye Leib.

The popularity of biblical names in English-speaking countries has eased the task of English and American parents, and there have been any number of Davids, Dans, Daniels, Jonathans and the like. Problems arose when the names were a little bit 'too biblical' or post-biblical. The tendency then was to give an approximate English equivalent: Reuben became Roy or Rex; Moshe, Murray or Morris; Aharon, Harry; Yehudah, Julius; Jacob, Jack; Abraham, Brian; Chaim, Charles. One still retained the Hebrew name as a stand-by: if not officially on the birth certificate, then at least for use on religious occasions such as the Bar Mitzvah, or on the

SIGNATURE OF BEARER.

The British passport of the leader of the Zionist movement and first President of the State of Israel, Chaim Weizmann

tombstone. The practice of giving children both a secular and religious name enabled parents to combine the wishes of relatives and the demands of tradition with their own predelictions: they could name their child, say, Rachmiel after some long-dead great-uncle and Gary, after the mother's favourite film star. Among

Jewish immigrants to England, parents eager to give their children a good start in life sometimes opted for royal names – George, Albert, William, Elizabeth or Victoria – only to discover that they were also working-class names. For a time there was a vogue for saints and disciples, of Johns, James's, Matthews and Marks. In recent years, however, the Prophets and the House of David have enjoyed something of a come-back.

In some communities, someone critically ill was often given an additional name like Chaim ('life') or Alter ('longevity') in the belief that a change of name could mean a change of fortune. The Talmud supported this view in suggesting that the name of a person determined his destiny. As a result, the full name of a person was sometimes a statement of his health record.

Jews were rather slow to adopt surnames, and in much of Europe, as in the orient, they tended to be known as the sons of their fathers. But in 1787, a royal decree forced the Jews in Austria to adopt surnames, and similar decrees were passed in France (1808) and in Prussia (1812). During the next few decades, the practice gradually spread eastwards into Poland and Russia, the main centres of Jewish population. In many cases, the Jews simply adopted their fathers' first-names as their surnames, hence Abrams, Isaacs, Jacobs or Jacobson, Davidson, Samuelson and so on. Sometimes they chose the name of their town or locality – Berliner, Wiener, Frankfurter, Schwartzenberg; their occupation – Becker (baker), Schneider (tailor), Drucker (printer), Lehrer (teacher); or names that were imposed on them – Garfunkle (carbuncle), Karger (mean), Schryer (noisy).

As Jews moved westwards out of Europe to Britain and America, there was a general tendency to westernize their names or adopt what they thought to be western forms: it was not uncommon for the various branches of, say, the family Katzenelenbogen to be known as Katznell, Katz or Kaye; one may come across grandfather Vinstein, son Winestone and grandson Winston. Cohens have been Cohned, Kahned, Conned and Conwayed; the ancient and honourable name of Levy has suffered variations and permutations as ingenious as they are numerous: Levine, Le Vin, Levian, L'Evine, Elvy, Velay, Evelyn, Elwes, Lovains, Leary and even McLevy. In Israel there has understandably been a reverse process Gruen has become Ben Gurion; Shimshelevitz, Ben Zvi; Shkolnik, Eshkol; Myerson, Meir; Shertock, Sharett; and Aubrey Eban Abba Even. To some extent, the different names adopted by different generations of a family indicate the various stages of its wandering,

overleaf The *pidyon haben* ceremony, by Bernard Picart (1673–1733)

Benedict Spinoza, the 17th-century Dutch-Jewish philosopher who believed that the circumcision ceremony alone could assure the survival of the Jewish people

but at the same time they tend to weaken the link between them.

The festive meal which follows the *brit* is often an all-male affair, with the women busy in the kitchen and the men at the table. There is much singing of hymns, and the occasion is rarely free of a sermonette by the rabbi or any other learned – or unlearned – guest. The speaker usually dwells on the link the *brit* constitutes between the generations and ends with the hope that the new arrival will be a credit to his family, his friends and the entire Jewish community. The father, who may still hear the cries of his infant ringing in his ears, is perhaps too shaken and bemused to take it all in – especially if it happens to be his first *brit* – and it is very much the grandfather's day. He has accomplished the supreme duty of perpetuating Judaism beyond himself, even unto the third generation. He has lived to hear the echoes of the past reverberating into the future.

Spinoza argued that circumcision alone could assure the survival of the Jewish people: it was a rite so ingrained that even those who rejected other religious practices tended to observe it, and it set the Jew apart from the rest of the world. This is hardly the case today. Circumcision is now widely favoured for medical and/or aesthetic reasons, and in many American hospitals the foreskin is automatically removed shortly after birth unless the parents insist that it be retained. It is the *arelim*, the uncircumcised ones, who are becoming the odd men out. It is therefore not so much the actual excision that counts as the ceremonies which surround it – the prayers and incantations, the wine, and even the festive meal and platitudinous speeches that follow.

Along with other Jewish rituals observed with due solemnity the *brit* has given rise to a good deal of humour, some of it verging on the ribald. Stories about *mohelim* with faulty eyesight or shaky hands, about over-developed infants, over-curious matrons or nervous fathers are so numerous that one might almost speak of foreskin-humour as a genre in its own right.

If the boy is the family's first child, he has to undergo a further, if less traumatic, ceremony on his thirty-first day: the *pidyon haben*, redemption of the first-born. The ceremony derives from a verse in Exodus: 'Every firstborn, the first birth of every womb among the Israelites, you must dedicate to me, both man and beast; it is mine' (Exodus 13:2). Some Bible critics have seen in this verse proof that Jews at one time indulged in human sacrifices, but it is merely a reminder that all that man and earth bring forth is the Lord's. In ancient times, the first-born were dedicated to Temple

The dedication of the Portuguese Synagogue in Amsterdam, by Bernard Picart

service – apart from the priestly tribe of Levites, who were all Temple servants – and from this evolved the ceremony of redeeming one's son.

It is a simple occasion without the large celebrations common to the *brit*. A *cohen*, meaning a descendant of the Temple priesthood, must be in attendance, and the father presents his son to him with the declaration: ' . . . this is my firstborn son and the firstborn of his mother, and the Holy One blessed be He has commanded us to redeem him . . .' He then places five specially minted pieces of silver before the *cohen*, and the *cohen* asks: 'Which wouldst thou rather give me, thy firstborn son, the firstborn of his mother, or five *selaim*?' It is a rhetorical question (though there have been fathers who later wished that they had handed over the son). The father passes the silver to the *cohen*, and the child is returned to him. The *cohen* holds the silver over the child's head and declares:

This is instead of that, this is the commutation for that, this is the remission for that. May this child enter into life, into the Law and the fear of Heaven. May it be God's will that even as he has been admitted to redemption, so may he enter into the Law, the nuptial canopy and into good deeds.

The two sides of a *pidyon haben* coin specially minted in Israel

The formula in the last line is the same one that was uttered at the *brit*. The child is hardly born and redeemed when his family is looking forward to his marriage!

The *cohen* closes with the traditional priestly blessing:

May the Lord bless you and keep you. May He make His countenance to shine upon you. May He lift up His face unto you and bring you peace.

The birth of a girl passes without celebration or fanfare, nor does one have to redeem a daughter even if she is the first-born. The father simply announces her name in the synagogue on the Sabbath after her birth. There is a greater eagerness to perpetuate the names of male relatives than female ones and if, as sometimes happens, there are not enough sons, the daughters have to bear their names. As a result, there are numerous female forms of decidedly masculine names – Davida, Isaaca, Simona, Daniela – while one knows of no male forms of female names.

All this may suggest that Judaism tends to disregard its daughters or to treat them as a weight and a burden. Some daughters may, indeed, become a weight and a burden, but they are often more cherished than sons, and fathers in particular tend to indulge them, as if to compensate for all the slights of tradition.

A Bar Mitzvah held in the synagogue of the Hadassah-Hebrew University Medical Centre in Jerusalem, under the famed Chagall Windows

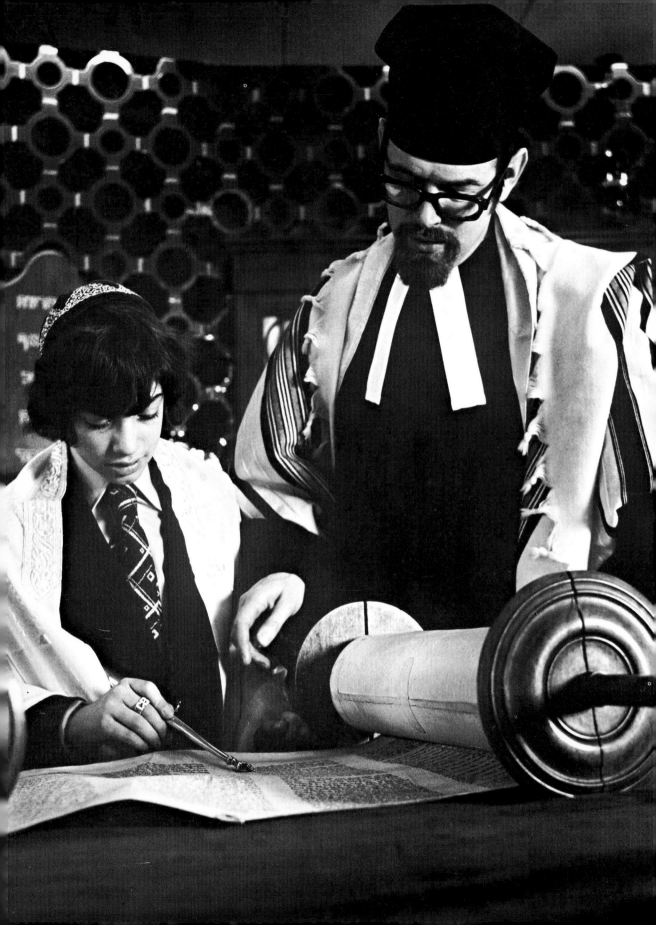

3 Bar Mitzvah

As Jewish ceremonies go, the Bar Mitzvah is something of an innovation, for it only goes back some 500 years. The term means 'son of the commandment' and marks the attainment of one's religious majority. If the *brit* initiates one into the Covenant of Abraham, the Bar Mitzvah signifies one's voluntary assumption of its burdens: at the *brit* one is done to; at the Bar Mitzvah one does.

Under Jewish law, girls reach their majority at the age of twelve and boys at thirteen. As long as a girl remained in her father's house, she could claim his support and protection, but technically the boy was on his own – financially and, more important, morally. It was not that minors were considered incapable of going wrong, but if they did, their parents were held responsible. Once they attained their majority, they were answerable for their own moral accounts.

Jewish legend ascribes great significance to the age of thirteen: Abraham, it was said, rebelled against his father's idol worship at that age; at thirteen years, Jacob embarked on a life of study and Esau on a life of debauchery. It is the age when a child becomes a man, an entity in his own right, a master of his own fate. Henceforward, he must don *tephilin* (phylacteries) with his morning prayers; he is old enough to make up a *minyan* (a quorum for prayer); he is obliged to observe the fast-days in full; and he may be called up to the Reading of the Law.

The most sacred part – the only sacred part – of a synagogue is the ark, which holds the Torah, the scrolls of the Law containing the Five Books of Moses. On the Sabbath and festivals, the Torah is taken from the ark, carried aloft around the synagogue and then read before the whole congregation. One begins with the book of Genesis and continues through each of the other books, week by week, portion by portion, until the scroll has been completed;

Reading from the Torah scroll at a Bar Mitzvah in London

then one starts again, in an ever-continuing cycle. The Reading of the Law forms the central part of the service. Each Sabbath seven or more people are given an *aliyah* – they are called up to the Reading – and each one says a short prayer to mark the honour:

Blessed art thou, O Lord our God, King of the universe, who hast chosen us from all peoples, and hast given us Thy Law . . .

Boys under thirteen are called up to the Reading together on Simchat Torah (a festival which celebrates the completion of the cycle of the Reading) at a ceremony known as *kol hana'arim* (all the youngsters) and they all make the blessing in unison; it is only when a boy reaches thirteen that he is called up in his own right. He is then symbolically received into the presence of God, and gradually there evolved the practice of marking the occasion with a formal celebration.

In an earlier age, this accession to manhood was more than symbolic. The Bar Mitzvah boy was virtually regarded as a man, for childhood was as contracted in times past as it is protracted in

Boys under the age of thirteen called up to the Torah together in the ceremony of *kol hana'arim* on Simchat Torah

our own. There are numerous references to early infancy in the Bible, but few to the period between that and maturity. It was as if a child were hardly out of the womb before he assumed many of the burdens of adult life. (Rebekah, according to legend, was only three when she married Isaac.) The Talmud urges a father to teach his son a trade ('he who fails to do so, teaches him robbery'), but it also lays down a strict regimen of study:

At five to Scripture, at ten to Mishna (oral law), at thirteen to the fulfilment of the commandments, at fifteen to the Talmud . . .

Some felt that five was too late an age and urged that instruction should begin the moment the child utters his first intelligible word. As the boy grew older, his hours of study lengthened, and as he approached Bar Mitzvah, they extended far into the night. With his growing knowledge came a growing awareness of the responsibilities he was assuming as a Jew: the manifold commandments – 613 of them – the injunctions and the prohibitions directing how he should conduct himself from the moment he rises until he settles

Two Chassidic children immersed in study

into sleep, what he should wear, how he should dress, which shoe he should don first, what he may eat and what he must avoid, which blessing to make over what, what tasks may be performed on a Sabbath and what on a festival, and what on the intermediate days of the festivals (*chol hamoed*). By the time he was thirteen, he may not have had the voice or the height of a man, but he had something of the appearance of one, as if his childhood somehow had been exorcised. The boy had become a man and already, at thirteen, stood in the shadow of the *chupah*. There are Jews living today whose fathers married within a year or two of their Bar Mitzvah.

From all this, one might get the impression that Judaism was impatient of childhood, but that isn't quite true. There are a great many ceremonies connected with the Sabbath and the festivals that are specifically designed to entice the child and to draw him into a love of Judaism. The *seder* on the first night of Passover, for example, the most colourful occasion in the Jewish calendar, was almost built round the child. The Book of Proverbs seems to have been addressed to children: 'Hear my son the instruction of thy father, and forsake not the teaching of thy mother,' but it was couched in adult language and presumes a relatively mature child. The Talmud abounds in legends and fables that seem to have been written for the edification of children, and there are many traditions, some of which still linger, that were designed to attract the child to the ways of his father.

In Germany in the Middle Ages, the child was initiated to his studies at a formal ceremony usually held during the Feast of Pentecost. He was dressed in his best clothes, laden with honey cakes, eggs, fruit and sweets and brought by his mother to the rabbi, who then led him to the synagogue dais where he heard the Ten Commandments being read. This was his first lesson. For the second he was led to the schoolroom, where a famous text from the Bible would be smeared on his slate in honey, and he would repeat it as he nibbled on his treat. This made study sweet to the tongue of the four- or five-year-old and established it as a habit while he was still young. There has always been a subtle connection between food and religion amongst Jews. (The way to a man's soul was through his stomach.)

But if Judaism is not fundamentally impatient of childhood, poverty certainly is, and, until our own times, the mass of world Jewry was poor. As families were larger, older daughters were obliged to look after younger children and sons had to help earn the family's daily bread. If the father was a shopkeeper, the son

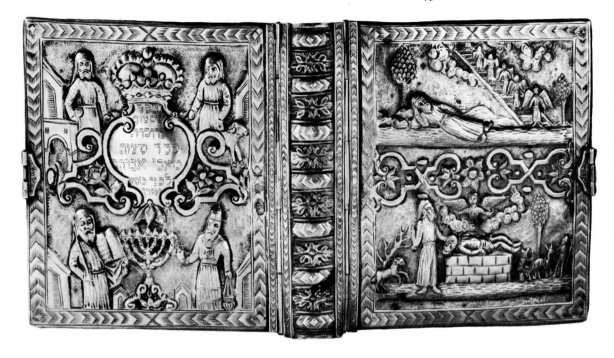

helped with errands; if a craftsman, the boy entered his craft, all at an early age. All this, coupled with the relentless stress on study, gave rise to a sort of precocious maturity. By the time a boy was thirteen, no matter how immature he seemed in physique, he was, to use a Yiddish phrase, an *alte neshome*, 'an old soul'.

Today there is the opposite tendency. Childhood is extended almost until the fringes of middle age, as if to compensate for all the childhood pleasures forgone in the past. People live longer, and there is a sheltering ring of parents and relatives – to say nothing of a more benign external society – who sustain one for many years. The protracted childhood, with all its little joys of sweetmeats, games, toys, nursery rhymes, fairy stories and legends, is primarily a middle-class privilege, and the majority of Jewry is too new to the middle class not to indulge or prolong it.

In an earlier age, a boy was able to devote himself to sacred study because, in most cases, secular education was closed to him. Today, a boy has the full curriculum of his day school to tackle, and the very years once spent in achieving a basic grounding in Jewish study are now devoted to grasping for the bottom rungs of the academic ladder. Yet there are boys who, in spite of the demands of their secular education, are somehow able to acquire a considerable degree of Jewish knowledge. They are familiar with Jewish law, can follow a page of the Talmud and at their Bar Mitzvah can

An 18th-century silver prayer book cover from Central Europe, one of the popular Bar Mitzvah gifts from father to son at the time. The *menorah* on the front cover (left) is flanked by Moses and Aaron; the back cover shows scenes of Jacob's dream (top) and the sacrifice of Isaac (bottom)

recite not merely some small paragraph of the Torah, but the entire portion of the week. And at the family dinner they will follow it all up with a Talmudic discourse, dazzling – to those few who can understand it – in its erudition.

Most Jewish families have a love of tradition, but some still retain a belief in the faith that gave rise to it. Boys from such families regard the Bar Mitzvah as a form of moral graduation; the others regard it as one of the travails of childhood, something to be got over with, like mumps or chicken-pox, but made somewhat more palatable by the compensations – gift-cheques, presents and possibly even a holiday in Israel. Many boys belong to the latter category for whom the Bar Mitzvah means a prolonged spasm of effort. It is something in which one takes special instruction, like dancing lessons. Indeed, many a boy has parallel courses in both. But the halting efforts of a semi-literate boy to utter the blessing over the Torah can give rise to a whole cycle of festivities – starting with a huge family dinner on the eve of the event, followed by a huge family lunch immediately after, and concluding with a banquet for perhaps 400–500 guests in the evening.

Although today there is less to celebrate at the average Bar Mitzvah than at any time in the past, something of the earnestness of the earlier occasions still attaches itself to the ceremony, and the Bar Mitzvah is always much more than a sacred excuse for a ball. There is a great concourse of relatives and friends – some of whom have crossed oceans to witness the event. The menfolk (in Orthodox synagogues) arrange themselves in the pews below, while the women are seated in the gallery above. The mother is flanked by the grandmothers and a whole phalanx of cousins and aunts, and with their heads craned forward for a better view, they gaze on the proceedings with moist eyes, their perfume rising from the assembly like incense to heaven.

In England, the father, who may normally come to synagogue (if he comes at all) in a bowler-hat, is now attired in a top hat. And if the son has not, to appearances at least, quite become a man, his father has definitely become a *baale bos* (a worthy burgher), and he plants himself on the synagogue dais at the side of the Torah while various relatives are given an *aliyah*. The last portion of the day is read by the Bar Mitzvah himself.

A Sabbath morning service can last for three or four hours and, understandably, the congregation does not remain silent during all that time; but as the boy's name is called out, voices fade away and one can hear a prayer-shawl drop. He ascends the platform – a

A Bar Mitzvah ceremony at Wilson's Arch, adjoining the Western Wall in Jerusalem, which has become a popular site for the occasion

The celebrations, toastmaster and all, after the ceremony in London are indicative of where the emphasis is placed in the contemporary Bar Mitzvah

slight, white-faced figure in a dark blue suit – and begins to chant in a clear, piping voice that rings through the synagogue. Mother and grandmothers reach for their handkerchiefs.

Among Sephardim, the Bar Mitzvah boy is showered with almonds, raisins and sweets as soon as he has completed his portion, and there is a *mêlée* of children diving to fill their pockets. In Moroccan synagogues, there is a loud ululation from the ladies' gallery while the boy is pelted with nuts, raisins and sweets.

Reform Jews feel that, whatever the traditions behind it, the age of thirteen represents no significant phase in the life of a boy, and a confirmation ceremony, generally celebrated at the age of fifteen or sixteen, has superseded the Bar Mitzvah in Reform congregations. The Bar Mitzvah is not without its critics even among Orthodox Jews, primarily because of the junketing that often surrounds it. This is not a recent complaint: in medieval Italy some Jewish communities tried to limit the scale of celebrations by imposing a tax on every guest at the table or an outright fine on every guest above a certain limit. There has not been an age in which the Rabbis have not denounced excessive display, even though rabbis themselves have sometimes been amongst the worst offenders.

Jews have always found it difficult to suppress their love of display, but greater than that is their pride in their children. The less a family is versed in things Jewish, the greater seems to be the achievement of the Bar Mitzvah boy, and the fact that he can read Hebrew at all may fill some relatives with awe. The very presence of their son as the cynosure of all is in itself a source of pride, and the extravagant feasting that follows derives in good part from a sense of thanksgiving, a generosity of spirit, a desire to share their joy with as many relatives and friends as their credit will permit. The Jew, moreover, has an extended sense of family, and no kinsman is so remote as not to feel entitled to a place at the festive table. As we shall further discover when we examine the Jewish wedding, hell knows no fury like a second-cousin overlooked!

The Bar Mitzvah is also a time for family reckoning. Parents suddenly realize not only that their child, so recently held wriggling and screaming at his *brit*, is approaching maturity, but that they are nearing – or may already have reached – middle age, and the celebrations which surround the event serve, in part, as their consolation.

When the Bar Mitzvah boy has completed his blessings, his father responds with another: 'Blessed is He who has freed me from the penalties due this one.' From then on, the misdeeds of his son

are no longer charged to his moral account. While Christianity
believes in original sin, Judaism believes in original innocence, but
on reaching the age of thirteen a boy (the girl gets there a year
earlier) acquires his very own *yetzer hara* (evil inclination), a sort
of private devil which urges him to do things he shouldn't. He
becomes prone to temptations unknown in childhood, and part of
the purpose of his religious training is to help him overcome them.
The *tephilin* that he is required to wear on his head and arm each
morning and the *tzitzit* (fringed garment) that he must wear under
his shirt every day are reminders of his new status and his new
responsibilities. A famous sage, Rav Eliezer ben Yaacov, said:
'Whoever has *tephilin* on his head and arm, *tzitzit* on his garment
and a *mezuzah* on his door is assured that he will not sin.' Unfortunately, it does not always work out quite like that, and sacred
vestments have often hidden a multitude of sins. But a lad accustomed to wearing *tephilin* each morning, if not always less
likely to go wrong, is certainly more aware when he has gone wrong.
If the properly trained Bar Mitzvah boy does not always become a
saint, he at least ceases to be an innocent sinner. If nothing else, he

The ancient art of making
tephilin

is imbued with a healthy sense of guilt, and guilt feelings are not something for which any tradition-minded Jew would apologize; it is part of Jewish belief that awareness of one's own deficiencies is half the way to correction. Unfortunately, as few Bar Mitzvah boys put on *tephilin* for much beyond their thirteenth birthday, and fewer still wear *tzitzit*, they lose their innocence without acquiring a lasting sense of guilt.

Almost any Jewish occasion is considered a time for presents, and the Bar Mitzvah more so than others. In the inter-war years a boy could expect fountain-pens from poor relatives and watches from rich ones. Now that every boy has a collection of ballpoints before he can write, he expects watches from poor relatives and perhaps a bicycle from rich ones. Straight cash is still always welcome, though in more Orthodox families it is usual to give learned works (some of which are so learned that they may be passed unopened from one generation to another), and many a boy is provided with the beginnings of a private library.

While some have questioned the value of the Bar Mitzvah, others considered it so salutary an experience that they felt girls, too, should benefit from it. And over the protests of Orthodox rabbis, in recent years there has evolved a Bat Mitzvah ceremony. The term Bat Mitzvah, which means 'daughter of the commandment', is in a sense a contradiction in terms. A girl, on reaching maturity, does not assume the religious obligations of a boy. She does not wear *tephilin*, is not required to pray or attend synagogue, does not – indeed, cannot – make up a quorum for prayer, nor is she called up to the Reading of the Law. The role of the Jewish woman will be discussed in some detail in a later chapter, but suffice it to say that the attitude of Jewish tradition to the woman is, at best, ambivalent. 'Nothing is of so much worth as a woman's mind well instructed,' said one celebrated Rabbi. To which another, equally celebrated, replied: 'To teach one's daughter Torah is to teach her frivolity.' On the whole, especially among the more Orthodox Jews, the latter view has prevailed.

The *cheder* and Talmud Torah, where the East European child received his Jewish education, was for boys only, but even in 1973, the rabbi of a large and fashionable London congregation felt compelled to suspend a lecture on the Talmud because a man had appeared in the audience with his wife. The *yeshivot*, the great centres of higher Jewish learning where the Talmud is studied intensively and in depth, have always been – and still are – closed to women. This does not mean that Jewish women were always

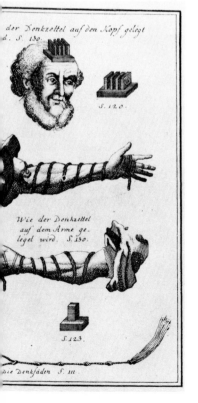

An illustration from the first issue of *Der Jude* (1768), showing the proper placement of the *tephilin*. *Der Jude* was published by an apostate Jew to familiarize Christians with Jewish life and rituals

left ignorant (though a great many were): they lived in a world with so much stress on learning that they were bound to pick up something – like scraps from a rich man's table. Indeed, some became scholars in their own right, in spite of the fact that every tradition was against them, but a knowledgeable woman was regarded as an exception, if not an outright freak. Except in the most rigid Orthodox circles, however, attitudes have changed, and in most Jewish communities the authorities have made extensive provision for the education of daughters as well as sons. The prospect of the Bar Mitzvah has always helped to keep the boy in class – if only for a couple of hours on Sunday morning and an occasional hour on week-day evenings – but the girl has had no such incentive; the Bat Mitzvah was introduced to provide it. It was hoped that it would combat the effects of centuries of neglect and give the girl a more positive role in the religious life of the community.

The exact form of the Bat Mitzvah ceremony has not yet been crystallized, and it tends to vary from community to community and even from congregation to congregation. In some places it is celebrated when the girl is twelve, in others when she reaches thirteen, or even fifteen or sixteen. As a rule, the girl, unlike her brother, does not have the day to herself: Bat Mitzvot are dispatched rapidly and in batches, like a graduation ceremony. All the girls in the congregation who have reached the age of twelve, thirteen, or whatever is customary in the locality, undergo a course of instruction in Hebrew, history and fundamental Jewish laws and practices, and on the appointed day they all dress in white and are brought before the congregation. The synagogue is generally banked with flowers for the occasion, and the girls in their crisp white frocks, white shoes and sometimes even white gloves are a sort of ornament in themselves. It is all very beautiful and sometimes moving. Each girl reads a passage from Psalms or from some appropriate Jewish teaching, and then they are addressed jointly by the rabbi.

One of the most taxing tasks of a rabbi is the address to Bar Mitzvah boys week after week. He must imbue them with the same message – the need to follow in the ways of their fathers – without repeating the same words. In the case of the Bat Mitzvah his task is eased somewhat by the wholesale nature of the proceedings, but, again, the message is always the same – the need to follow in the ways of their mothers and that the Jewishness of a Jewish home rests with them.

The girls' ceremony tends to be more decorous and solemn than

The Bat Mitzvah of an American girl held at Masada, the famed fortress above the Dead Sea where Jewish zealots held out against the Roman legions after the fall of Jerusalem in AD 70

the boys', but it has none of the antiquity, none of the echoes of the past, and consequently does not have the same capacity to stir memories. The Bat Mitzvah is, at best, a 'poor man's Bar Mitzvah'. The celebrations which surround it will be less expensive, colossal or prolonged. Relatives will not feel compelled to cross continents to attend it, and it will rarely call forth the same expensive presents.

In Orthodox congregations the Bat Mitzvah ceremony is barely tolerated and if it exists, it is called *Eshet Chayil* or *Bat Chayil* ('woman of valour' or 'daughter of valour') rather than Bat Mitzvah, in case anyone should confuse it with the Bar Mitzvah or attribute to it the same significance. Such congregations, moreover, tend to hold it in the synagogue hall rather than within the sacred precincts of the synagogue itself and treat it as a social occasion tempered by Psalms and a sermon.

In Israel, the Bat Mitzvah has taken firm root. In religious kibbutzim, for example, it is celebrated with the same pomp and ceremony as a Bar Mitzvah. But in Israel, Judaism is so much a part of normal, everyday life that its progress cannot be checked in the same way as in the Diaspora.

4 Maidens

In Sir Walter Scott's *Ivanhoe*, the Jewess, Rebekah, is depicted as the embodiment of every female virtue. This was not out of an eagerness to do justice to a maligned race, but because that was the not infrequently held impression of Jewish womanhood. The Jewish woman was synonymous with purity, nobility and high-mindedness. One can see something of this in an article on the young Jewish woman published in 1869 in the London *Jewish Chronicle*:

> Our girls, the brightest flowers in the garden of the world whose very ingenuousness is refreshing to those who mingle with the mighty throng of daily life . . . Trustful because they are themselves trustworthy, self-sacrificing, for their pride in those they love; they weave around our hearts a mystic chain, until our thoughts and feelings arise and unite with theirs . . . the influence of woman is still as strong, as ennobling, and as elevating as ever . . .

Grace Aguilar, the English novelist who wrote *The Women of Israel*

Until the ghetto walls collapsed in the aftermath of the French Revolution, Jewish communities, though not uninfluenced by trends in the outside world, were able to perpetuate their own mores, and the ideal of womanly purity remained intact (as it still does among the ultra-Orthodox Jews in the voluntary ghettos of New York, London and Jerusalem). As time wore on, they found themselves in a continuing conflict between the restraints of the past and the attractions of modern life. These problems were, to some extent, delayed, for throughout much of the nineteenth century, especially in Victorian England, Jewish mores were almost identical with those of the outside world; and whether or not the Jewish ideal of womanly purity helped to inspire the romantic revival, it was certainly in keeping with it.

In 1889, Grace Aguilar, a minor – though in her day, widely

An 1846 lithograph of a 'Jewish woman of Pera' from Sir David Wilkie's *Sketches in Spain . . .'*

read – Victorian novelist, wrote a book called *The Women of Israel* to illustrate 'the past history, present duties and future destiny of the Hebrew females, as based on the word of God', in which she enlarged on the worthy qualities of the Jewish woman as depicted in the lives of its principal heroines. In the case of some of the heroines – Sarah, Rebekah and Rachel for instance – she was kinder than the Bible itself, but she did portray a fine gallery of virtues. (Tennyson's Genevieve would have been entirely at home among them.) Judaism and Victorianism thrived on one another, perhaps reinforced one another.

The nineteenth century was the golden age of the family, and it was no accident that it was also the age in which the Jewish family came into its own. To this day, where Jewish family life is at its most Jewish and traditional, one senses nuances of nineteenth-century life. The discipline, the deference to one's parents, the formal mealtimes accompanied by prayer, the self-restraint, the very size of the families – with the father at the head of the table, the mother at the other end and two, three or even four children on *each* side – all evoke a bygone age.

One of the most fundamental aspects of Jewish tradition – which also may be going the way of other Victorian virtues – is the great significance attached to virginity. It appears in Judaism as early as the verse in Genesis, referring to Eliezer's encounter with Rebekah: 'And the damsel was very fair to look upon, a virgin, neither had

Eliezer taking leave of Abraham to fulfil his mission of finding a wife for Isaac, from the 6th-century illuminated manuscript known as the Vienna Genesis

any man known her' (Genesis 24:16) and is a recurring theme throughout the Bible, especially with regard to the laws governing betrothal, marriage and divorce. Virginity was so essential a quality in a woman that a man had an automatic right to divorce his wife if he found her to be otherwise. In Babylon (up to about the fifth century AD), where the Rabbinical court generally met on Thursday, it was usual for marriages to take place on Wednesday, so that if the bride's condition did not tally with her claims, the marriage could be dissolved without delay.

On the other hand, to suggest that a woman was not a virgin without adequate proof was the vilest calumny that a man could perpetrate against his bride:

If a man take a wife and go in unto her, and hate her, and bring up an evil name upon her, and say: I took this woman, and when I came nigh to her, I found not in her the tokens of virginity: then shall the father of the damsel, and the mother, take and bring forth the tokens of the damsel's virginity unto the elders of the city (Deuteronomy 22:13–15).

If the elders found the proof convincing, the husband had to pay 100 shekels to the outraged father, 'because he hath brought up an evil name upon a virgin of Israel.' But that was the minor part of the husband's punishment. He also forfeited all right to divorce and remained tied to his wife till the end of his (or her) days.

A pen and wash sketch of a Moroccan maiden in 19th-century dress, by Alfred Dehodencq (1822–1882)

The 'tokens of virginity' were the blood-stained sheets that the bride presumably handed over to her parents after her first night of marriage. Among the Jews of North Africa, the elders of the congregation waited outside the bridal chamber until the groom emerged with the sheets. A similar custom existed among the Jews of Kurdistan, but in Persia, the female relatives waited about the chamber, until invited inside to examine the bridal bed. The sheet was then passed around for closer inspection and finally deposited with the bride's parents. This was no empty ritual: a woman other than a virgin (unless widowed or a divorcee) was not thought to be a fit member of a Jewish household.

Not that non-virgins were unmarriageable – some of them proved to be more readily marriageable than their maiden sisters – but they were regarded as 'damaged goods' with less value and less standing in the community, and they often married into a class beneath them. In the *ketubah*, which, among other things, records the financial obligations that a man undertakes towards his wife, the minimum guarantee to a virgin is 200 zuzim, while the minimum to a non-virgin is 100.

In ancient times, the High Priest was not allowed to marry a non-virgin, and to this day a descendant of the priesthood (most *cohens* consider themselves to be so descended) cannot, according to Jewish law, marry a divorcee nor a victim of rape. Similarly, a *cohen* cannot marry a convert: it is presumed that any gentile female above the age of three is by definition a non-virgin. Furthermore, a Jewish woman taken in captivity cannot marry a *cohen*, for while she was held among non-Jews she might have been raped.

There is a natural male instinct to explore new worlds and unknown lands, and marrying a virgin is about man's only hope of doing so. That is why almost every society – and certainly those dominated by men – has laid particular stress on female chastity. Judaism's stress on virginity was twofold: first was the belief in chastity as an end in itself, for the person who was pure in both body and spirit came that much closer to his Maker; second was the extent to which sex entered into the ritual of several Near Eastern cults, especially those connected with Baal, and fornication, thus interpreted, constituted a form of idolatry. One began with strange women and ended with strange gods. When Potiphar's

Joseph and Potiphar's wife, portrayed on a 16th-century enamel casket from Limoges

wife tried to seduce Joseph, he recoiled with the plea: 'How can I do this great wickedness and sin against God?' And the Rabbis, through the ages, spoke of it in like terms: adultery was an affront to God.

But virginity also had its defenders on plain social grounds. It was believed to strengthen marriage and establish a sense of mutual respect that formed the basis of family life. A virgin, it was suggested, often falls in love with the first man she sleeps with, and her virginity thus establishes an emotional bond that might not otherwise exist. Jewish tradition sees it as a fulfilment of the prophecy made to Eve after the expulsion from the Garden of Eden: '. . . and thy desire shall be to thy husband, and he shall rule over thee' (Genesis 3:16). In a woman other than a virgin that desire is less pronounced. The tradition of premarital chastity, moreover, gave to marriage an intense sense of liberation, the sudden freeing of yearnings long suppressed. One possible reason for pre-arranged marriages having worked out so well was the complete innocence of bride and groom. Marriage represented the first sexual experience for both and their mutual discovery formed a firm bond. Premarital chastity was regarded as one of the elements basic to marital bliss. To the chaste, marriage thus constituted an adventure; to others it was an anticlimax. Until the end of the eighteenth century, it was customary for the groom to recite a blessing the moment he he had consummated his marriage and found that his bride was indeed a virgin:

Astarte, the fertility goddess widely worshipped by the Canaanites – and sometimes by Israelites straying from the fold of Mosaic Law

Blessed art Thou, O Lord our God, King of the universe, who has planted a nut-tree in Eden. Lily of the Valley, let not a stranger have dominion over the sealed fountain wherefore the hind of love has preserved her purity and has not transgressed the statute. Blessed be He who has chosen the seed of Abraham.

There is no definite, outright condemnation of fornication between unmarried, unrelated men and women in the Bible, but the sense of disapproval is evident in every page. The Israelites were frequently warned against the abominations of 'the land of Egypt in which ye have dwelt and the land of Canaan into which I bring ye'. These abominations were not explicitly defined but everyone knew what they meant. When the Israelites were offered the Torah on Sinai it was said that they hesitated over the seventh commandment: it was one thing not to covet one's neighbour's ass, but quite another not to commit adultery. Nevertheless they felt prevailed upon to accept, and Maimonides noted sagely – and

גמילות חסדים להכנסת כלה
"יד אליהו"
FREE LOAN SOCIETY to HELP POOR BRIDES
"YAD-ELYAHU,,

Lest penury be an obstacle to marriage, to this day there are funds to help a young bride on her way. This sign in Jerusalem is evidence of one still in existence

sadly – that 'no prohibition in the Torah is as difficult to keep as that of forbidden unions and illicit sexual relations'. Brachya, his contemporary, agreed that the prohibition, if irksome, was necessary, for sexual indulgence had 'evil results . . . causing pain to the loins, reducing strength, injuring the quality of the blood in man, inducing pain in the sides and weakness of the stomach'. In a word, it pulls down the constitution entirely and causes the break-up of a man's body. It is a consequence of these evils that wise men utter the warning: 'Give not thy strength unto women' (Proverbs 31:3).

But that could arise from over-indulgence even within marriage. Indulgence outside it had even graver consequences, for the fornicator 'becomes a creature defiled, loathsome, unperfumed, and unclean . . .':

Such a man moreover, reduces his home to ruin, and goes on corrupting his way and making his paths abominable, as it is said, 'When I had fed them to the full, they then committed adultery and assembled themselves by troops in the harlots' houses' (Jeremiah 5:7). Hence it happens that he does not have a legitimate son by his own wife as he acts towards others, as it is said 'If mine heart have been enticed by women . . . then let my wife grind unto another' (Job 31:9).

There was, noted the Talmud, 'no guardian against unchastity'. Tacitus, who was a close social observer of the many peoples under Roman rule, described the Jews as a particularly sensual brotherhood. It was a view with which Rabbis on the whole concurred, and they felt compelled to make allowances for it. Adultery was thus regarded as a capital offence only when a married woman was involved. Men – married or single – were all cautioned to be chaste, but where they were overwhelmed by desire, they were ordered to be at least discreet. They should garb themselves in black, go to a place where they are unknown and do their dirty work there. But it was understood that an upright man shouldn't, and, on the whole, upright men didn't. In this respect, available evidence suggests that later generations of Israelites have been rather more upright than earlier ones. The Old Testament not only condoned polygamy, but, where the propagation of children was concerned, positively commended it. Thus, Abraham had two wives, and Jacob four. There were, of course, certain prohibited relationships, but if a woman was not in that category and was not married nor betrothed, the sanctions against intercourse with her were slight. There were, however, penalties if she happened to be a virgin:

When a man seduces a virgin who is not yet betrothed, he shall pay the bride price for her to be his bride. If her father refuses to give her to him, he shall pay money according to the dower of virgins (Exodus 22:16–17).

All this applied even to a married man who, besides primary wives, might have secondary wives (or concubines) and tertiary wives in the form of female slaves. The Rabbis were prompt to limit such excesses, but example was perhaps more important than prohibitions, and once we pass into post-biblical times, polygamy becomes rare. In the entire Talmud there is no instance of a Rabbi who took a second wife, and in the tenth century, polygamy was declared illegal among Jews through the interdict of Rav Gershom, one of the outstanding sages of post-Talmudic times. His authority was, however, accepted only by western Jews; among oriental Jews, polygamy, or at least bigamy, though not common, was not unheard of, and among the immigrants from Arab lands who settled in Israel after 1948, there were a few who arrived with more than one wife.

The Rabbis were aware of the immense strains that chastity imposed, and they sought to ease them as much as possible by limiting the areas of temptation. Primarily, they segregated the sexes as much as the practicalities of day-to-day life permitted. They found particular allurement in a woman's voice, and mixed choirs are not permitted in Orthodox synagogues to this day; Jewish women might be seen, but not heard, and it was better still if they were not seen either. In the Temple, women could observe – though not participate in – the religious ceremonies from their own court-yard, the *ezrat nashim*, and in Orthodox synagogues they still sit separate from the men. At ultra-Orthodox weddings, apart from

Segregated festivities at an ultra-Orthodox wedding

the bride and groom, male and female guests sit at separate tables – if not in separate rooms. 'Men and women shall neither rejoice nor mourn together,' decreed the Rabbis. On Purim, the one occasion when Jewish law tolerates a certain degree of merry-making and levity, a type of masked ball became common in some communities. This, too, caused a measure of concern, for it could result in a mingling of the sexes. 'Everyone who fears God will exhort the

The residents of Mea Shearim, an ultra-Orthodox quarter in Jerusalem, caution visitors in English, Hebrew and Yiddish of local standards of modest dress

members of his household, and those who defer to his opinions, to avoid such frivolities', wrote a medieval scholar. There were frequent warnings against teaching boys and girls together (including some against teaching girls at all), and ultra-Orthodox communities abide by this principle to the extent of sponsoring separate nursery schools.

Likewise, there have been prolonged debates on modesty in dress. Most Rabbis agreed that arms and legs constitute an unseemly form of enticement and should be kept out of sight, but no firm

attitude was established vis-à-vis the face. In eighteenth-century
Metz, women were not allowed to appear in the synagogue with
their faces uncovered; and about the same time, the Rabbis of
Amsterdam attempted – one knows not with what success – to
prevent engaged girls from appearing unveiled in public. In biblical
times women kept their heads covered, and although there is no
explicit injunction to do so, tradition dictated that no chaste or
modest woman would allow herself to be seen in public with her
head exposed. The Talmud (the compilation of Jewish tradition
completed about the sixth century AD) goes so far as to allow a man
to divorce his wife, without repaying her dowry, if she appeared in
a public place with her head uncovered. Some Rabbis argued that
to be seen in public with a naked head was the same as being seen
with naked genitals. The *Shulchan Aruch* (a synopsis of Jewish
law first printed in 1565) is quite specific on the point and states
that 'daughters of Israel, whether married or not, should not go
in the street with hair uncovered, but young girls are permitted.'
This law has been allowed to lapse even in Orthodox families, but
among ultra-Orthodox Jews no married woman will be seen in
public with her hair uncovered. She will wear either a hat, a
kerchief or a wig.

Today, a wig – or *shaytl*, as it is called – can often outshine the
glory it is meant to shade, but it is still regarded as the ultimate
symbol of wifely modesty. When the *shaytl* first appeared in the
eighteenth century, some rabbis protested that, although it con-
formed to the strict letter of the law, it merely sought to ape
contemporary fashion and, as such, was anything but modest. But
as the fashion died out, Rabbinic criticism was silenced. Now that
wigs are once again in style, it is difficult to tell the ultra-Orthodox
matron from the ultra-fashionable 'swinger', and the criticism of
the eighteenth-century rabbis may again be valid.

Jewish courting-couples were expected to court from a distance
or through an intermediary, though most authorities felt that it
was better not to court at all and leave such matters to one's parents.
Young people, however, were inclined to be wilful in such matters,
and the Rabbis decreed that the least they could do was to conduct
themselves with circumspection. 'A man should ever avoid women,'
advised the *Shulchan Aruch*. 'He should not wink to them, nor jest
with them, nor be light-headed among them. Nor should he gaze
too long at their beauty. If he find himself behind a woman in the
street, he should not continue to follow her, but take another
direction.' One was allowed to look closely at one's fiancée, but

'not with lascivious eyes', and one had to avoid any intimacy 'that leads to embracing and kissing'. To be on the safe side an engaged couple should only be together in the presence of a chaperon. A respectable maiden had to be careful about her reputation: it was in order to be with a man of good character in the presence of another, 'but only in town, and during daylight'. At night, or in a field, she had to have two chaperons, both of good character. Such safety in numbers applied only to women: 'A man', continued the *Shulchan Aruch*, 'should not be alone with many women'. He was further warned not to come within three yards of a house of ill-repute.

The Old Testament is rich with cautions against the wiles of the harlot, and they are particularly frequent in the Book of Proverbs:

> My son, attend unto my wisdom,
> and bow thine ear to my understanding:
> that thou mayest regard discretion,
> and that thy lips may keep knowledge.
> For the lips of a strange woman drop as a honeycomb,
> and her mouth is smoother than oil:
> but her end is bitter as wormwood,
> sharp as a two-edged sword.
> Her feet go down to death;
> her steps take hold on hell.
> Lest thou shouldst ponder the path of life,
> her ways are movable, that thou canst not know them.
> Hear me now therefore, O ye children,
> and depart not from the words of my mouth.
> Remove thy way from her,
> and come not nigh the door of her house (5:1–8).

Joseph Kimchi, an eighteenth-century London Talmudist, warned his readers in much the same terms:

How much better it is to caress a lioness than a senseless woman! Better to kiss the lips of an adder or scorpion than foolishly to kiss her lips! You may think it pleasant to have her company to your heart's content, but understand that you'll have a full share of shame and disgrace to follow.

Such words of caution were not always heeded, but once Jewry was in exile it behaved with greater circumspection than in its own land and, as we have seen, the Jewish woman became the model of modesty and chastity.

It cannot be said that Jewish men were seen quite in the same light, and one finds warnings in the Talmud against the tendency to consort with gentile women. A similar tendency existed amongst the Jews in Renaissance Italy, and it is here that one begins to sense the roots of what might be called the 'shiksah syndrome'. The shiksah is the young gentile woman (as distinct from the goya, who is the old one). If the Jewish man could see a Jewish woman only under numerous prescribed conditions, he was not allowed to see the gentile one at all. She, therefore, had a double allure of being doubly prohibited and, at the very same time, subject to fewer inhibitions.

For a long time there was no middle ground between the pure virgin and the fallen woman. One rabbi warned that a daughter who was not married off in her youth – that is by the age of twelve – might become a harlot. At the end of the nineteenth century, the great westward movement of Jewry resulting from Russian oppression caused the wholesale disruption of family life. Innocent girls, who had rarely stirred from the family hearth, found themselves unsheltered and alone – or, at best, lodged with thoughtless relatives – in great cities like London and New York. Their very upbringing made them easy prey for seducers, and they succumbed to temptations that in normal times every instinct would have induced them to resist. Once seduced, they felt themselves unfit for anything but the streets, and some in fact took to, or were ensnared into, prostitution. A good Jewish girl who goes astray does so with abandon.

In the intervening period between Waterloo and the Franco-Prussian War, there developed a recrudescence of anti-Jewish feeling in Prussia, Austro-Hungary and France. Jews in those countries enjoyed an almost unbroken period of tranquillity and progress: they entered the professions in vast numbers; they dominated the intellectual life of the Continent; and they prospered in commerce and industry. The abandonment of their Old World attitudes was not a necessary precondition for acceptance into the new life style, but even so there was an *en masse* desertion from traditional Judaism. But here and there in small towns and large one found snug pockets of tradition, of life as it was lived; this was beautifully captured in a series of canvases by the German painter Moritz Oppenheim. The scenes, like Grace Aguilar's *Women of Israel*, were more than a little romanticized, but they captured beautifully the closeness, the tranquillity, the attention lavished on children and the wealth of ceremony in Jewish life. It was a tragically brief golden

Yet another generation being raised to live with Old World attitudes, as expressed by the garb and hair styles of these Chassidic children

age, for it was followed by harassment, persecution and extinction. In England, traditional ideals lingered a little longer. The fact that English society at large was so tradition-conscious helped to sustain traditional Judaism and impeded the rate of assimilation. Victorian primness, however, remained intact in the Jewish family long after it had faded from other areas of English life.

In America, the situation was different. There, the Jew was not encroaching on a society with settled traditions and ways, he was a newcomer among newcomers, and the unique challenge of this new and open society made it difficult for him to preserve the customs he had practised at home. Instead, he tended to develop a new type of pragmatic Judaism, which borrowed something

'Beginning of the Sabbath' by the German painter Moritz Oppenheim (1800–1882)

The nature of American Jewish life has changed drastically since the great wave of immigration at the beginning of this century, symbolized by this engraving from the *London Illustrated News* (1892)

from the Reform Judaism flourishing in Germany from the mid-nineteenth century, but evolved ways of its own. The restraints that had helped to keep Jews Jewish, such as Sabbath observance, the dietary laws, the ritual purity laws, were jettisoned. Among the teeming Jewish masses of New York, Boston and Chicago there was a doctrinal reaction against the inhibitions and impositions of Judaism. This was no mere backsliding but a conscious revolt, for to them traditional Judaism represented all the agonies and humiliations of life in the *shtetl*. They were in a new world, among free men, with new opportunities, and they cast off all the old constraints as inhibiting progress and a fuller life. This included the ideal of womanly purity. In this new setting it was also no longer a matter of Jewish attitudes being influenced by outside ones, for the outside world was in no small measure influenced by the Jewish newcomers. In some instances, the Jews were the pace-setters for the very trends that their more tradition-minded brethren consistently resisted.

The idea of segregating the sexes, in some ways not merely acceptable but actually congenial to the English and Anglo-Jewish mind, could not take root in America; and most Jews who attend synagogue sit next to their wives and daughters. The innocence and puritanism that still lingers in some American areas of the South and Midwest was never particularly evident in the great cities like New York. The restraints that Jews brought from Eastern Europe, with the exception of a few scattered families, were neither preserved nor transmitted. Few question whether a boy and a girl might be together, but the degree of their togetherness: at which point necking could stop and petting begin, and when petting could give way to full-blooded fornication. Today, a mother's prime concern is when to broach her daughter on the subject of the pill. Chastity is not the virtue it once was; and upon observing the tempo of modern times, one may conclude that it is not merely outmoded, but downright quaint. Promiscuity is regarded in some circles as the birth-right of every American – and every American Jewish – child. There was a time, if Philip Roth be a sufficient witness, when Jewish young men, like their counterparts in Europe, went in for *shiksahs* because they were thought to be more yielding than Jewish girls. Today it is generally agreed that some American Jewish girls yield to no one in their readiness to yield.

Yet one can sense the stirrings of a reaction. Many young women have begun to feel that promiscuity, which at first seemed to be a mark of liberation, was, in fact, exploitation. They are more inclined to reassess old attitudes in a more sympathetic light, without, however, necessarily subscribing to the beliefs that gave them force. There have always been American Jews who refused to compromise with the times and have always done things *their* way, but they were more or less confined to their small reservations, and it was all done at a price: they had to establish and maintain their own schools and were inclined to insulate their sons and daughters from the surrounding environment, even to the extent of keeping them away from college and thus out of the professions. Now, however, many young couples who have been exposed to the full blast of the outside world, who did go to American schools and universities, who have qualified in various professions, and who would have been expected to enter wholeheartedly into the spirit of their swinging times, have instead reverted, not so much to the ways of their fathers – for their fathers had themselves departed from tradition – but to those of their grandfathers. The young among them may no longer shun women, but they will approach them with a basic respect and, to use an 'archaic' expression, with 'honourable intentions'. Chastity is making a come-back, and virginity may no longer be a source of self-reproach.

5 The Go-between

According to Jewish tradition, once God made the earth and saw it was good, he drew breath and turned at once to make it better – by getting the single married. Thus, God was the first matchmaker. And as man was created in God's image, so is he involved in this Godly undertaking, and there is hardly a Jewish event that is not an occasion to conspire to find a man a wife or a woman a husband. Yet, if God was the first matchmaker (*shadchan*), the later ones did not have the pure motives of their Creator: if they discharged a necessary function, they discharged it with excessive flair, tempering fact with fancy, and far from being honest brokers and trusted go-betweens, they became the first exponents of the 'hard sell'. The *shadchan* was, for many centuries, a central figure in Jewish life. He fell out of employment in recent years and was threatening to become extinct, but of late he has been making a come-back.

In extenuation, it should perhaps be added that *shadchanim* worked on commission – on a 'no-sale no-fee' basis – and were often required to match the unmarriageable with the unapproachable. No Jewish father can be convinced that his daughter is less than beautiful, and no wealthy father that she is less than a princess. There is the story of a wealthy gown merchant who had the highest expectations for his daughter, who, though well endowed physically, was rather better endowed financially. No proposal put to him was good enough, until one evening he was approached by a *shadchan* with 'something special'.

'There's this young man, good looking, nice family – one of the nicest in the land – good education. Went to Cambridge, did very well. He was an officer in the Navy. One day he'll be an Admiral, I shouldn't be surprised. And he's pleasant, sociable, charming, well-spoken. Believe me, I wouldn't want anything better for

A scene of a betrothal in a Jewish home by the 19th-century German artist Hermann Junkker

my own daughter – if I had one.'

The merchant listened patiently, puffing his cigar. 'And where's the catch?' he said.

The *shadchan*, caught off guard, admitted that there was, indeed, a catch: the boy wasn't Jewish. 'But,' he quickly added, 'for a girl like your daughter who wouldn't be converted?'

'And what's his name?' asked the father.

'Prince Charles.'

The father continued to puff at his cigar, and after a minute or two nodded. 'OK, it's all right by me.'

'Excellent,' said the *shadchan*, rubbing his hands, 'excellent. Now for a word with Her Majesty . . .'

The stress put on marriage and procreation; the anxiety of Jewish parents to have their children married, not only within the right faith, but within the right family; coupled with the wandering of the Jewish people all across the face of Europe made it necessary for some intermediary to maintain contact between the scattered groups. The term *shadchan* came into use in the twelfth century, after the Crusades, and it usually referred to a merchant entrusted by parents to find a partner for their children. But the function of the *shadchan* was known much earlier.

After the destruction of the Second Temple in AD 70, Jewish exiles founded great colleges of learning in Babylon. The heads of these colleges were often approached to recommend suitable husbands for the young girls in their community, and when there were none in their own college, they would correspond with the head of another. The Maharal, a famous fourteenth-century German rabbi, travelled widely as a *shadchan* and used his fees to establish colleges of learning. But gradually the calling passed from sacred hands into commercial ones, and the *shadchan*'s status declined to that of a strolling minstrel. He usually received about two per cent of the dowry if the parties were near, three per cent if they were distant, and was usually over-eager to earn his commission. 'Whenever you are arranging a marriage between parties, never exaggerate but always tell the literal truth,' urged a seventeenth-century writer. As we have already implied, such counsel usually fell on deaf ears. There was a fateful tendency to embellish, and as almost anything a *shadchan* said was discounted as an exaggeration, he was obliged to exaggerate further. And where there were no qualities to exaggerate, one could depend on him to underplay the faults.

The story is told of an anguished young man who, on being

confronted with his prospective bride, quickly pulled the *shadchan* aside:

'You told me she had the appearance, the bearing, the grace of a queen. Look at her. She's pimply, cross-eyed and hook-nosed. She slobbers her food, she limps, and she's hunchbacked.'

'No need to whisper,' said the *shadchan*, 'she's also deaf.'

Then there is the story of another anguished young man – or possibly the same one – who pulled his *shadchan* aside with an even graver list of complaints:

'What are you trying to do to me? You said she's of good family; her father's a woodman and her mother a fishwife. You said she's got a sunny, golden temperament; she's a scold and a shrew. You said she's cultured; she can't read. You said she's as innocent and pure as our mother Rebekah; she's got the worst name in town. You said she's beautiful; her face could stop a clock. You said . . .'

'And who's perfect?' shrugged the *shadchan*.

It was generally the father of the bride who commissioned the *shadchan*, though the first *shadchan* in Jewish history (apart from God Himself) was employed by the father of the groom. Abraham, as we have seen, dispatched his servant Eliezer to find a wife for Isaac, and it was Eliezer who came laden with a dowry, not, as later became common, the bride. The father of the groom provided the dowry for the very sound reason that in taking a bride one acquired not merely a wife, but a palpable, vendible asset. The bride left her father's house and joined that of her husband and – tradition being strictly patrilineal – any children resulting from the union remained part of the father's tribe. In the circumstances, the father of the bride felt entitled to some compensation. This took the form of the *mohar*, or 'bride price'. The size of the *mohar* tended to vary in relation to the standing of the groom's father, although as in the case of the modern engagement ring, it could also be taken as a measure of the groom's affection. The appearance and character of the bride and the standing of the family also entered into it: the more beautiful the bride or the more exalted her family, the higher the *mohar*. Sometimes a homely bride from a lowly family could also exact a high *mohar*, if only to indicate that she was not as homely or as lowly as she appeared. The effect of all this was rather inflationary, and in some Jewish communities there were attempts to limit the *mohar*, which was liable to reduce some families with greater pretensions than wealth to penury.

Gradually, as men became scarce and as daughters became less of an asset and more of a liability, the *mohar* gave way to the *nadan* (dowry). But this was not a gift for the husband to use as he wished, and if the marriage broke up the wife was entitled to the recovery of the full sum. Poor brides were provided for out of communal monies, and most communities maintained a fund (*hachnassat kallah*) for that very purpose. If the girl's father died, the brother or next of kin was expected to provide a dowry. In the main, however, dowries are associated with wealth, and particularly in Eastern Europe, there evolved a tacit alliance between cash and culture. A man who had built up a fortune would seek out, with the help of a *shadchan* or his rabbi, a young scholar for his daughter and would keep him as an *eidem af kest* – roughly translated as a son-in-law in residence – for the first year or two of the marriage. On occasion, if the son-in-law were particularly renowned and the father particularly wealthy, this arrangement could last for life. This practice seems to have been fairly well established by the Middle Ages, as one can see from the following marriage contract drawn up in 1249:

> The father gives his daughter Zeuna in marriage, promising a dowry of ten marks at the time of the nuptials and a further sum of five marks a year later. He will provide both with weekday and Sabbath apparel, and give them ample food and lodging. He will support them an entire year in his house, furnish them with all they require, clothe them and shoe them and discharge their talliage, if any be imposed on them during the aforesaid year.

That particular groom must have been an exceptionally raw young man, for the father-in-law, who appears to have been a Santa Claus in mufti, further undertook to 'engage a teacher to instruct the husband during the twelve months after marriage'.

Sometimes fulfilment fell well short of promise and on occasion the groom refused to go through with the marriage. In some towns, the Jewish community had a special fund to help the father out at such a time, but it was sometimes abused, and in 1618, the Rome community ruled that no father who promised his daughter for more than 200 scudi (or the equivalent) was eligible for help. Jews were subject to numerous feudal impositions, including a marriage tax and domicile tax, and many marriages could never have taken place without some sort of help from the parents. Nor was it a bad thing if a wealthy untutored father supported the studies of a learned impecunious son-in-law. Study, in particular

Detail of the 15th-century Second Nuremberg *Hagadah* showing a wedding ceremony

limudei kodesh (sacred study) was regarded as an end in itself, ennobling and elevating both the student and his patron, but the system was left wide open to abuse. Scholarship was not as widespread as the desire for scholars; eligible scholars were not as numerous as eligible brides. Instead of a prodigy of learning, one often ended up with an eternal student, and there evolved a type that is far from extinct even today: the professional son-in-law.

Jewish communities have nearly always been affected by a shortage of males: in the many massacres and pogroms, women and children were sometimes spared, but the men were usually slaughtered; male infants generally proved to be less hardy than females, and when infant mortality was high, comparatively few boys survived their infancy. The male was also more venturesome than the female, and more mobile: he might enlist or be conscripted into the army, or stake out a new life abroad. Between

1881 and 1914, the years of mass emigration from Eastern Europe, there was such a large-scale movement of young men to the West that something akin to a male famine developed in Russia and Poland. Fathers exerted themselves to scratch together any money they could in order to draw in any available male; where none were close at hand, they commissioned a *shadchan* to snare one from some more distant place. Scholarship, family background and financial status were all forgotten. It was enough that he was a man. The situation gave rise to some dreadful tragedies. The Talmud warned against postponing a marriage in the hope of a better match, and the warning may have been too closely observed. Thus, young men who had lived in England or Western Europe and had picked up something of the gloss of Western life travelled to Eastern Europe, attended synagogue, made their presence felt and found themselves assailed with offers of marriage. Parents, too impressed by the appearance of the young men and too anxious about the prospects of their daughters, failed to make the usual inquiries, and the visitors often came away with the prettiest girls in town. That was the last anyone heard of them. The slick young men were white slave-traders, and when they reached Paris or London, they trans-shipped their young wives to Buenos Aires or Bombay.

Although all Jews within a community tended to be thrown into contact with one another, there was no great mobility of class. Money tended to stick to money and poverty to poverty, unless, as we have mentioned, one had some compensating attainment. Ben Sira, in Ecclesiasticus, describes marriage for money as 'hard labour and a disgrace'. But if a girl was endowed with wealth and not much else, it was not altogether undesirable for her to make use of her sole attraction and, given an able *shadchan*, it was not difficult to convince a young man that she had others.

The *shadchan* had to have a smattering of Jewish learning and more than a smattering of piety in order to get access to good Jewish homes. He generally combined his calling with some religious duty, such as rabbi or cantor of a small synagogue, or *shochet*, but whatever his profession, his bearing tended towards the ecclesiastic, though it often came with the histrionic gifts and ambling gait of a travelling minstrel. He followed the immigrant westwards – a slightly bizarre figure, rarely, even in hot weather, without his black overcoat, Homburg and umbrella in hand. He was not the sort of man one could overlook or forget, but as the newcomers assimilated into their new surroundings, he was elbowed further and further backwards into the realm of lore.

The child of the immigrant scorned the go-between. Romantic love was part of the Western way of life and the youngster adopted it as part of his birth-right. Even where parents felt compelled to challenge this, in the end they usually had to give in. Yet, if the professional *shadchan* became obsolete, the need for *shadchanut* (the art of matchmaking) did not suffer a similar fate, and his function was taken over by amateurs – sisters, cousins, aunts, neighbours – though naturally without his direct approach. The straightforward offer gave way to elaborate conspiracies, and *shadchanut* became, and, to a large extent still is, the principal Jewish pastime.

The dance-hall also dabbled in neo-*shadchanut*. For example, the establishment maintained by Messrs Black and Fleck in Grand Street, New York, in the early decades of this century, was advertised in the Yiddish press as the Automatic Marriage Bureau. 'In our establishment,' they declared, 'you simply pay fifty cents each Saturday night, or twenty-five dollars per year, and you have fine entertainment, meeting people who are eager to meet you and have the same ideas as you have. You pay when you come and you don't have to worry about brokerage fees when you find your mate.' It was a sort of self-service affair that worked fairly successfully, though in the course of their existence, they were sued by one disgruntled patron who had paid his $25 and after a year of attendance had failed to find his mate. These commercial undertakings were run mainly for the benefit of immigrants and eventual-

'Mrs Rosenfield's marriage ceremony according to the Orthodox Hebrew ritual' from a 19th-century American publication called *Frank Leslie's Illustrated Newspaper* (1877)

ly were replaced by charity fund-raising groups who ran their own dances. They do not call themselves the Automatic Marriage Bureau, they make no promises, but their stated function of fund-raising is often secondary to their unstated one of matchmaking. The Jewish resort hotels in the Catskill Mountains of New York or in Bournemouth, England, are also unofficial marriage fairs. The old go there to relax, while the young are eager to prospect.

In many families, marriages are still arranged by the parents – sometimes with the aid of a *shadchan*, sometimes through rabbis pulled in as intermediaries, much as in nineteenth-century Poland. Among the ultra-Orthodox, the *shadchan* was never obsolete, so the novelty in the present situation is that he is making a come-back among the up-to-date, though perhaps not in his traditional guise. He now operates as a 'matrimonial agent', sometimes with the aid of a computer.

The Jewish press in Eastern Europe used to be full of matrimonial advertisements, as were journals catering to immigrant readers in the West. In time, both readers and papers felt that such notices were not particularly respectable, and even if readers were prepared to insert them, some papers refused to take them. The London *Jewish Chronicle*, the oldest and most prestigious British Jewish paper, will now accept advertisements from matrimonial bureaux, but not from individuals, but other papers have fewer qualms in this matter. The Israeli mass-circulation evening paper *Maariv* has almost cornered the market and carries a full page of such advertisements every Friday. One finds them also in the New York *Jewish Press*:

MOTHER introducing son, Bachelor 40, handsome 6 ft, Business executive, looking for intelligent girl, up to 30 years and financially secured. Object matrimony.

Or in more down-to-earth terms:

PLAIN gentleman, 37, 5'10", never married, seeks plain lady, never married for companionship and marriage.

Such notices are by no means confined to Jewish papers. The *New Statesman* of London, which has been in the forefront of liberal English thought for the past half-century, has rarely been free of its weekly quota of spouse-wanted advertisements:

JEWISH, slim, attractive, blonde divorcee, 42. Educated, lively person-ality, enjoys life, wide interests. Wishes to meet financially secure gentle-man 45–55 . . .

MOST YOUTHFUL WIDOW, incredibly late fifty, non-practising Jewish, with house of unique charm, and driverless car, wishes to meet unattached gentleman, 58–64 . . .

COMPUTER DATING. Only connect through Dateline, Britain's best-known, best-conducted computer introduction service . . .

MARRIAGE AND ADVICE BUREAU. Katherine Allen (ex-welfare officer Ministry of Labour, War Office, Foreign Office). Personal introductions . . .

People are more rootless and mobile, and marriages are less permanent, and if people still hope to fall in love the first time round, they are generally ready to invoke the help of a *shadchan* the second or third time.

According to Jewish lore, to be married is the one assured form of bliss, and even if it isn't, to be single is a lasting misfortune to which any conceivable – or at least any permissible – alternative was preferable. The *Shulchan Aruch* states 'It is the duty of every Jewish man to marry a wife in his eighteenth year, but he who anticipates and marries earlier is following the more laudable course, but no one should marry before he is thirteen.' A great many people did, however, and a twelfth-century writer who had lived through a prolonged period of calamity explained why: '. . . persecutions are more frequent every day, and if a man can afford to give his daughter a dowry today, he fears that tomorrow he may not, and his daughter would remain unmarried forever.' Marriage was a form of security in an insecure world. In the seventeenth century, after a series of further calamities in which whole communities were devastated, many Jews saw in their suffering proof that the Coming was nigh, and they rushed their children into marriage in the hope that the Messiah might issue from them.

There is such stress on marriage in Jewish life that Jewish society has never quite adapted itself to the thought that some must of necessity remain single. The thought that a healthy, normal individual would actually opt to remain single was inconceivable, and it was somehow taken for granted that celibacy (if, indeed, the single were celibate) was involuntary. One could just as well speak of a voluntary leper. Celibacy was the ultimate calamity against which every father had to guard his child, and every community its members. But if, after every effort, the worst did happen and a woman remained single, she fell back into the safety of her father's house – as a refuge, not as a duty. The idea that one daughter of the family, usually the youngest, remained single in order to look after her aged parents, common in middle-class English households up to a generation ago, never took root among Jews. Children were expected to help out their parents, but no Jewish child was ever expected to forgo a chance of marriage; if a daughter ended up remaining at home, it was, alas, because she had no alternative.

It was only in this century that Jewish women could think of careers or of simply going out to work, but even if they did they would invariably return to the family hearth in the evening. And if they outlived their parents, they generally moved in with a married brother or sister. It was unthinkable, until our own times, for the single Jewish girl, or even a mature woman from a traditional Jewish home, to live on her own. The maiden aunt, as she became, was the supernumerary home-help – travelling to her married sisters to help out during their pregnancies, coping with this nephew or that niece, on hand at times of sickness or grief. She was not thought of – nor did she think of herself – as having a life of her own. As she grew older, she tended to become eccentric – for was not being single an eccentricity in itself? – the source of some amusement, from time to time an object of concern and pity and a living warning to her young nieces.

Today, the Jewish girl, even from a traditional Jewish home, is more emancipated. She still regards marriage and motherhood as her primary goal and will go to very considerable effort to attain it, but she will not marry for the sake of marriage, and if the right man should not appear she will reconcile herself to being single with equanimity. But her relatives and friends will never entirely abandon their efforts, and she will rarely be invited out for an evening or a meal without being confronted with an elderly widower or divorcee, but she is no longer a floating appendix to the families of her married kin. She may have a career – a factor which in itself makes her more selective and, therefore, more prone to remain single – and she will almost certainly have an income of sorts to enable her to lead a fairly independent existence. But more important, she is no longer singular in her singleness, no longer dependent on her married contemporaries for companionship. She is now part of a large community of the unmarried – single girls, divorcees, widows – from whom she can choose friends and among whom she can find happiness.

But if there is stress on the importance of marriage, there is special stress on marriage to the right person, into the right family and the right circle. Jews of all classes were brought together in

opposite An illuminated *ketubah* from Ancona, Italy (1791)
overleaf A Jewish wedding as portrayed by the Dutch painter Joseph Israels (1828–1911)

the Temple, and in later years in the synagogue, but Jewish society was far from classless. And as a result of the fact that classes could mix freely, considerable care was taken that such mixing did not lead to any permanent relationships. People of good stock were anxious to keep their stock good and married through the agency of a go-between; even where they met on their own and had formed a romantic attachment, a go-between was still brought in for appearances' sake.

'One should marry an estimable woman of respectable family,' urged the *Shulchan Aruch*. And it went on:

> By three traits is Israel known, modesty, compassion and charity and it is improper to form an alliance with one devoid of these. One should not take a wife so immodest in conduct that it lead to her divorce. If she be respectable one may marry her, even if one was drawn to her by her money . . .

Money was in itself often taken as a sign of respectability, but not always. 'Marry your children, O my sons and daughters, as soon as their age is ripe, to members of respectable families,' counselled Eleazar of Mayence, a fourteenth-century Jew, but he cautioned: 'Let no child of mine hunt after money by making a low match for that object, but if the family is undistinguished only on the mother's side, it does not matter, for all Israel counts descent only from the father's side.'

Everyone was concerned for *yichus*, meaning not only connections, but the right connections. What constitutes good stock can vary, and has varied, from age to age. Traditionally it was learning, today it is mainly money – though learning still counts for something in Jewish life. The ideal is the millionaire scholar, and if he should have some claim to pedigree, it is better still. But ancient lineage is not taken very seriously, as most claims to it are made lightly and, if not lightly, are generally spurious. Genealogy has never become a popular pastime among Jews, but many families do claim descent from King David or famous rabbis of old. Among English Jews antiquity means descent from the Spanish and Portuguese grandees who settled in London in the seventeenth century. Among Americans, the German Jews who came after the 1848 revolution were considered the aristocracy. In Israel, they are the pioneers of Ben Gurion's generation who settled in Palestine before the First World War. To an immigrant generation anyone actually born in the country is regarded as an old settler. One man's blueblood was another man's *greener*.

A group of amulets from Persia (16th–18th century) designed to ensure love and luck in marriage

The greater the *yichus* of a family, the more difficult it was for its children to be matched. This is well illustrated in the legend of Nadab and Abihu, the sons of Aaron, who perished in a fire while offering up a sacrifice. According to Rashi, one of the reasons for their tragic death is that they had refused to marry. 'Our father's brother is a king,' they declared, 'our mother's brother is a prince, our father is the High Priest – what woman is worthy of us?' Presumably, there was a paucity of female cousins in their immediate family. If one's family was particularly exalted, one had the choice of either marrying out of one's class or, as often happened, into one's own family. The *yichus* principle thus became a mandate for inbreeding, and one could see it in operation already in the time of Abraham. His directions to his steward Eliezer were '. . . that thou shalt not take a wife unto my son of the daughters of the Canaanites, among whom I dwell. But thou shalt go unto my country, and to my kindred, and take a wife unto my son Isaac' (Genesis 24:3–4). When Esau, Isaac's son, grew to manhood, he married Beeri and Basmath, two local girls 'which was a bitter grief to Isaac and Rebekah' and, as if to make amends, he went on to marry a cousin, Mahalath, daughter of Ishmael. Rebekah was anxious that Jacob should do better and dispatched him to her brother Laban where, after numerous trials, he met, wooed and married his cousins Rachel and Leah.

The *Shulchan Aruch* laid down that it was 'mandatory for one to marry his niece, whether the daughter of his sister or his brother'. Where nieces were not available, it was desirable to marry cousins. 'One of the good methods which I desired for maintaining the family record', wrote Judah Asheri, a fourteenth-century merchant, 'was the marriage of my sons to members of my father's house . . . it is a fair and fit thing to join fruit of vine to fruit of vine.'

This tendency to marry into one's own family continued down the ages, and it meant not merely that one married among one's peers, but it kept wealth flowing within the same limited circle. The exalted Jewish banking clans of France, Britain and Germany who made their names and fortunes in the post-Napoleonic years were great proponents of this practice. They all came to be inter-related, and the nineteenth-century Jewish grandee virtually could not marry within his faith without either marrying into his family or out of his class. Marrying one's kin perpetuated the familiar, the known and the traditional, and excluded the alien. It meant that one reared one's children within the same social framework,

and that one grew old among familiar scenes and familiar faces.

Inbreeding – and here we must introduce yet another untranslatable Yiddish expression – meant an easy relationship with *machatonim*. (*Machuton* [in Scotland it is sometimes pronounced McNaughton] is the male form; *machateniste* is the female form.) *Machatonim* is the plural and refers to *them*, the other side, one's children's in-laws – not merely the immediate family, but the outer periphery of uncles, aunts, and even second-cousins twice-removed. Thus, for example, Bethuel was Abraham's *machuton*, and Laban was Isaac's; and when the Prince of Shechem later sought to marry Jacob's daughter, Dina, his sons found the match unacceptable, partly because they could not see themselves as *machatonim* with the King of Shechem. When families lived in close propinquity and were likely to encounter one another at circumcisions, Bar Mitzvot, weddings, funerals and the thousand other occasions at which families get together, it was useful for the *machatonim* to get on, to speak the same language and find in one another company that was both congenial and respectable. *Machatonim* are, of course, linked to the *yichus* principle. One married not merely a husband or wife but the entire family, and the worth

Nathan Meyer Rothschild, of the famous banking clan, founder of the English branch of the family

of a son-in-law was dependent not only on his personal qualities (in childhood marriages, they were often not yet evident), but on those of his relatives, both living and dead. The latter can be as important, if not more important, than the former, and distinction in a dead relative is often accepted as compensation for deficiencies in a living one (and as the good that men do lives after them, it is usually easier to find distinction in the dead than in the living). *Zechut avot al banim* is a Hebrew expression that may be roughly translated as 'the apple does not fall far from the tree.' This belief in heredity is still largely extant, although the Rabbis were aware of exceptions: Abraham had his Ishmael, Isaac his Esau, Eli his Hophni and Phineas, and David a whole household of delinquents. But they still argued that, as a rule, a man could hope for no better start in life than having a saint as a father or, failing that, as a grandfather – though a sainted mother could also help – and that Israel was the Chosen People and awarded the Promised Land as a result of the merits of Abraham, Isaac and Jacob.

The young Moses Montefiore, a leading member of the Anglo-Jewish 'aristocracy' and the first to break the taboo against marrying into an Ashkenazi family when he wed Judith Cohen

The *yichus* principle is sometimes stretched a bit far, and if even dead relatives cannot be of aid, distant ones are sometimes evoked – like cousins, uncles, aunts; the apple may not fall far from the tree, but it can also be made to fall sideways. And when there is no *yichus*, even in the outer family, there is one final resort – *lantsleit*, one's countrymen. In Eastern Europe, Polish Jews looked down upon their Galician brethren, Russian Jews upon Polish Jews, and Lithuanian Jews upon everyone else. German Jews, for their part, regarded the whole of East European Jewry as *die Ostjuden*, only partly civilized. In Israel, Yemenites look down upon Moroccans, Moroccans upon Yeminites and Iraqis look down on both; Sabras (Israel-born Jews) look down on newcomers, Ashkenazim upon Sephardim, and Anglo-Saxons – a loose term including English, American and South African Jews, most of whom are of European origin – tend, without necessarily inferring that anyone is inferior, to regard themselves as decidedly superior. One will always find *yichus* somewhere, for underlying the whole *yichus* principle is the tendency to make a virtue out of what one is, or failing that, out of what one was.

All this can affect one's attitude to a prospective partner. No *Litvak* (as the Lithuanian Jews are called) will today tear his hair if his daughter marries a Moroccan, but he would much prefer someone nearer home, even a *Galitzyaner* (a Galician Jew). In eighteenth-century England, the Elders of the Sephardic community imposed painful sanctions against those of its members who married one of the despised Tudescos (as the Ashkenazi Jews were known). The barrier was not lifted until 1812, when Moses (later Sir Moses) Montefiore married Judith Cohen, the daughter of a wealthy Ashkenazi merchant who was also the father-in-law of Nathan Mayer Rothschild.

The very rich and the very poor have always been above – or below – such barriers. With the poor it was a slight matter, but the rich tended to establish precedents that others followed. Thus there was great consternation in the Anglo-Jewish community, for example, when Emma Rothschild married Lord Rosebery in 1877. Rosebery was noble, exalted, rich, handsome, distinguished, a rising politician who was soon to become Prime Minister, but, alas, he was not Jewish, and the feeling of anguish and dismay was well voiced by the *Jewish Chronicle*:

> If the flame seized on the cedars, how will fare the hysop on the wall? If the leviathan is brought up on a hook, how will the minnows escape? . . . was there amongst the millions of brethren in faith all over Europe no one of sufficient talent, sufficiently cultured, sufficiently high-minded to be deemed worthy to be received into the family circle, that this honour must be bestowed upon one who must necessarily estrange the partner from her people? A sad example has been set which, we pray God, may not be productive of dreadful consequences.

Lady Rosebery (Emma Rothschild), who left the Anglo-Jewish community undone when she married Lord Rosebery, a future Prime Minister but, alas, not a Jew

It may seem, from the foregoing, that the idea of romantic attachments rarely entered into a partnership. 'He may not be much, Mother, but I love him' was not the sort of recommendation a daughter could bring to a parent. One often reads in the Bible how this or that man loved this or that woman, but one rarely discovers how the woman felt. Her feelings were possibly beside the point, for Jewish women were thought to be almost immune to passion or, if not immune, they kept themselves under close control. Courtship was an entirely male prerogative. Eve, says the Talmud, was moulded from a part of Adam and, as a result, Adam has eternally gone in search of his mate. 'That the woman should display pre-nuptial love,' wrote Israel Abrahams, a celebrated Anglo-Jewish scholar, 'was repulsive to the Jewish conception of womanliness.' 'The outstanding feature in the attitude of members of society towards arranging a match', Professor Jacob Katz, a modern historian, has written, 'was the cold, calculated approach with which they weighed the pros and cons. Personal compatibility, not to speak of romantic attachment, was not taken into account at all.'

This did not mean that a man could marry off his daughter

against her will. The Talmud is fairly explicit on this: 'A man must not betroth a daughter while she is still a minor; he must wait till she attains her majority and says, "I love this man."' Nor could a son be forced to marry against his will, or even without his definite assent. Bride and groom, however, often caught their first sight of each other only under the *chupah* when, before the marriage was officially solemnized, the bride's veil was formally raised to allow the groom a close look. At this stage, both parties, in keeping with Talmudic dicta, were still free to change their minds – but there is no known instance of anyone having done so. In any case, young men and young maidens were kept so carefully segregated that few of them had any clear idea of what to expect in a prospective partner.

If the idea of pre-nuptial love in women was repugnant to Jewish tradition, it was not entirely welcome in men. If one searches among the biblical commentaries, one can see that they were not entirely dismissive of romantic love – Jacob's affection for Rachel has always been held up as a model of everything that true love encompasses: selflessness, devotion, reverence and, of course, patience – but no

'The Youngest Married Off' by the American painter Saul Raskin (1886–1966)

one felt that love was something that should be allowed to affect the choice of a husband or wife. Love came later, if at all. When the Talmud said that a daughter could not be forced to marry against her will, it was understood to mean that she could not be compelled to marry a man she hated. Love was regarded as a bonus, and not expected as a right. One Rabbi, the sagacious Rav Chiyah, urged that one should not expect too much out of marriage or a wife. 'It is enough if they give us children,' he said. Judaism was by no means unique in this for, until relatively recent times, romantic love was regarded as the stuff of poetry and drama rather than of real life.

Despite it all, most of these marriages lasted. Jewish divorce laws are liberal and simple, but there is no evidence that in those times divorces were common. The reason for this may have been a result of a combination of factors: Jewish divorce law may be simple, but Jewish tradition abhors it; Jewish parents will suffer any agonies rather than jeopardize the happiness and welfare of their children; people had a higher pain threshold and were prepared to suffer a degree of unhappiness which today would have been found intolerable; and, in the main, it seems fairly clear that Jewish marriages lasted because they were happy. All this in spite of the fact that marriages were arranged between the parents with, or without, the help of an intermediary, and in spite of the fact that the couple may have met for only one or two heavily chaperoned occasions prior to their marriage, and sometimes not even that.

The whole basis of Jewish family life as it has evolved since post-biblical times presumes monogamy and fidelity. The Jewish husband is faithful to the point of being uxorious. If he is more abstemious than those around him, it is because he is less relaxed; the Jew has always been aware of the hostile attention of his neighbours, and Jewish puritanism is, in part, a product of Jewish exile. One can see this puritanism well displayed in the laws and customs surrounding the betrothal.

Today a betrothal is thought of merely as an engagement, an informal understanding that a couple are bespoken to each other with a view to matrimony and are no longer accessible to third parties. The purpose of the traditional Jewish betrothal was basically the same – a means of reserving one's prospective mate – but it was almost as binding as a marriage and could not be broken without severe penalty. The Rabbis regarded it as a necessary preliminary to marriage and argued that anyone who sought the latter without the former should be flogged. In the Middle Ages it became customary to accompany a betrothal with *tenaim* ('conditions'), a written contract between the parents on such details as the size of the dowry, the date and place of the marriage, and the penalty for any breach of promise. It did not, however, mean that the parties, once committed to one another, could enjoy any form of intimacy. A betrothal, in fact, meant the worst of both worlds: one had neither the liberty of being single, nor the pleasures of marriage. The betrothed woman was at a greater disadvantage: she was liable to all the pains and penalties to which her married sister was subject, without any of the privileges. Even her fiancé could not come near her, as is made clear in the following contract drawn up in the Middle Ages:

I, Aaron ben Ephraim, solemnly agree, on my oath, that from this day forward it is forbidden for me to go to the residence of my intended. I will not go there at any time, whether by day or by night, until my wedding. If I infringe this undertaking, I am to be adjudged as one who breaks his oath and I shall become liable to every penalty, fine, censure and contempt.

The strain of a long betrothal, the impossible demands imposed on the young couple, the frustration of pent-up yearning, led to a narrowing of the gap between the betrothal and the wedding, until eventually they were held on the same day. The former was celebrated in the morning and the latter in the afternoon, each with due ceremony and a festive meal comparable to a banquet. Two banquets in one day proved to be too much both for the pocket of the host and the stomachs of his guests and, in time, betrothal and marriage merged into one. Today the *erusin* ('betrothal' in Hebrew) is part of the marriage ceremony proper.

But there was still an eagerness to announce and to celebrate the fact that one's daughter or son was bespoke for marriage, hence the modern engagement. This is an entirely social affair, devoid of any religious significance and celebrated without the benefit of clergy. It is usually preceded by an announcement in the local paper (such announcements are the mainstay of the Jewish press) and is the occasion on which the young lady displays her prospective husband and her engagement ring to relatives and friends.

The engagement ring, unlike the wedding ring, has no religious or legal significance, though it usually costs a great deal more and has a curious history. Engagement rings were initially worn by men rather than women and were generally a gift from the father of the bride. The bride received her ring as a gift from the groom only on the morning of the wedding. Some of the rings had elaborate artefacts, crowns, turrets, lion-heads and even weather-vanes; some had huge stones, or small golden replicas of the Temple; some were large enough to serve as bouquet holders – and possibly were intended as such. Nearly all were too cumbersome to be worn. In Italy (where both men and women received engagement rings) there were times when the ring fashion ran away with itself, and in the fifteenth century, the Jewish community issued a by-law declaring that 'no man shall bear more than one gold ring, which he may place on any finger of either hand. No woman may put on more than two rings on the same occasion, or at the most she may wear three rings.'

An 18th-century silver and enamel ring from North Africa used in the wedding ceremony, but not worn thereafter as a wedding ring is today

Today the value of the ring (and the size of the stone) are sometimes regarded as the measure of the young man's fervour (or his father's worth), and it sometimes happens that the intentions of a young man who approaches his fiancée with too small a stone are regarded as less than honourable. Worse, it suggests that he may not be able to keep his wife in the manner to which she feels she should become accustomed. There has been a tendency in some Jewish circles to 'outstone' one another, with the result that a reaction may have set in. Many young people are dispensing with at least the ring, if not the engagement, altogether.

There has also been a growing decline in the importance attached to the fact that a girl has been engaged. Rav Elijah of Wilno argued that, rather than break an engagement, a man should marry his fiancée and then divorce her. It was apparently less of a stigma to be an ex-wife than an ex-fiancée. In some Jewish circles a broken engagement rendered a girl almost unmarriageable and she had to be dispatched to a grandmother or an aunt to hide her grief and shame. Today, in most Western countries, a girl can get engaged two, three, or even four times without the slightest reproach, though she may feel the need for a change of scene between each break: a girl from the provinces will generally go to the big city, and girls from the big city go abroad.

The English-style engagement, the idea of being bespoken, did give a couple the opportunity to get to know each other. It was a golden, sunny time of mutual discovery without the pains and embarrassments of a honeymoon. Today, in most Jewish circles, young people require nothing as formal as an engagement to get to know one another, but their respective families still need an opportunity to become acquainted and, if young couples no longer need engagements, the *machatonim* certainly do!

6 The Wedding

Now for that great moment anticipated at every milestone in a child's life. As early as the *brit*, a Jewish boy receives his first intimation of what he may expect when the assembled relatives declare: 'Even as this child has entered into the Covenant, so may he enter into the Law, the nuptial canopy and into good deeds.' The child is hardly out of the womb and they are yearning to see him married!

And there he stands – as if in fulfilment of everyone's wishes – under the *chupah*. In Britain, he appears, Ascot-style, in grey top hat and morning coat, pacing impatiently up and down, as if waiting for the race to begin. His father and best man, both in similar attire, are by his side, as the ushers, likewise in Ascot dress and clutching white gloves in their sweating palms, busily direct the guests to their seats.

The *chupah* was originally the bridal chamber in which the groom, in princely attire, awaited his bride, and to which the bride was led in solemn procession for the consummation of the marriage. Today it consists of an ornate canopy atop four poles; if the bride's family's finances run to it (and even if they don't!), it is garlanded with flowers, roses, carnations and perhaps even orchids. Flowers also bedeck the approaches to the *chupah*, the ladies' gallery and the surroundings of the ark, and the whole synagogue is a little like the Garden of Eden. There is a certain symbolism in this, for many rabbis have described marriage as an admission to paradise.

Outside there is much tooting of horns and frantic gesticulations as late-comers seek the parking place which isn't there, and unsuspecting travellers trapped by the crush of oncoming traffic try to get out to the main road.

Within the synagogue most of the guests are already seated, and there is an expectant murmur as they await the bride. A young

A member of the Inbal Dance Theatre in costume for her performance in a Yemenite Jewish wedding. Note the myrtle in her hands as prescribed in Yemenite custom

cousin or two, wearied by the wait, begin crying. Under the *chupah* the groom stops pacing and chats uneasily with the best man. The usual jokes are exchanged: 'She's had cold feet . . . She's run off with the postman.' The rabbi holds the *ketubah*, the marriage document, like a college diploma and taps it impatiently against his palm. The *chazan* has his tuning fork to his ear and eyes on the door. The organist and choir in the loft wait for the signal to begin. Suddenly she appears. All heads crane forward. *Chazan*, organ and choir strike up together. The tune is traditional and may vary from place to place, but the words are ancient:

> Blessed be the bride that cometh in the name of the Lord: we bless you out of the house of the Lord.
> O come, let us worship and bow down; let us kneel before the Lord, our Maker.
> Serve the Lord with joy, come before Him with exulting.

The bridal party advances slowly, like a flow of lava: the bride in white, on the arm of her father, her face flickering with mixed feelings – pride, apprehension, joy, bewilderment. Behind her, an array of bridesmaids in pink or yellow organza hold the bridal train – sometimes tripping over it – and behind them a maid of honour, also in organza, keeps them all in line, like a mother hen with her chicks. Then the two mothers, the *machatenistes*, appear. Whatever may follow thereafter, now they are as one, in step shoulder to shoulder, sending up a glow of pride and joy, of sheer *naches*, which almost illuminates their passage. And somewhere in the procession are the grandmothers, with mink wraps over their ample shoulders, made uncommonly erect by their moment of joy, smiling one minute, weeping the next.

The bride is now under the *chupah* with the officiating clergy and the principal relatives – a mass of top hats and tulle. The *chupah* is not a spacious contrivance, but somehow everyone finds room beneath it. The *chazan* continues: 'He who is mighty, blessed and great above all things, may He bless the bridegroom and bride.' He then steps back and the rabbi steps forward to address the young couple. There is no set form to his address, no 'Dearly beloved, we are gathered here . . .' It is a sermon that dwells briefly – or at length (usually at length, for few rabbis can resist the temptation of a large congregation) – on the joys and obligations of matrimony and the meaning of a Jewish home. Somewhere in the course of his address he will evoke the example of the bride's and the bridegroom's parents (it has to be both sets of parents or none); where they are not too exemplary, he may evoke the grandparents; and failing that he may hark back to Abraham, Isaac and Jacob, the purpose being to instil an appreciation of one's inheritance. Just as no bride is ever ugly on her wedding day, no wedding sermon is every quite banal, for the congregation, to say nothing of the bride and groom, are under the influence of the very solemnity of the occasion and tend to be especially receptive to homilies. A good sermon under the *chupah* can reverberate for the rest of the couple's married life and actually affect their conduct. After the rabbi has had his say, the ceremony moves on to the sanctification, which sounds better in Hebrew than in English, and is better sung than read:

Blessed art Thou, O Lord our God, King of the universe, who hast sanctified us by Thy commandments, and hast commanded us concerning forbidden marriages; who hast disallowed us to those who are betrothed, but hast sanctified unto us such as are wedded to us by the rite of the canopy and the sacred covenant of wedlock. Blessed art Thou, O Lord, who sanctifiest Thy people Israel by the rite of the canopy and the sacred covenant of wedlock.

And then to the high point of the ceremony, the act that binds bride to groom. He places the ring, handed to him by his best man, on the forefinger of the bride's right hand and declares in a loud voice, so that the entire gathering can, if need be, act as witness: 'Behold thou art consecrated to me by this ring, according to the Law of Moses and Israel.'

The rabbi then unfurls the *ketubah* and begins to read. *Ketubah* literally means a written document. It originated among the Jewish exiles in Babylon and is still handwritten on parchment (a generally fine example of calligraphic art) in Aramaic, the lingua franca of that country. It was designed principally for the protection of the wife and transcribes in basic terms the basic settlement to which she is entitled from her husband, plus any special provision on which they have agreed between them. The husband pledges:

I shall work for thee, honour, support and maintain thee in accordance with the custom of Jewish husbands who work for their wives and honour, support and maintain them in sincerity.

In effect, the *ketubah* was a protection against the powers of arbitrary divorce possessed by the husband. These powers have since been whittled down, but the *ketubah* is still necessary as the Rabbis regard a marriage without it as concubinage. If it is burned or lost, the husband must provide a new one, otherwise he cannot –

The reading of the *ketubah*
during the wedding
ceremony

or at least should not – live with his wife. In American Conservative congregations (which stand to the left of Orthodox synagogues but to the right of Reform ones) bride and groom empower the *Beth Din* to dissolve the marriage in the event of a civil divorce, and their agreement is contained in the *ketubah*. Reform synagogues have dispensed with the traditional *ketubah* altogether.

After the *ketubah* is read both in Aramaic and English, there follow the *sheva brachot*, seven benedictions, which are treated as a virtuoso piece by the *chazan*. The last of the seven is fairly lengthy and the language bursts with exultation:

Blessed art Thou, O Lord our God, King of the universe, who hast created joy and gladness, bridegroom and bride, mirth and exultation, pleasure and delight, love, brotherhood, peace and fellowship. Soon, O Lord, our God, may there be heard in the cities of Judah and in the streets of Jerusalem, the voice of joy and gladness, the voice of the bridegroom

and the voice of the bride, the jubilant voice of bridegrooms from their canopies, and youths from their feasts of song. Blessed art Thou O Lord, who makest the bridegroom rejoice with the bride.

Then, with the voice of the *chazan* still ringing in their ears, the beadle steps forward and places a glass at the foot of the bridegroom, which the latter promptly shatters with his heel, to loud cries of *mazel tov*! – good luck! – from the assembled congregation. The ceremony is over. Bride and groom leave the synagogue as man and wife.

The cracking of the glass is related to the second part of the final blessing – the remembrance of Jerusalem. Even in moments of jubilation the Jew has to be mindful of the destruction of the Temple and the fall of Jerusalem. Jerusalem has been recovered, but the Temple is still not rebuilt, and the symbolic remembrance endures –

A Chassidic groom, outfitted in his *kittle*, being taken to the *chupah* on the arms of his *unterfuehrers*, a custom that hearkens back to Polish-Jewish tradition and would endure even if the Temple were rebuilt, for Judaism abounds in ceremonies which have outlived their original purpose. Not everyone at the wedding is mindful of the symbolism, and the common joke is that the cracking of the glass represents the last time the groom will put his foot down!

All of which would be typical of a middle-class Jewish wedding in England. (There is no such thing as a working-class Jewish wedding in the English-speaking world. Everyone becomes middle class, if only for a day.) The details of the ceremony vary from place to place and have varied through time, but the essentials remain the same. The most important part – the formula 'Behold thou art consecrated to me with this ring . . .' – uttered even without the benefit of clergy, in the presence of competent witnesses, is sufficient to bind the couple, and they would require a divorce should they wish to separate.

Among the ultra-Orthodox, the bride is not led to the *chupah* by her father, as it is felt that paternity is never a matter of absolute certainty, but by the mother. Among them, too, the groom will wear a special garment, a *kittle*, presented to him by his bride at the time of their engagement. It is white in colour and generally made of linen or cotton, and he will wear it in the synagogue on Yom Kippur (the Day of Atonement), as well as at the time of his interment, for the *kittle*, though often prettily finished with flutings and lace, is a shroud. It is also customary at such weddings for the bride to circle the groom seven times (sometimes with a candle in hand). If the groom is robust it can be quite a walk, and wags have been known to suggest that she use a bicycle. The custom, which dates back to the Middle Ages, was intended to exorcise evil spirits, and lately it is done even at fashionable weddings.

Among the ultra-Orthodox, the festivities do not stop with the wedding feast, but continue for a full week (unless the bride is a widow or divorcee, in which case they last three days) with a festive meal, usually provided by relatives or friends of the couple, at a different house every night. This custom is known as *sheva brachot*, from the seven benedictions sung at the wedding and repeated at each of the festive meals. Where bride and groom become intimately acquainted only after the wedding, the continuing celebrations and the constant gatherings of relatives and friends may ease the embarrassment they may find in each other's company in the first days after their wedding. The week also provides a period of grace between the excitement of the wedding and the rigours of the honeymoon.

'Les Amoureux' by Marc Chagall
overleaf 'The Wedding' by the French artist Mané-Katz (1894–1962)

וכב הנמצא יהבו לחם נשיס מתפט ומבטל תומת זו
נשיאל רבי יהוד מדעשנא לרבי יוסף למה רובני על ההדם ים
והשריעי רובך גלהחם סו
שוטה שלם וישלי ומבלת

אהה יי אהינו מלך הי
העריוה ראסר לגו א
ידי חובה וקהגשין ב
חובה וקהגי
וילו ה
הרי אב ביקוד
ומיחרן שעערי
וחב הורן ה
הכת

נשכות קועה של מאות-
ועליה מנמך וחפנרן
קלהינודלעת ה החוחר
ימך עיהברי ומוך לתו
תוות המחעד יפלה הת וסאות

In biblical times bride and groom wore special attire and both were crowned, usually with garlands of myrtle. The bride remained veiled until after the ceremony, and the ornaments about her were so many and ostentatious as to become proverbial: 'And Zion will adorn herself with her newly returned children as a bride with her ornaments' (Isaiah 61 : 10). The nuptials were generally held under an open sky, as they are today among the ultra-Orthodox even in the midst of an English or North American winter.

In Talmudic times, the bride required a year to prepare her trousseau for her wedding (today some girls take even longer) and the celebrations began on the Sabbath before the wedding with a great feast in her father's house. On the day of the ceremony she was carried in a litter to the *chupah* – which was an elaborate pavilion usually draped in white with gold and purple crowning – where the groom, in attire as colourful as the *chupah* itself, awaited her. Before her went drummers announcing her progress; behind her, a long line of relatives who stopped short in front of the *chupah*. In the Middle Ages, the nuptials were gradually transferred from the courtyard and the home to the synagogue. Clans had become larger, as did the number of those who felt entitled to a place at the wedding, and by this stage, the bridal pavilion had given way to the *chupah* we know today. The idea of leading a bride to the groom and waiting by his tent until the marriage was consummated was considered indelicate by European Jews. In ancient times, moreover, the march to the groom's tent symbolized the transfer of the bride to the groom's family; by the fourteenth or fifteenth century, it was the groom who often joined the bride's household.

In Poland, which from about the fourteenth century until the Holocaust remained the principal centre of Jewish life, weddings assumed an extravagance that was a source of concern to the Rabbis, but that they were helpless to suppress, partly because, as with the Bar Mitzvah, they themselves were amongst the worst offenders. The celebrations began well before the wedding and continued for some time after, so that the actual ceremony itself was almost lost in the midst of them. *Klei zemer* (musical instruments or *klesmer*, as they were called in Yiddish) insinuated themselves into the proceedings – fife and drum, fiddle and cymbal – along with the *badchan*, or professional jester. An intimate family occasion developed into an extended spectacle that would throw a whole community out of gear for a week and beggar the father of the bride for life.

The proceedings began on the Sabbath before the wedding,

A portrayal of a betrothal from the 15th-century Rothschild Miscellany

when the groom was called up to the Reading of the Law. His approach was announced by the *chazan* in an especially sonorous voice, and as he ascended to say the customary blessings, he was showered with raisins and almonds by the ladies in the gallery, and the waiting children indulged in a wild scramble to fill their pockets. There followed a reception in the groom's house at which he treated relatives, friends and virtually the entire community to cakes, herring, wine and schnaps. About the only person absent was the bride herself. It was considered both improper and unlucky for the bride to see her groom so soon before the wedding. (During this period, too, friends were required to keep the groom company, for at such a time he was not thought to be quite himself, and it was feared that he might come to mischief if left alone.)

The bride and groom each appointed a married couple as *unterfuehrers* (guides) who would lead them to their respective places under the *chupah*. They were generally chosen from amongst close relatives and friends and had to be reasonably solvent, for they were expected to pay for the honour with lavish presents and generous tips to the *klesmer*, *badchan* and cook. It was the *klesmer* and *badchan* who began the day by going from house to house with fiddle and fife to summon the guests, who followed them to the synagogue like children behind the Pied Piper. Bride and groom, plus *unterfuehrers*, appeared somewhat later in separate coaches with bells on the harness and garlands in the horses' manes, while children and onlookers cheered them on their way. The bride was first to arrive, in a white veil extending almost to the floor, and was ceremoniously seated on an ornate chair covered with white sheets and decorated with flowers. This ceremony of *bazetzen di kalle* ('enthroning the bride') was accompanied by lachrymose music from the *klesmer*, who drew rivers of tears from the bride and her attendant womenfolk. The *klesmer* and *badchan* then called on the groom to invite him to *badeken di kalle* ('cover the bride'). As he arrived, he was received by the rabbi, and each took a corner of a silk kerchief, provided by the two mothers, and placed it delicately over the bride's face. There then followed a *mitzva tantzel* (sacred dance) performed by the bride and her attendants in one room, and the groom and his attendants in another. It did not continue for long, for the wedding day was treated as a sort of joyous Day of Atonement by ultra-Orthodox couples, and both bride and groom did not eat until they became man and wife.

Finally came the ceremony itself. The groom – preceded by the ubiquitous *klesmer*, who buzzed here, there and everywhere like manic hornets, and led by his *unterfuehrers*, each firmly holding an arm, as if he might attempt to escape – approached the *chupah*. The music was so solemn that he indeed might have felt he was being led to the scaffold. As he waited for his bride in the synagogue courtyard he was sometimes pelted with snowballs by boys in the crowd, and he had to duck as best he could, until the bride – also preceded by *klesmer* and steered by her own *unterfuehrers* – appeared. From then on the proceedings substantially followed the familiar pattern of today.

In some Polish communities it was customary for the bride and groom to attempt to stamp on each other's foot at the close of the ceremony to see who would dominate whom. The bride, though hampered by the length of her dress, tended to be rather more fleet of foot. In Persia, wheat and nuts were scattered in the path of the bridal pair; in Turkey a cock and hen were let loose before them; in Morocco they were served with lavish portions of fish – all fertility symbols. In other oriental communities, the couple jumped back and forth over a bowl of live fish – again for the same reason. 'May you be as fertile as a fish' was a common blessing.

At weddings, as at other ancient ceremonies, there was always the fear that evil spirits might spoil the day, and the people went to great lengths to confound them: among Yemenite Jews the bride had her hands painted with henna on the eve of her wedding and, for good measure, was fed seven times in the course of the

A Yemenite bride having her hands painted with henna

twenty-four hours; in Afghanistan, a private wedding ceremony was held on the night before the announced day; in Kurdistan, the officiating rabbi cautioned guests against casting spells. In some places it was thought that evil spirits were vulnerable to the sound of cutting, and a relative would sometimes be stationed in the synagogue to cut paper or cloth for the duration of the wedding ceremony. The fear of evil spirits was also one of the reasons why Jewish weddings grew to be of such inordinate size: there was no telling if some wicked person, left out of the festivities, might not cast an evil spell on the bride and groom.

In modern Israel, weddings have assumed a more simplified form. All the traditional rites are followed, and they are conducted with due solemnity, but there is less pomp, less extravagance in dress, no sermon, and the festivities are generally less protracted.

Within a family, the wedding is one of the three great periods of assembly, the others, of course, being the Bar Mitzvah and funeral. It can be either a reconciliation feast for those members of the family who have quarrelled on earlier occasions, or it can be the source of new quarrels. It is very easy to slight a relative: an invitation sent out too late, a minor role in the proceedings (or none at all), a place at the table too remote from the top or among insignificant guests, can lead to a form of displeasure peculiar to Jewish families. This is known as *broiges*, a combination of pique, high dudgeon, low dudgeon, *amour-propre* and simmering wrath, and given the Jewish memory for slights, it can be kept going through three generations – though usually it need not last much more than twenty or twenty-five years. There is, as a rule, no reconciliation till death, not necessarily of the principals, but of someone held in common affection.

In some Jewish families there is a practice known as 'Joy Sunday', the Sunday before the wedding, at which time the bride and her family are at home to visiting relatives and friends who come to view the wedding presents. It is uncertain whether the joy refers to the prospect of the presents or the wedding. The practice of sending presents possibly dates from the venerable tradition of *hachnassat kallah*, when neighbours and friends tried to help the young couple set up home. Today the presents tend to be in inverse proportion to the needs of the couple; to him that hath much is much given. There are certain types of gifts which have an immediate appeal to the imagination and purses of guests – table-knives, table-mats, bottle-openers, cake trowels, carving-knives, sugar-tongs. A bride receives scores of these, and she may spend the first year of her married life exchanging them at the shops, or the next ten years passing them on as wedding presents to others. Nowadays many brides have wedding lists in one or another of the big department stores and thus can avoid duplication, but the richer the bride the more expensive the store and the higher the level of expectations.

The scale of the celebrations does not always bear a strict relationship to the means of the parents. Men of great wealth are able to get away with modest affairs; men of lesser wealth – lest word should spread that their wealth is even less than it is – are compelled to offer something more elaborate. But large weddings are often necessitated by the very size of one's family, the anxiety to reciprocate all previous invitations and by the desire to avoid making enemies for life by overlooking someone who felt he and his wife (and possibly their children) had a right to be invited. This is a necessarily thankless task, for one's rights in the matter depend not on one's relationship to the celebrants, but on who else has, or has not, been invited, and the greater the number of guests the greater the circumference of displeasure. 'Make a feast,' goes an old saying, 'and make enemies; have a funeral, and make friends.'

The lavish fare at some Jewish weddings is in some ways affected by the great exertions made by some guests to be present. One cannot fob off a relative who has travelled 3,000 – or even 30 – miles with a cup of tea and a bun. And again, like at the Bar Mitzvah, there is a deep spirit of gladness and thanksgiving and an eagerness to share it with one's friends. The character and scale of some Jewish Bar Mitzvot, engagements and weddings are not always easy to defend, but at the bottom of it all lies a tradition of hospitality that

below The entire 'extended family' joins the celebrations after the wedding ceremony on a kibbutz *overleaf* A Jewish wedding feast in Eastern Europe as portrayed by the Polish artist Leopold Pilichowski (1869–1933)

goes back to Abraham and that makes it possible to forgive the extravagance, the ostentation and even the vulgarity which often surrounds them.

A seven-course banquet is usual at Jewish weddings. They are often preceded by a reception, which is a meal in itself, and are sometimes followed by a buffet and a ball. The inner circle of guests is invited to all three, the outer circle to the first or the last. Again, it is easy to make enemies by confining to the outer circle guests who felt entitled to a place in the inner one. It is one of the recognized hazards of giving away a daughter in marriage.

Another is the speeches. Whenever three or four Jews gather to celebrate almost anything, someone always feels called upon (one doesn't know by whom) to say a few words; *a por* (few) in Yiddish means many. As a rule, the more Orthodox the company, the longer and more numerous the speeches. At ultra-Orthodox weddings the speeches generally take the form of learned discourses and moral exhortations; at less Orthodox weddings the rabbi or a learned guest might feel moved to offer a learned discourse, but there is more often an attempt at humour, which does not always come off. In the main, however, the speeches take the form of flattery and praise: the bride will be described as beautiful, the groom as brilliant, the fathers as men of standing and public benefactors, the mothers as women of valour and 'true mothers in Israel'), the grandparents as builders of the community (if living) or as saints (if dead). There will be much stress on pedigree, on *yichus*, and no one is so ill-endowed as to be devoid of a grace that cannot be enlarged. Speakers sometimes get carried away by their own eloquence – so much so that they sometimes leave their audience far behind – but as a rule the sublime qualities ascribed to the celebrants are sincerely meant. Weddings bring out the most generous feelings in everyone – or at least in the speakers, if not always in their listeners – and there is a tradition, which goes back to Hillel, that one speaks nothing but good of the newly-wed. One could, he said, call a bride beautiful even if she was ugly – to which he added, all brides are beautiful.

Every Jew who has had a traditional Jewish upbringing undergoes a baptism of words and takes speeches for granted, as an integral part of any festive occasion – if not as a pleasure, then at least as a tolerable ache to which one becomes hardened in the course of time. But Christians, who increasingly find themselves at Jewish affairs, sit through the speeches with looks of glazed stupefaction, wondering whether it is normal for Jews to mortify themselves

This 19th-century *ketubah* from Meshed, Persia, written in Persian in a local mosque, was for public consumption only. The couple's true *ketubah* was written in Hebrew at home

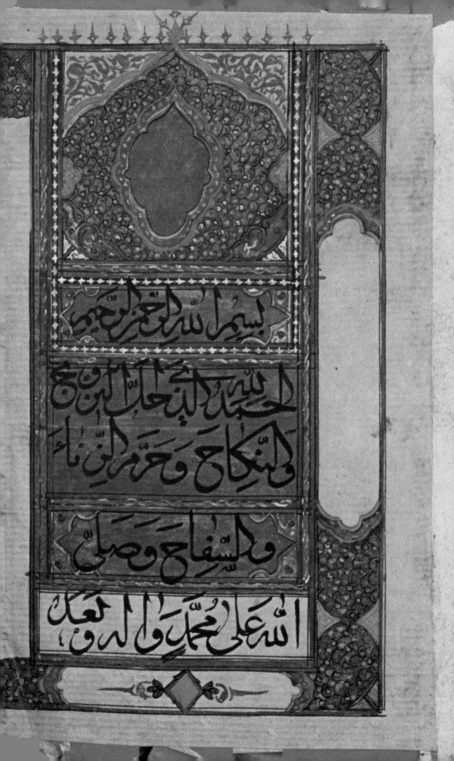

بسم الله الرحمن الرحيم

الحمد لله الذي جعل النكاح وحرم الزنا

والسفاح وصلى الله على محمد وآله وعلى

in this way even in the course of a celebration. And the ample fare placed before them is not always sufficient compensation for what they have to endure. The speeches, in fact, answer a common feeling among Jews that a meal is only a meal, but that an appropriate word or two raises it to the level of an occasion. Simeon, a contemporary of Hillel, said that when three men sat at a table without a word of learning between them, it was as if they had eaten of the entrails of the dead. The word elevates; not every word uttered at Jewish weddings has this effect, but it is basically an attempt to grace the gross.

The Jew, moreover, has an almost Irish love of words, though – especially at happy occasions like a wedding – people are perhaps more readily moved to speak than to listen, and the speeches one hears are more often the product of an overflowing heart than an acute mind. But sincere feelings, even if clumsily put, have an eloquence of their own. Speeches do add something to a wedding, and in some Jewish circles it is felt that a marriage could not be properly consummated without them.

To the parents, the marriage represents the happiest hour of their lives, the occasion to which they looked forward for many years. *Ich zol em nor zehn unter di chupah* ('I should only live to see him under the *chupah*') was the traditional wish of the Jewish mother – and it still is. In earlier years it was a question of mere physical survival. Infant mortality, especially among boys, was high, and the average life expectancy was short; no one took it for granted that the child would survive to maturity or that his parents would survive to see him mature. With a daughter there was an added worry: whether she would find a husband at all! And her father began saving for her dowry almost from the day she was born. When the Yiddish author, Sholem Aleichem, wanted to depict a sort of cheerful Job – buoyant, irrepressible and indestructible in the face of calamity – he created Tevye the Milkman and gave him five daughters.

If a father can make the blessing *baruch shepatrani*, 'Blessed be He who hath freed me from the responsibility for this child' on the Bar Mitzvah of his son, he has to wait for the wedding till he is free of responsibility for his daughter. There used to be a popular Yiddish song with the refrain: *Nor yitster ken mir leben/Di muzinke is oisgegebn* – 'Now we may start to live, our youngest one is spent.' But by the time she was, her parents too were almost spent. And if not, they were overtaken with a new yearning – to see their grandchildren under the *chupah*!

top Bridal belts from Holland and Germany 17–18th century), part of the traditional wedding costume in these two countries
bottom A bridal box of silver-engraved niello from Farrara, Italy (15th century). The engravings portray the duties of a Jewish wife

7 Daughters of Israel

'A man', says the Talmud, 'should look on the birth of a daughter as a blessing from the Lord.' There is almost a tone of admonition in these words, as if many men did not share this view and, as we have seen, the birth of a daughter is not attended with any of the ceremonies or feasting that greets the birth of a son. Little girls creep unnoticed into this world, and many Rabbis would prefer that they remain unnoticed – but then again it depends on which Rabbi one quotes. For almost every misogynist there is a philogynist, but the balance of accepted opinion has been largely negative.

Take, for example, a Rabbinic legend concerning the birth of Eve:

God said: I will not create her from the head, that she should not hold up her head too proudly; nor from the eye that she should not be a coquette; nor from the ear, that she should not be an eavesdropper; nor from the mouth that she should not be too talkative; nor from the heart that she should not be too jealous; nor from the hand, lest she be too acquisitive; nor from the foot, lest she be a gadabout; but from a hidden part of the body, that she be modest.

But women are frivolous, said one Talmudic sage; to teach them the Torah, said another, is to teach them lasciviousness; 'Ten measures of speech were given the world,' said a third, 'and women took nine'; 'The more women,' said a fourth, 'the more witchcraft.' Yet another Rabbi warned: 'He who gossips much with women brings evil upon himself and will inherit a place in Hell.'

One hears of the occasional woman, like Bruriah, wife of Rabbi Meir, one of the foremost Talmudic sages, who was a great scholar in her own right and went so far as to give opinions on law. One hears of Bruriah so often, and so rarely of anyone else, that clearly she was regarded as a woman in a million, the exception who

A sixth-century bowl from Iraq inscribed with an Aramaic incantation against evil spirits that was chanted at the time of childbirth

The creation of Eve, from Michelangelo's ceiling for the Sistine Chapel proves the rule. And as if to demonstrate that even Bruriah was not quite as exceptional as was generally believed, Rashi relates that after she had ridiculed the Rabbinic belief that women were light-headed, her husband sent one of his scholars to seduce her. At first she ignored the advances, but finally she succumbed. Rabbi Meir had proved his point, but his wife, according to legend, killed herself.

When a woman tried to engage Rav Eliezer ben Hyrcanus on some fine point of scholarship, he became impatient with her. 'A woman has no learning except about the spindle,' he declared. 'Let the words of the Torah be consumed in fire, but let them not be transmitted to a woman.'

The devout Jew to this day includes in his morning prayers the words: 'Blessed art Thou, O Lord our God, King of the universe, who hast not made me a woman.' Many authorities have gone to great pains to explain that these words were merely an utterance of thanksgiving for being accorded duties from which women were exempt. And it has been suggested that women indeed were freed of many duties incumbent on men because their household tasks were considered sacred, and that, in a way, a well-prepared meal is in itself a form of prayer. This argument is not entirely convincing, for the duties, or *mitzvot* as they are called, are eagerly sought privileges to be performed with joy, and to be excluded from them is therefore a disability. Moreover, it is perfectly possible nowadays (and was possible in prosperous homes in the old days) for Jewish women both to discharge their household duties and undertake the same *mitzvot* as their menfolk, but they are still not allowed to do so. They cannot, for example, lead a congregation in prayer (in fact, they dare not be heard at all); they cannot make up a quorum, or be called up to the Torah. Finally, a woman's exclusion from religious duties starts long before she has assumed any domestic responsibilities.

There is, for example, the verse in Numbers: 'You must make tassels on the corners of your garments, you and your children's children,' from whence is derived the commandment to wear *tzitzit*, but it is interpreted to refer to boys – who wear it from earliest infancy – and not girls. When a boy becomes Bar Mitzvah he wears a *tallit* (a large, fringed prayer-shawl) and *tephilin* for his morning prayers. Great significance is attached by the Rabbis to the *tallit* and *tephilin*, but especially to the latter (God himself wears *tephilin*, claims the Talmud). The *tallit* over the shoulders envelop one like a cloak, and the *tephilin* round the arm and head

A scene that is lost from Jewish life: a street peddlar selling *tallitot* in Cracow, Poland, three years before the outbreak of the Second World War

are necessary aids to meditation and prayer and can induce a gravity of mind even in the most frivolous individuals. But women are not required to don them, nor can they do so even if they want to. To which traditionalists might argue that women can do without these, for their disposition is more religious. It is true that women are more meticulous in their observance and more loyal to usage than their menfolk, and in many homes the women are the ones who preserve the last vestiges of tradition. Few Jewish fathers today don *tallit* or *tephilin* for their morning prayers – or say prayers at all – or make the customary blessings over bread and wine at the Sabbath table, but there are few Jewish mothers who will not light Sabbath candles and intone the words:

Blessed art Thou, O Lord our God, King of the universe, who hast sanctified us by Thy commandments, and commanded us to kindle the Sabbath lights.

The dietary laws, with all their complications, are almost entirely in the woman's hands: it is she who has to keep separate sets of cutlery and crockery; it is she who has to buy the kosher meat, salt it and drain it; and as Passover approaches it is she who has to turn her entire household upside down to make sure that there is not a speck of leaven about the place. There was a more-or-less tacit separation of duties between the men and the women in the Jewish household, with the latter looking after this world and the former the next. Today there is almost a reversal of functions. Women still do perform all the necessary household tasks they did before, but now religion has also fallen into their lap, and if the Jewish home is still a temple it is the mother who is usually the priestess. As a result, something of a dichotomy has developed in Jewish life. Thus, many eat kosher at home, but non-kosher out; one may experience something of the Sabbath while at home, but nothing of it when one is away. For the very many for whom Judaism is a vague jumble of sentiments, the most essential part of their creed are the recollections of mother and home.

It is comparatively rare for a Jewish girl to marry out of her faith – though there are communities where it is rare for a Jewish boy to marry within it. Jewish women tend to be more conservative, more amenable to religious influences, more sensitive to the effects of their actions on relatives and friends, and more cautious, even though, as far as Jewish law is concerned, exogamy on the part of a woman entails fewer complications, for her children are Jewish whoever or whatever her husband might be.

A woodcut of the blessing of the candles, a familiar portrayal of the Jewish woman's ritual role in her home

The Rabbis envisaged no role for the woman outside the home. Thus she was utterly dependent either on her father or husband and they made careful provisions for her maintenance. The *ketubah* stipulates in specific terms the material responsibilities that a husband assumes towards his wife. If she brought a dowry to her marriage, as she often did, she could not be divorced without it, and if her husband died intestate she could reclaim it from his heirs. The Rabbis also sought to ease some of the burdens affecting the Jewish woman. Thus, under Mosaic Law, a jealous husband – whether his wife's conduct gave him grounds for jealousy or not – could submit her to ordeal by trial. He brought her to the Temple with a meal-offering in her hand, and there her ordeal began:

And the priest shall set the woman before the Lord . . . and uncover the woman's head, and put the offering of memorial in her hand, which is the jealousy offering; and the priest shall have in his hand the bitter water that causeth the curse. And the priest shall charge her by an oath, and say unto the woman, If no man have lain with thee, and if thou hast not gone aside to uncleanliness with another instead of thy husband, be thou free from this bitter water which causeth the curse. But if thou hast gone aside to another instead of thy husband, and if thou be defiled, and some man have lain with thee besides thine husband: Then the priest shall charge the woman with an oath of cursing, and the priest shall say unto the woman: The Lord make thee a curse and an oath among thy people, when the Lord doth make thy thigh to rot and thy belly to swell . . . And when he hath made her to drink the water, then it shall come to pass that if she be defiled, and have done trespass against her husband, that the water that causeth the curse shall enter into her, and become bitter and her belly shall swell, and her thigh shall rot; and the woman shall be a curse among her people. And if the woman be not defiled, but be clean; then she shall be free and shall conceive seed (Numbers 5:16–28).

There was no penalty on the husband if his suspicions proved unfounded. Such trials were familiar in antiquity, but the Rabbis were troubled by the whole procedure and abolished it after the destruction of the Second Temple.

There are still areas of Jewish life where the girl is anything but emancipated, where she can leave her father's house only to be married. This is especially true of oriental families, and when Israel introduced a law to conscript girls for national service, it caused a political upheaval and threatened to cause serious social strife. Finally, a compromise was reached in which girls who could prove they were Orthodox – the fact that they came from an Orthodox home was not enough – could claim exemption from military service.

In biblical times, a woman whose husband died without issue had to marry his brother. This was the levirate law as defined in Deuteronomy:

If brethren dwell together and one of them die, and have no child, then the wife of the dead shall not marry without unto a stranger; her husband's brother shall go in unto her, and take her to him to wife (25:5).

The purpose of the law was to perpetuate the name of the deceased so 'that his name be not blotted out in Israel', and to keep his property within the family. It applied whether the surviving brother was married or not. If he refused he had to give the widow *chalitza*:

And if the man like not to take his brother's wife, then let his brother's wife go up to the gate, unto the elders, and say, My husband's brother refuseth to raise up unto his brother's name in Israel, he will not perform

Jewish domestic life in Morocco ran the gamut from high sophistication to a life-style more reminiscent of the Patriarchs than of the 20th century. This photo of a woman from Tissint, Morocco, drawing water from a water-skin was taken in the early 1950s

the duty of my husband's brother. Then the elders of the city shall call him and speak to him: and if he stand to it, and say I like not to take her; then his brother's wife come into the presence of the elders, and loose his shoe from off his foot, and spit in his face, and shall answer and say, So shall it be done unto that man that will not build up his brother's house. And his house shall be called in Israel, The house of him that hath his shoe loosed (Deuteronomy 25:7-10).

The Rabbis adopted this ritual in order to circumvent the whole levirate law, and today a man cannot marry his brother's widow even if he should want to. *Chalitza* has become mandatory and is followed substantially as set down in Deuteronomy, though the expression 'spit in his face' is interpreted to mean 'in his presence', and in fact she spits on the floor.

The *chalitza* ceremony, from *Kirchliche Verfassung* (1784), a primer on Jewish rituals by the German Protestant theologian Johann Bodenschatz

According to Mosaic Law, a man could divorce his wife almost at will, but the Rabbis hedged this right with many qualifications, and today one has to show good cause why the marriage should not continue. The law still stands that only a man may grant a divorce, but a woman can sue for divorce through the Rabbinical courts on any number of grounds. If a man is 'wounded in the stones', said Maimonides, he should not marry an Israelite woman, and she can sue for divorce if he should prove impotent; if he suffers from a loathsome disease, such as leprosy, or has a loathsome occupation, such as tanning, or denies her conjugal rights, or puts unreasonable restraints on her movements (as, for example, when she wants to attend a wedding or funeral and he does not), or if she wants to settle in the Holy Land and he does not, a woman has substantial grounds for divorce. In Israel today, the *Beth Din* (Rabbinical Court) has the backing of civil authority, and if a man refuses to grant a divorce that they consider is justified, he can be incarcerated for contempt of court. But complications can arise even in Israel. One recalcitrant has spent a considerable part of his life in jail for contempt because he is determined, come what may, not to give his wife her freedom, and she remains an *agunah* ('chained') unable to divorce and not free to marry. A deserted woman is in much the same position, and outside Israel any woman whose husband refuses to give her a *get* (divorce), or whose brother-in-law refuses to undergo the *chalitza* ritual, is likewise tied and cannot remarry according to Jewish law. Reform congregations have dispensed with both the *chalitza* and the *get*. A non-Orthodox woman has no problems (unless she is living in Israel, where the Rabbinical courts have complete jurisdiction over such matters), and unless she happens to believe that the Jewish law is supreme, as a great many Jewish women do, there is nothing in English or American law that prevents an *agunah* from remarrying.

Apart from the handicaps of law, the Jewish woman suffered from the fact that she was never quite taken seriously. The great Elijah of Wilno recalled in old age: 'Throughout my life, whenever I read my prayers, I felt as though I still stood as a child before my dear pious mother, who dictated every word to me,' but he too could not escape the feeling that there was something essentially trifling in a woman's disposition. He told his wife and daughter not to go to synagogue 'for in synagogue you cannot avoid scandal and frivolity', that is to say, in the women's section, where, he complained, the talk was all of fashion and clothes. 'Women are temperamentally light-headed,' states the Talmud – an opinion which has been widely quoted and with which Maimonides concurred. A Jewish woman could have her vows annulled by her father or by her husband for, as Maimonides explained: 'Women are easily provoked to anger owing to their greater excitability and weakness of mind, and their vows, if entirely under their own control, would cause great grief, quarrels and disorder in the family.' All Jewish authorities are vehement in their condemnation of gambling in every form, but women in their last weeks of pregnancy are allowed to play cards. Similarly, although one is required to follow the reading of the weekly portions of the Torah in the original, the Rabbis allowed translations to be made 'for the benefit of the unlearned, women and children'.

The Rabbis regarded all literature that did not bear directly or indirectly upon the Holy Law as necessarily profane and to devote any time to it at all was *bitul zman*, a waste of time; but, again, allowances were made for women, and much of the secular Jewish literature of past centuries was designed largely or exclusively as reading matter for wives and daughters. The Yiddish expression *wiberse meises* ('wives' tales') came to refer to romances and other

As the centuries passed, each tradition and ritual tended to develop its own special apparatus. This is a special *chalitza* shoe used in the ritual ceremony in Germany a century ago

Moses Sofer, the leader of Jewish orthodoxy in post-Napoleonic Europe, who gave his daughters license to read what they chose – as long as they read it in Yiddish!

light material to which women seemed to be addicted; and another expression *bobbe meises* (grandmothers' tales), which referred to the stories of the supernatural favoured by older women, passed into the language as the word for wild fantasies. Some of the earlier books were sort of bowdlerized versions of the Bible translated into Yiddish with all the passages that might be 'disturbing' to a delicate temperament erased and biblical figures like Sarah, Rebekah, Rachel and Leah raised to a stature not always accorded them by the Bible. The most famous of these works was the *Tzenerene* (a corruption of the Hebrew *z'ena ur'enna*, 'go out and see'), which wove together Bible stories, legends, biblical commentaries and homily into a continuing narrative, intended both for instruction and uplift. Written in Yiddish, it first appeared in the seventeenth century and since then has been republished in over 200 editions. It is still not entirely extinct, although now it is read only as a literary curiosity while then it was the constant companion of the East European Jewish housewife, both for the synagogue and the home. Jewish women, where they were literate, were avid readers. Moses Sofer, a leader of Jewish Orthodoxy in post-Napoleonic Europe, forbade his daughters both in his lifetime and in his will from reading German novels, but by then a wide range of reading matter was available in Yiddish, including even Boccaccio's *Decameron*.

Beyond that was the belief that no matter how innocent her own disposition (a point on which some Rabbis had their doubt, for example, Rabbi Akiva, who counselled that one should never arrive upon one's wife unannounced), a woman, even a good woman, could lead men to mischief almost in spite of herself. 'Whosoever gazes at a woman intently,' warned the Talmud, 'is as though he lay with her.' Jesus made much the same point: '. . . whosoever gazes at a woman with desire has already debauched her' (Matthew 5:28). As a result, it was regarded as sinful even to look at a woman, or indeed, at anything which might bring a woman to mind – like her attire, even if it wasn't being worn – and the pious Jew, like the pious Christian, went on his way with eyes on the ground. Even that assured no freedom from hazard, for it was wrong for a man to follow a woman, especially over a river, even if she happened to be his own wife (nor could he, of course, walk alongside of her). And when making a purchase, he had to take care when he took change lest their hands touched. Near or far, touched or untouched, the woman was an object of desire and had to be kept out of sight and out of mind.

Yet in spite of such attitudes, and in spite of the disabilities imposed upon the Jewish woman by custom and law, the Jewish family, for much of its history, has been a matriarchy. The woman was loved, respected, placed on a pedestal, almost worshipped. Even in the golden age of patriarchy, as demonstrated in the lives of Abraham, Isaac and Jacob, the woman, whatever her formal status, could get pretty well what she wanted. There is a certain uxoriousness in the Jewish male which makes it difficult for him to refuse anything to his wife and daughters. Moreover, the very handicaps from which women suffered induced them to greater effort; sometimes they were compelled to greater effort by the very inertia of their menfolk. It was very rare for a Jewish woman to find herself with a drunk or a ne'er-do-well on her hands, but what was not uncommon among Jewish men was a certain dilatoriness, an unhurried, unflurried disposition. In some cases this was a by-product of the scholastic tradition, in some a result of excessive faith that the Lord will provide, and in some a simple world weariness:

What profit hath a man of all his labour which he taketh under the sun. One generation passeth away, and another generation cometh; but the earth abideth forever (Ecclesiastes 1:3–4).

The Jew who wanted to rest from his labours, who indeed preferred to desist from labour altogether, could find sufficient sanction for his attitude in the Bible. The woman tended to be of sterner stuff, if only because she had to be. The very paucity of males, the widespread fear of fathers that unless daughters took what males there were, they might – Heaven forbid! – be left single, meant that Jewish women often married beneath them, not merely in the social or economic sense, but in calibre. The woman may have been pulled back by social convention, but she was propelled forward by strength of character. Someone in the family had to face reality. She not only looked after the house, but she was often the bread-winner. She reared the young, and in spite of her indifferent health – arising out of her many pregnancies – and her indifferent education, she somehow found time to look after their Jewish education. The burdens that she assumed would have crushed her had she not believed that she was thereby freeing her menfolk for the higher duties of life, and that something of their holy pursuits attached to her lowly ones and gave her equal standing in the sight of God.

טריבחרהש

8 Sex and the Married Woman

Rashi (1040–1105), foremost of all biblical commentators, described sex as a *yetzer hara*, an evil inclination, but added sagely: 'If it were not for the evil inclination no man would build a home or marry.' This perhaps sums up the difference between the Jewish and Christian attitudes to sex. The one regarded it as an evil to be suppressed, the other as an evil to be harnessed – naturally to the sublime purpose of marriage. But even in marriage it did not mean that a man was free to indulge his sexual appetites to the full. Among Jews this form of bodily pleasure is subject to as many restraints as any other. One was first of all obliged, even in the very depths of passion, to maintain some awareness of its higher purpose. A man, said the *Shulchan Aruch*, 'should train his mind on pure thoughts and sacred ideas and not be light-headed'.

According to some authorities, 'a man may do with his wife as he pleases,' but only if she so pleases. He cannot approach her against her will and sometimes, as we shall see, not even at her will. The *Shulchan Aruch* itself insists on dignity and modesty in the marital relationship and, to this end, prohibited intercourse by daylight, moonlight or lamplight. The couple had to be alone in a darkened room, and even at such a time a man could not approach his wife 'in a spirit of levity, or befoul his mouth with ribald jests'. The wife, for her part, was expected to show constant modesty and restraint. On the other hand, she should not be afraid to entice her husband, and the husband should not be averse to being enticed:

It is the duty of one who observes that his wife is trying to please him, and to appear as attractive as possible to gain favour in his eyes, to lie with her even outside the hour set aside for the regular performance of his duties.

But, continued the *Shulchan Aruch*, she must not go too far: 'If she

A woman immersing herself in the *miqvah* before joining her husband in their conjugal bed, as outlined in the laws of *niddah*, from the 15th-century illuminated Hamburg Miscellany

approaches him verbally, her behaviour is brazen and his obligation lapses.' In this, as in most other matters bearing on family life, the initiative must come from the man, but again it must not come too often. 'One should not be too familiar with one's wife except at the times regularly appointed for sexual intercourse.' But times – preferably at night – *should* be appointed and, in so far as it lies within one's powers, one should keep to them. One is never at liberty to neglect one's wife, even if she is pregnant or nursing.

Healthy, prosperous men of strong constitution, whose business does not take them away from home, 'should perform their duties nightly'. The settled labourer has to perform his duty twice a week, itinerant labourers once a week, commercial travellers on short trips, once a week, on distant trips once a month, 'while the time appointed for a scholar is from Friday eve to Friday eve.' Friday eve, indeed, was a time when the wife had a special claim on the attentions of her husband, and to this end he was required to eat garlic, for, in the words of the Talmud, 'garlic promotes love and arouses desire.'

But there are times when a man cannot approach or even touch his wife under any circumstances – according to some authorities, he may not even be in the same room with her – and that is during her periods of 'impurity', as defined in Leviticus:

> And if a woman have an issue, and the issue in her flesh be blood, she shall be in her impurity seven days (15:19).

The sanctions against anyone approaching her during this period were extremely grave:

> And if a man shall lie with a woman having her sickness, and he shall uncover her nakedness – he hath made naked her foundation, she hath uncovered the fountain of her blood – both of them shall be cut off from among their people (Leviticus 20:18).

The Rabbis therefore surrounded the scriptual enactments with a whole complex of laws. The seven days of impurity were extended to twelve, and as they felt that one cannot be absolutely sure that bleeding from other causes is not intermingled with menstrual blood, they defined all vaginal bleeding – even though it should leave a stain 'no bigger than a mustard seed' – as menstrual; thus, for example, the virgin bride becomes impure from the moment the marriage is consummated and must remain separate from her husband for the next twelve days. (The prospective bride must calculate her wedding date to fall outside her unclean days, otherwise she must

A page from a 1728 edition of '*Seder Birkat Hamazon*', from Moravia, illustrating the benediction over the candles and the custom of sitting on a low stool as a symbol of mourning

בָּ״אֲ״מֶ״ה אֲקֵ״בֵּ״וּ לְהַדְלִיק נֵר יֶ״של שֵׁבַּת ‪❖‬ (מן י״ע זאגט מן דיא
לְהַדְלִיק נֵר יֶ״של יוֹ״ט ‪❖‬ (און יוֹם כֵפוּריֶ״ם) לְהַדְלִיק נֵר יֶ״של יוֹם הַכִּפּוּרֵי״ם
(על שֵׁמוּעוֹת רְעִית קוּמֵד)

בָּרוּךְ אַתָּה יְיָ אֱלֹהֵינוּ מֶ״ה רַיִן הֵאֱמֵרֵת ‪❖‬

keep her distance from her groom even under the *chupah*.) Similarly, a woman is rendered impure by a pregnancy or miscarriage, or indeed through any injury to her reproductive organs that may give rise to bleeding. She must keep a careful record of her periods and should not cohabit on the day she is due in case bleeding should result during intercourse. If her periods are delayed or irregular, one *niddah* period is hardly over before she has to reckon for the onset of another. Women who for one reason or another are prone to frequent or irregular bleeding are unable to cohabit at all and, according to some authorities, their husbands should divorce them.

Before the destruction of the Second Temple, the laws of *niddah* were interpreted so strictly that women were treated as virtual lepers during their menstrual periods and kept in quarantine away from the rest of the household. An ancient work, *Baraita deNiddah*, took the matter further and argued that the *niddah* be prevented from lighting the Sabbath candles or entering a synagogue, and if her husband as much as followed her step, he too should be debarred from synagogue. A descendant of the priesthood could not make the priestly blessing if his wife, mother, or daughter were menstruous; one could not benefit from the work of a *niddah*; one could not stop to inquire after her health, for her breath was poisonous, her glance was harmful, and she polluted the very air about her. She was regarded as the ultimate in corruption, a walking, reeking, suppurating pestilence. Something of this attitude remains, and even today the strictly devout Jew will avoid any physical contact with his wife, or any actions that could lead to physical contact. As laid down in the laws of the *Shulchan Aruch*, the burden of caution lies largely on the wife:

During her unclean days she should wear special clothes as a reminder that she is a *niddah*. She may prepare food and drink for her husband, but not in his presence, and may not prepare anything for his toilet, nor may he serve her with any beverage. If her husband falls ill and she has no one else to attend to him, she may raise him up or lay him down, or support him, but not with bare hands. And if she should fall ill he may likewise look after her, but only in times of absolute need when there is no one else available.

They should not sit together on the same couch, and if they are at the same table (something which is not really encouraged), they must take care not to pass articles – the salt-cellar, for example – to each other. And of course, however powerful their self-control, they will not sleep in the same bed. Thus the double-bed is unknown

A linen cloth from Russia embroidered and painted sometime in the late-19th or early-20th century with motifs from 6th–10th century Jewish iconography. Many of the same motifs appear on archaeological finds from the Holy Land that were uncovered years after the cloth was made, which says much for the strength of Jewish tradition in exile

An engraving of the Amsterdam *miqvah* by Caspar Jacobsz Philips (1732–1789)

in ultra-Orthodox homes, and some Rabbis have written of such beds as symbols of depravity.

After the necessary term of separation is completed, the woman remains prohibited to her husband until she has immersed herself in a *miqvah*, a pool specially constructed for this purpose, though one may also use a spring, river, or bathe in the sea. The main provision is that the waters must be moving and free of any discolouring matter; the *miqvah* must be large enough and deep enough to enable a fully grown woman to immerse herself completely, and it must be leakproof. The immersion laws have nothing to do with physical cleanliness – one is, indeed, required to have a bath before one goes to the *miqvah*. They are entirely a means of spiritual purification and are regarded as so essential to the spiritual well-being

of the family that, according to Jewish law, one should not live in a town without a *miqvah*.

The *miqvah*, incidentally, though used largely by women, is not intended exclusively for them. Chassidim use it on the eve of the Sabbath and festivals, and it was customary in some communities of Eastern Europe for the bodies of great rabbis to be immersed in the *miqvah* before they were prepared for burial. This practice stopped only after the local women threatened to boycott the *miqvah*.

A woman must count five days from the beginning of her period, and if by the end of the fifth day she is satisfied that she has no show of blood, she begins to count a further seven during which she must examine herself twice daily to be sure that there has been no further show. 'A virtuous woman should not be lax in this matter,' writes the *Shulchan Aruch*, 'but should examine herself well throughout the entire seven days.' If she does not, her immersion is not counted as an immersion, and she remains a *niddah*. If she has found a further show, no matter how slight, during those seven days, she must, even if she found it on the seventh, begin her count anew. If seven consecutive days have passed without a sign of blood, she prepares herself for the immersion by combing her hair, paring her nails and washing herself thoroughly from head to toe. It is imperative before entering the *miqvah* that nothing intervene between her person and the water. If she has make-up, a plaster or dentures, she must remove them; if she has any clot of blood on her skin, she must rub it off; she must pick her teeth – dentists who have ultra-Orthodox women as patients are often kept busy removing temporary fillings; the slightest thing, a touch of paint to the lips, an ink-stain on the finger, would be sufficient to make the immersion invalid.

When the woman has finished her necessary preparations, she disrobes and enters the *miqvah* till the water comes over her head. (There is always a female attendant present to make sure it does.) She must stoop slightly to make sure that no part of her body is closed to the water, and when she rises for air, she makes the benediction: 'Blessed art Thou O Lord our God, King of the universe, who has sanctified us with Thy commandments and commanded us concerning the laws of immersion,' and then goes under twice more.

Although the laws of *niddah* may seem arduous, and perhaps even bizarre, to the general reader, the effect on the believing Jew is one of rejuvenation and introduces an element of the sacred to an area of life that one might think is necessarily profane. It perhaps weighed most heavily of all on the Rabbis, for the laws of *niddah* are very

overleaf Judaism's hostility to birth control and the resultant large size of Jewish families in ages past may have been one of the factors that preserved the Jewish people from extinction. This is a portrait of the family of Joseph Elias Montefiore, whose son Moses (with the book) became the most famous Jewish philanthropist of his time

complex and when a woman is in doubt she has to consult 'not some old wife', as the *Shulchan Aruch* put it, 'but a man expert in the law'. In *My Father's Court*, the novelist Isaac Bashevis Singer describes how a regular succession of women would call on their rabbi, clutching undergarments to their bosom, to determine whether some stains they had discovered were due to bleeding or some other cause. Neither they nor the rabbi showed any more embarrassment in the matter than a gynaecologist interviewing a patient. The idea that any aspect of life might be too private or too intimate to discuss with one's rabbi was never considered. Indeed, the more private and intimate it was, the more likely the advice of a rabbi would be sought, for he was regarded not merely as a wise man himself, but as one who had immediate access to the wisdom of the ages.

It is clear from the Rabbis' great attention to the laws of *niddah* – they occupy an entire tractate of the Talmud and whole libraries of commentary – that over the centuries these laws were considered basic to the existence of the Jewish family. One can see something of the importance attached to it in the last will and testament of a fourteenth-century German Jew:

My daughters must obey scrupulously the laws applying to women; modesty, sanctity, reverence, should mark their married lives. They should watch carefully for the signs of the beginning of their periods and keep separate from their husbands at such a time. Marital intercourse must be modest and holy, with a spirit of restraint and delicacy, in reverence and silence.

The laws of *niddah*, according to many writers, were the rock on which the integrity of the Jewish family was based. It assured the mutual reverence and respect vital to domestic stability. It protected the woman, wrote Dr J. H. Hertz, a former Chief Rabbi of Britain, 'against uncurbed passion . . . and taught her to view marital life from the aspect of holiness'. (It could be added that it also protected men against the excessive demands of their wives – and as men often married women much younger than themselves, it was a necessary protection.)

The performance of a *mitzvah*, a divine commandment, is in itself a source of joy to the devout, and the more demanding the *mitzvah*, the more arduous its performance, the greater the joy. But on a more mundane level, the monthly separations and reunions do introduce a continuous touch of novelty to married life and help to prevent the marital relationship from degenerating into a mere routine. A wife fresh from the *miqvah* often feels like a wife renewed and, by law, has an immediate claim on the attention of her husband – even more pressing than on a Friday night. The husband may stay separate from his wife at a time of famine or hardship, but not on the night of her immersion. The fact that one's wife is inaccessible for a considerable part of the month, and sometimes longer, can in itself add to her attractiveness; as the Sabbath seems the sweeter for the privation of the weekdays, so do the reunions seem the richer for the abstemiousness of the *niddah* days. There is a considerable body of medical evidence to show that the devout Jewess is less prone to uterine cancer than the non-Jewish woman of the same social group and that the laws of *niddah* have pronounced physical benefits, but these, where they exist, are considered incidental to the essential purpose of ritual purification.

One does not know how far the *niddah* laws are observed even amongst those Jews who call themselves Orthodox. The number of ritual baths normally available in most Jewish communities suggests that they must be few. The Reform and Conservative synagogues in America have dispensed with the *miqvah*; in England, the United Synagogue, the leading Orthodox institution in the country, pays towards the upkeep of baths maintained by the ultra-Orthodox groups, but provides none itself. This is not to say that the practice of ritual immersion is dying out; if anything it is enjoying a revival. The rite was, in the main, associated with the immigrant generation, and apart from being inconvenient it was also unfashionable. It had an aura of dowdiness, homeliness and lack of sophistication about it, and the baths themselves, though not unhygienic, tended to be in cheerless, dingy surroundings. Thus, to some, the *miqvah* represented an immersion in a dark and oppressive past, and no matter how hard mothers tried to impress their daughters with its importance to their moral and physical well-being, they preferred to forgo the benefits. All that has changed. Both the *miqvah* and clientele are different. One cannot say that it has become the symbol of elegance and fashion – it would have failed in its purpose if it was – but neither is it regarded as a quaint hangover of a quaint past.

If Judaism has raised the marital relationship to the level of a sacrament, it does not regard sex, even within marriage, as something to be enjoyed for its own sake. Sex is sacred only if sought for the purpose of procreation, and there are authorities who argue that it is wrong to cohabit with a barren woman or even with one who, though once fruitful, is past child-bearing age. Judaism is entirely hostile to birth control, more so, in some ways, than the Catholic Church, for Rabbis do not recognize the 'safe period'; if

The woman at the hearth, the idealized vision of *shalom bayit*, by the Palestinian artist Joseph Butko (1888–1941)

they did, they might have been disposed to ban cohabitation while it lasted. But it is more lenient than Catholicism in its attitude to the life and health of the mother. Thus, abortions are prohibited except if there is a risk to the health of the mother. Then, in the words of the Talmud, the embryo may 'be cut out limb by limb'. For the same reason, Judaism is prepared to tolerate some birth-control devices, but never the male sheath, which Jewish law regards as a form of masturbation, a particularly heinous offence. The attitude derives from the story of Onan who, under the levirate law, was required to marry his brother's widow, but refused to consummate the union:

And Onan knew that the seed should not be his; and it came to pass that when he went in unto his brother's wife, that he spilled it on the ground . . . And the thing which he did displeased the Lord; wherefore he slew him (Genesis 38:9–10).

The female contraceptive is considered less reprehensible, and the pill comes near to finding favour because it does not interfere with the male partner but with the ovular cycle. But in the last analysis, the purpose of every birth-control device is to control birth, something which is not entirely acceptable in Jewish law – except, as was pointed out, if the life of the mother is at stake. There are Orthodox authorities who are prepared to take a more lenient course and also permit birth control where *shalom bayit* (the harmony of the household) is concerned: if the increasing size of the family and the increasing burden on the wife may affect the relationship between her and her husband. One also may limit the size of one's family at times of need, not through birth control, however, but by abstention. But even then, the *Shulchan Aruch* points out, the right to abstain is limited:

> If there be a famine, Heaven forbid, or if the land is in distress from any other cause, one may diminish one's conjugal pleasures, except on the night of her immersion, or if they are childless.

Thus, the childless couple after ten years of marriage are regarded by some authorities as living in sin, for the wife is either capable of bearing – in which case she should have borne – or she is not – in which case she should have been divorced. To the ultra-Orthodox, the very thought of resorting to any form of birth control is alien, and families of ten, eleven, or even twelve children are not uncommon. Elsewhere in Jewish life, families are small and getting smaller, and nowhere is Jewish practice so far removed from Jewish law as in the matter of family planning. And it is not a subject on which

Far from serving their apprenticeship in housewifery, these teenage girls from the Israeli Chassidic village of Kfar Habad appear to be immersed in the more trivial preoccupations of young girls in the 1970s – a sign of the influence of the times on even the most conservative bastions in Jewish life

many Orthodox Rabbis can exhort their congregations, for they often have amongst the smallest families of all (possibly because they have amongst the smallest incomes of all). A family with two children is common, three is considered large, four is regarded as bordering on the irresponsible.

The compassion and the energies with which the Jewish mother is equipped was, perhaps, meant for bigger things: spread over many children, they were warming and benign; concentrated on a few, they can be suffocating. It is possible that some of the neuroses evident in Jewish life may be due to the fact that most Jewish families are too small. The rituals and ceremonies of Jewish life presume a certain material sufficiency and minimum numbers. In the case of the former those with a surplus helped those with a deficiency, but there is no helping out with numbers. Small families can and do coalesce for an occasion like the Passover *seder*, but at the Sabbath table, which also calls for sizable assemblies, they form bleak little groups. Not only are children few, but they are far between and are separated from each other by four, five or even ten years. (The usual norm is to have two in quick succession and then mark the onset of middle age with a third.) They are thus less likely to find pleasure in one another's company and more likely to seek the company of contemporaries outside the family. In small families, too, the children often feel over-exposed to the anxious attention of their parents, and this, too, tends to drive them away from the family. Sometimes the fewer children one has, the less one is likely to see of them and the less control one has over them. Logically, the contrary should be true: the very numbers within a large family should make it impossible for parents to give each child the attention it needs; but within the Jewish family there evolves a hierarchy of siblings, with the older children looking after the younger. Daughters in particular thus served an apprenticeship in housewifery that prepared them to be complete mistresses over their own household from the day they married. The large family is thus a more viable social unit than the small. It calls for selflessness and definite organizational skills, but the effort is usually more than outweighed by the reward.

Judaism, or at least Orthodox Judaism, does not consider the wider question of whether it is socially responsible, given the present trends to overpopulation, for people to have many children. Such matters are left to the Almighty. If one believes that to 'be fruitful and multiply' is a divine command, then one has no fears that the world can become too small for its inhabitants.

9 Queen Mother

Shalom bayit, or *sholem bayis* in Yiddish, simply means 'peace in the house', or connubial bliss. It refers to the idea of serenity sought in the Jewish household and the compromises necessary to the creation of a happy and stable family life.

'Never quarrel with your wife,' urged a medieval sage. 'If she asks you for too much money, say to her: "My darling, how can I give you what is beyond my means? Shall I, God forbid, acquire wealth by dishonesty and fraud?"'

'Make allowances for the weakness of thy wife,' said another. 'If thou canst not raise her to thee, do thou stoop and speak encouragingly to her.'

'Be ever zealous for the honour of thy wife,' said a third, 'for there is no blessing in a man's house which comes not through his wife.'

As we have seen, a man should not consort with his wife against her will, nor should he be 'unduly familiar with her at times set aside for the performance of his marital duties'. Only a wife could free her husband of his obligations – 'provided he has already performed the precept to "be fruitful and multiply"'. A wife, on the other hand, also had her obligations, and if she refused to cohabit, she was known as a 'rebellious' woman and could be divorced without the compensation set forth in her *ketubah*. The Talmud laid down the procedure to be followed:

If the court finds that the woman is at fault and her rebellion is without meritorious cause, then for four successive Sabbaths it is made public in the synagogues that a woman named so-and-so has deliberately rebelled against her husband. After the expiration of the four Sabbaths, the court inquires and if there is no reconciliation and the woman persists in her ways, a divorce may be issued at the pleasure of the court.

Her conjugal obligations comprised her primary duties, but the

'Mother and Child' by the contemporary American painter Max Band

secondary ones were by no means unimportant: the Talmud declared that it was the duty of the wife to wash her husband's face, hands and feet daily, to pour the drink into his glass and prepare his bed, even if her husband was wealthy and she was surrounded by servants. Maimonides enlarged the list: she was obliged to grind corn, wash, bake, cook, suckle her young, feed the cows and clean the table at which her husband eats; if she failed in such duties as preparing his meals on time or washing his feet, he had a right to beat her. Maimonides spent his entire life in Moslem lands and was no doubt influenced by oriental customs. Most Rabbis regarded wife-beating with abhorrence. 'This is a thing not to be done in Israel,' declared Rabbeinu Tam, a twelfth-century teacher, and Rabbi Meir of Rottenburg, writing a century later, was able to observe with some satisfaction: 'Jews are not addicted to the prevalent habit of ill-treating wives.' But if wives were not ill-treated, they were kept sternly aware of their duties, as one can see from the following 'Ten Commandments' that a seventeenth-century writer urged upon the wives of Israel and that have been quoted with approval since:

The first, my dear daughter, is to beware of his anger, lest you enrage him. When he is cross do not be jolly and when he is jolly do not be cross. And when he is angry smile at him and answer him with kind, soft words . . .

The second, my dear daughter, concerns his eating and drinking. Search, consider, reflect about his food . . . Try to have his meals ready at the proper time, for hunger does nobody any good . . . Should he get drunk, don't tell him what he did or said in his drunkenness; and if he tells you to drink, drink, but not to the point of getting drunk, lest he should see you in such a state and learn to hate you.

The third, my dear daughter, when he sleeps, guard his sleep that he be not wakened, for if he doesn't get a good night's rest he may become very angry.

The fourth, my dear daughter, try to be thrifty . . .

The fifth, my dear daughter, don't be anxious to know his secrets . . .

The sixth, my dear daughter, find out whom he likes and like him too, whom he dislikes and dislike him too . . .

The seventh, my dear daughter, don't be contrary with him. Do everything he tells you . . .

The eighth, my dear daughter, don't expect anything of him which he considers too difficult . . .

The ninth, my dear daughter, heed the requests which he may make of you, awaiting in turn that he will love you if you do so, and will be your slave and serve you.

The tenth, my dear daughter, be very careful to guard against jealousy. Don't make him jealous in any way. Don't say anything that might hurt him, and let him have his own way in everything. Make an effort in all things to do what pleases him and avoid doing what displeases him . . .

In other words, be his slave! The whole piece may have been a satire, or an exercise in wishful thinking by a particularly down-trodden husband, for although it appears to have been taken seriously by some commentators, it was a formula for grief. Jewish law and Jewish tradition may have been less than equitable to the Jewish woman, but she was very far from a doormat. A man could lord it in the house of prayer, the house of study or the counting-house, but at home the woman was very much in charge. It was her domain, if not by right, then by male resignation: 'I never called my wife "my wife,"' said a Rabbi, 'I called her "my home"'; 'A man without a wife is but half a man,' said another. No one went so far as to call his wife the *better* half, but all agreed that she was the indispensable half.

In Psalms, domestic bliss is depicted as the privilege of the pious:

Happy is the God-fearing man who walketh in the way
When thou createst the labour of thy hands.
Happy art thou and it is well with thee.
Thy wife, like a fruitful vine in thy house,
Thy sons like olive plants around thy table,
Behold, thus is the man blessed who feareth the Lord (128:1-4).

A good wife was the reward for wholesome living, and there could be no wholesome life without her; it was she who created the environment for earthly bliss. 'He who has no wife,' said a second-century Rabbi, 'remains without good, and without a helper, and without joy, and without a blessing and without atonement.' Through her, one fulfilled the most basic of all com-mandments – procreation – and through her, lusts, if not killed, were at least stilled. She bore the children, weaned them, fed them, clothed them, cleansed them and, although this was not her function, taught them – certainly through their early years and, in the case of daughters, often through to their late ones.

A man might be a merchant and travel far on business, or a scholar who spent all his days and half his nights in the *Beth Midrash*, the house of study; during the week the house might be a chaotic place from which he was happy to retreat, but came the Sabbath and festivals, there was a transformation. Even a man who lived

Kazimejz, Poland, one of the hundreds of small towns throughout Eastern Europe remembered as the *shtetl*

in a hovel – as most Jews once did – would return from the synagogue to find a palace – the table laden, the rooms gleaming, his wife and daughters in their best clothes. One can understand how, in time, it became customary for men to intone these lines from Proverbs on Friday night:

A woman of valour who can find?
For her price is far above rubies.
The heart of her husband does trust in her,
And he hath no lack of gain.
She doeth him good and not evil,
All the days of her life.
She seeketh wool and flax,
And worketh willingly with her hands.
She is like the merchants' ships;
She bringeth her food from afar.
She riseth also while it is yet night,
and giveth meat to her household,
And a portion to her maidens.
She considereth a field, and buyeth it;
with the fruit of her hands she planteth a vineyard.
She girdeth her loins with strength,
and strengtheneth her arms.

She perceiveth that her merchandise is good,
her candle goeth not out at night.
She stretcheth out her hand to the poor;
yea, she reacheth forth her hands to the needy . . .
Strength and dignity are her clothing;
and she shall rejoice in time to come.
She openeth her mouth with wisdom;
and in her tongue is the law of kindness.
she looketh well to the ways of her household,
and eateth not the bread of idleness.
Her children rise up and call her blessed,
her husband also, and he praiseth her:
Many daughters have done virtuously,
but thou excellest them all . . .   (31:10–29)

The words were partly sung, partly chanted by the husband, while the womenfolk busied themselves with last-minute preparations – finding the cover for the *challot* (the bread baked especially for the Sabbath), the wine bottles and the wine cups for *kiddush* – and then,

The generation whose parents left the *shtetl* for Western Europe and America inherited a radically different way of life, but the tradition of putting out one's best to greet the Sabbath held firm

A silver *kiddush* cup, for making the blessing over wine at the beginning of the Sabbath meal from Nuremberg, Germany (1761)

A 19th-century ceramic plate from Poland showing a family celebrating the *kiddush*

with everything in place, the whole family joined in the singing of *Shalom Aleichem*. According to tradition, two angels accompany the Jew home from the synagogue on Friday night, and *Shalom Aleichem* is the formal greeting sung to them. There are different tunes at different times of the year and in different lands, but the words are always the same:

Peace unto you, ministering angels, angels of the Most High, of the supreme King of kings, the Holy One, blessed be He. Come in peace, ministering angels . . . Bless me with peace, ministering angels . . . Go in peace . . .

The parents then blessed their children: for the sons they asked that 'God make thee as Ephraim and Menasseh', and the daughters that 'God make thee as Sarah, Rebekah, Rachel and Leah.'

This was the hour in which *shalom bayit*, or the lack of it, was most acutely felt. At other times, an unhappy man could escape his home; on the Sabbath he was a prisoner.

For the housewives the Sabbath eve was the denouement of the most hurried day of the week – in the winter, when the days were short, it often began the night before. They would go to bed late and rise early to continue at a breakneck pace – scarlet-faced and scarlet-tempered amid steaming saucepans and frying fish. At such times, husbands either kept carefully out of their way, or were pulled in to help; they crowded the markets with their baskets, less prone to shop around, less inclined to haggle, less able to tell good fruit from bad, but helpful. They busied themselves with other chores as the Sabbath approached, getting busier still as the day declined, until both husband and wife became frantic, rushing here, pushing there, putting a final pinch of salt to the soup, a final touch of polish to the floor, cutting up paper for the lavatory (for one dare not tear on the Sabbath), polishing boots, paring nails, arranging flowers. Then, dusk came and the Sabbath descended – peace. Mother covered her head and lit the candles. Then, father and sons, in their Sabbath best and gleaming boots, started out for the synagogue in the declining light of day, while the women retired to wash and change.

For the males of the household the Sabbath was a complete day of rest. It began with the large repast after synagogue and the *zemirot* (table-hymns) between each course. There are hundreds of *zemirot* in circulation and each community has its own choice selection. One that was frequently sung in Eastern Europe is the twenty-third Psalm: 'The Lord is my shepherd; I shall not want.

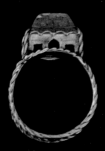

He maketh me to lie down in green pastures . . .' Jewish liturgy is often unintelligible to the less-than-learned, but somehow when sung, it attained meaning for all. All the family joined in – the young with greater gusto than the old – and their voices echoed through the surrounding streets. At the close of the meal, and immediately before the grace, another Psalm was sung:

> When the Lord turned again the captivity of Zion,
> we were like them that dream.
> Then our mouth was filled with laughter,
> and our tongue with singing:
> then said they among the heathen,
> The Lord hath done great things for them (Psalms 126:2–3).

In the deep winter evenings, when the nights were long, one went over that week's portion of the Torah to be read the next morning in the synagogue – possibly falling asleep in the course of it, to awaken in a darkened room with the fire dying in the fender, and the candles spluttering their last effulgence, casting long shadows on the wall.

For the housewife, the Sabbath could be more exacting than a weekday. There were meals to prepare, tables to be cleared, dishes to be cleaned – frequently more so than usual, for there was often a guest at the table; indeed, the Sabbath was not quite complete without one. Time to rest did not come, if it came at all, until after lunch, when the dishes could be left in the sink until the Sabbath was over; then the woman of the house could retire for an hour's sleep. It was at this hour that the Sabbath was at its most peaceful and Sabbatical. The whole village slept: shutters were shut, streets were deserted – save for small boys and dogs – the very eaves of the houses sagged with sleep.

As darkness fell, the *havdalah* ceremony, with candle, wine and spices, separated the holy day from the profane week. There was a song sung in Poland at this hour:

> The holy Sabbath is over,
> The time of gladness is past.
> The heart is chilly and sad.
> Once more to the rags,
> Once more to the bags,
> Once again to the black, heavy iron.

The party was over, but the mood was not quite as desolate as these lines implied. One emerged from the day reinvigorated –

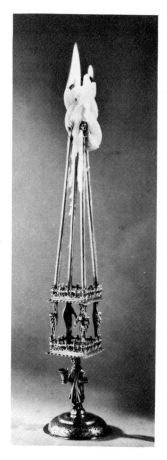

An 18th-century silver candle stick from Germany used to hold the candle in the *havdalah* ceremony

Seventeenth-century wedding rings of gold from Italy

The traditional opening of
the Sabbath, the wife
blessing the candles, the
husband blessing his
children, from *Der Jude*

unless one indulged too liberally in the heavy Sabbath fare – and braced to face another week. And the housewife had a lot to face!

The wife endeavoured to make the household economy as self-supporting as possible. One bought nothing that could be made at home, and to an able housewife – a *baale boste*, as she was called in Yiddish – *everything* could be made at home. Things were bought when they were in season and cheap and were preserved for when they were out of season and expensive: fruit was made into jam, milk into cheese, cabbages, cucumbers and onions into pickles; fresh herrings were made into sour herrings, and salt herrings into pickled ones; flour was bought already milled, but bread and cakes were baked at home. But the greatest industry and skill revolved around the sewing-machine. The typical Jewish household bought cloth rather than clothing, and if a ready-made article of apparel was bought – such as an overcoat for the father – in time, it was turned upside down and inside out with the help of the sewing-machine to serve each of the sons and most of the daughters. Sheets, pillows and bedding were all the products of the sewing-machine. And when the machine was silent, one found the mother cutting, stitching or ironing, usually in the evening, by lamplight, after the children were in bed, humming or grumbling to herself as she worked (for she had much to grumble about), or at her husband, if he was about.

The fact that there are three statutary services to the day (morning, afternoon and evening) and that the Jew was expected to devote any free time he had (and ideally all his time) to sacred study, gave the husband holy cause to be away from home almost any time he chose. A wife had to carefully choose her occasions for unloading her pent-up frustrations. And when she did nothing, she knitted – socks, scarves, gloves, sweaters, antimacassars, bed-covers. When a man married, he not only took a wife, he acquired an industrial complex.

It could perhaps be argued that because the Jewish mother was overworked in past generations she is being over-indulged in our own. In fact, it is not at all certain that she is being over-indulged, but if she is, the difference is due less to the attitudes than to circumstances. The *Shulchan Aruch* urged a husband to provide his wife with the fare and apparel 'common to her standing in life', and ornaments 'according to his means'. And if his means increase, so should his spending on his wife because 'the Lord has blessed him for her sake'. Some sages went further and counselled: 'Let thy

A Bokharian family
celebrating the Sabbath

table be considerably within thy means, thy dress and appearance
according to thy means, but the comfort of thy wife and children
beyond thy means.' Many acted on the last part of the precept more
than the first. Most Jews were optimists, as indeed they had to be,
and tended to regard themselves as prosperous individuals in tem-
porarily reduced circumstances. Such optimism may have been
due to a very real desperation – the feeling that things could not
get worse – coupled with a belief in the Lord as the ultimate provider – so that one bought first and worried about paying for it
afterwards. Even a pessimist was inclined to enjoy this world while
the going was good, and if the going was not so good, he borrowed
to make it better – the Jewish economy was based on credit long
before banks or bankers were invented. The inclination to do the
best for one's wife and children was, therefore, always there.
What was sometimes missing was the money. If the Jewish housewife
of an earlier age was a tireless workhorse, it was because she had to
be; and if she is somewhat more relaxed now, it is because she can
afford to be, and because she is part of a more relaxed class.

Until two or three generations ago the mass of world Jewry was working class. They may not have thought of themselves as such, they may not have had working-class ways, but they had working-class incomes, and sometimes not even that. If a show of sufficiency could be made on the Sabbath it was partly because the family starved themselves the rest of the week. As they ascended to the middle class, Jews acquired middle-class attitudes; or rather, they always had the attitudes, but now had the means to support them. As advancement came with clear memories of early privation, there was a tendency to over-compensate for what was lacking before and to enjoy through one's children what one had denied oneself.

This perhaps was the basis of complaints that Jewish daughters are too pampered and that they expect too much from their prospective spouse. In every land and in every age that Jews became sufficiently established to enjoy a modest prosperity this problem arose, and there were frequent warnings against it. 'Most strongly I beg,' urged a father in a testament written in 1357, 'that the daughters of my house be not, God forbid, without work to do, for idleness leads to sin, but they must spin, or cook, or sew and be patient and modest in all their ways.' As we have seen, in some communities local laws were passed limiting ostentatious consumption and ostentatious wear. In fifteenth-century Italy, the community decreed that brightly coloured fur-lined jackets should not be fringed with silk; in 1432, a synod of Spanish Jews forbade Jews over the age of fifteen to 'wear any cloak of gold thread, olive-coloured material, or silk', or any cloak trimmed with such materials, except on very special occasions. The trouble was that Jews were inclined to regard almost any occasion as special and such laws had slight effect.

Jews who made fortunes rarely felt so secure as to invest them in land (in many cases they were not even allowed to buy land), and their money tended to go to externals, which, apart from anything else, had the useful quality of being portable in a crisis. Moreover, many Jews who reached a certain stage of affluence could not quite believe in their own good fortune and wanted evidence of it in the attire of their wives and children and in the appearance of their home. (Those few who were born to wealth were far less ostentatious.) Beyond that was simple, unthinking affection, the desire to lavish loved ones with everything one has – especially when one isn't too sure how long one will continue to have it.

10 Faith, Hope and Charity

No Jew ever discovers the full extent of his family until he comes into money. Thereupon, he will be assailed with greetings from distant cousins in distant lands with daughters to marry and sons to educate and not a penny to their names. Every poor relative is a reproach to a rich one, and every rich one, a source of reassurance to a poor one; it is almost as good as having money in the bank. The Jewish papers in Eastern Europe used to be full of stories about the Rothschilds, Goldschmidts and other banking clans. It made the masses feel that even if they were poor themselves, they had rich relatives to whom they could turn in a crisis.

Jewish law, Jewish tradition and the whole Jewish way of life gave those who hadn't an automatic claim upon those who had. Wherever a Jewish community was formed, the first institution established was a burial society, and the second was a *gemilut chesed*, a mutual aid fund that was never quite mutual – or rather, in which some members were more mutual than others; in every community there were those who gave and those who received, and their roles were rarely reversed. In eighteenth-century London, half the Jewish community lived on the generosity of the other half.

Charity is regarded as a Godly attribute; its practice draws one near the Heavenly throne. Simeon the Just, High Priest at the time of Alexander the Great, said: 'Upon three things the world is based: upon the Torah, upon the Temple service, and upon the practice of charity.' With the fall of the Second Temple one could argue that there are only two left. There are several Hebrew words for charity, for charity has various forms, but the one most frequently used is *tzedakah*, meaning righteousness, or justice, and Jewish tradition regards a continuing redistribution of wealth as nothing more than that. 'Give unto Him of what is His, seeing that thou and what thou hast are His.' Giving was an imperative command-

An early 20th-century silver charity box from Turkey

ment, bestowing grace on both giver and receiver, though the giver perhaps received the greater share. 'The poor man does more for the rich man in accepting, than the rich man does for the poor in giving,' said the Rabbis. The Talmud tells the story of a pauper who came to the door of a Rabbi and asked for a meal. 'Certainly,' said the Rabbi, 'what do you usually have?'

'Fatted chicken and old wine,' said the man.

The Rabbi blinked. 'But are you not worried that you're a burden on the community?' he asked.

'Do I eat what is theirs?' said the man. 'I eat what is God's.' He got his fatted chicken and old wine.

One Talmudic sage argued that charity is as important as all the other commandments put together. One did not have to be destitute to have a claim on others, one only had to have much less than others; one who himself lived on alms was still obliged to give alms to others. Charity was an obligation from which none was exempt.

The minimum required to be set aside from one's income was one-tenth, but in practice it often came to more than that. Every community was expected to feed the hungry, clothe the naked, offer hospitality to the wayfarer, help the sick and comfort the

Although the custom of setting aside a minimum of one-tenth of one's income for charity has died, this 'soup kitchen' in Tel Aviv serves as evidence that both poverty and charity are still with us

Leon Israel's view of Hester Street, the heart of New York's Lower East Side, where many a family's 'black sheep' found himself relocated

bereaved. Those not-quite destitute had to be helped to celebrate the Sabbath in festive style. There was a primary duty to marry off any poor girls in the community, that is, they had to be provided with a dowry. Many communities – especially those round the Mediterranean shore, which were prone to invasions by pirates – had special funds for ransoming captives. But all this was merely part of the responsibility for co-religionists; the family was another matter. There was a primary obligation towards the inner circle of relatives, a secondary obligation to the outer circle – but an obligation. Every sizable Jewish enterprise had to grow quite large before it ceased to be a family affair. What might have been regarded as nepotism elsewhere was regarded as mere *chesed* among Jews – the right thing to do. A relationship, no matter how remote, was a recommendation – though the more remote the relationship the more one had to exhibit secondary qualities, like ability or stamina. A cousin or nephew who was considered too wild or incompetent might be shipped off to some distant country (which is how almost every major Jewish family has a cadet branch in North America), but everyone not much less than mediocre was looked after unto the third or fourth generation. This was true even

overleaf A roof garden on New York's Lower East Side was one answer to relieving the poverty-stricken Jews from their crowded living conditions. This is a painting of the garden in Rutger's Square in 1896

for one who married into the family. A Jew who marries a rich wife is expected to allow himself to be supported in the manner to which she's been accustomed, which in part explains the phenomenon of the professional son-in-law. There is but one remedy for the embrace of wealthy in-laws – flight!

Families with established wealth were supremely conscious of the generations to follow. Among the Cohens, the Waley Cohens, the Goldschmidts, Montagus, Montefiores and Franklins, who were part of the late nineteenth-century Anglo-Jewish ruling class, every father felt obliged to leave to each of his children as much as he was left himself. Capital was considered sacrosanct; one tampered only with the interest. Punitive death duties put an end to that tradition, but, in any case, only the old, established families thought in terms of wills and posthumous hand-outs and sometimes tied up their endowments in such intricate trusts that the lawyers got more out of them than the heirs. Most Jews were anxious to see the benefits of their generosity with their own eyes and passed on what they had in their own lifetime. The effect of all this was to generate a continuing redistribution of income. This was felt, to a greater or lesser degree, as one approached or receded from the centres of wealth, but the consequences reverberated throughout the community as well.

The observances and ceremonies of Jewish life presumed a certain minimal sufficiency. The education of children, the festive Sabbath board, the *matzot* on Passover, the booths and *arba minim* on the Feast of Tabernacles, the wine for *kiddush* and *havdalah*, to say nothing of such happy occasions as a *brit*, Bar Mitzvah or wedding, all cost money. But somehow it was nearly always found. 'All Israel is responsible one for the other,' said the Talmud. Am I my brother's keeper? Yes – and my cousins'.

All this tended to give an exaggerated view of Jewish well-being. It was generally accepted that the 'Jews have no beggars' and 'no poor'. A book on *The Present State of the Jews*, published in the seventeenth century, showed that there was a considerable number of both, but that the regular distribution of charity 'much concealed the level of poverty'. The fact that, over many centuries, rich and poor were compelled to live in close proximity in crowded ghettos also helped to obscure reality. The poor seemed less poor for their more prosperous neighbours, as if something of their prosperity had rubbed off on to them – as it often did. There is an epitaph to a Jewess who died in the Thirty Years' War that illustrates something of the concern shown for those in need:

The aged were also the object of community charity in the New World as well as the Old. This portrayal of a New York Home for the Aged by W. A. Rogers goes back to the end of the 19th century

She supplied scholars with Bibles, and the plundered with prayer books.

She ran like a bird to weddings, and often asked the poor to dine with her in her home.

She clothed the naked, herself preparing hundreds of shirts for distribution among the poor.

Mere generosity was not enough; there had to be personal involvement. To give money or goods to this or that cause was hardly more than paying taxes; one had to give of oneself. Distant charity was less than charitable, as expressed in the refrain of this popular Yiddish song:

Orm is nit gut
Orm is nit gut
Mir tor zich nit shemen
Mit eigene blut.

'It's not good to be poor/ it's not good to be poor/ yet one must not be ashamed of one's own blood.' If a poor niece got married, it was not enough to send a generous present, one had to attend the wedding. It often happened that families fell out, and that brother would not speak to brother, or cousin to cousin, but not because one was rich and the other poor. If anything, their different situations helped to keep them on good terms.

Financial help was usually preferred in the form of *gemilut chesed*, an interest-free loan, rather than an outright gift, and every community maintained a fund for that purpose. Frequently, it was used to help small businessmen over a lean period. In the first instance, one turned to brother and cousins – and if a Jew went bankrupt, it was a fairly clear indication that his relatives were in a poor way. Sometimes he would pull them down with him, for cousin not only enriches cousin, he sometimes beggars him. In every family there is a Menachem Mendel, the *Luftmensch* created by Sholem Aleichem, who was aflame with ideas on how to make his, and everyone else's, fortune, and who pauperized everyone in the process, including his hapless kinsman Tevye. On the other hand, the interconnections of family and the tradition of mutual help had obvious commercial benefits. The story of the Rothschild network, with brothers and cousins in every major European capital, is well known, but there were many lesser families who applied the same principles of interconnection on a lesser scale. If many Jews prospered in the import-export trade, it was because one cousin imported what another exported. Many a man in the textile trade in Lodz (Poland) prospered by discovering a relative in the textile trade in Manchester. Every immigrant who established himself in the West cast out lifelines to relatives in the East; he traded with them if they were in trade, or brought them over to work for him if they were in need of employment. The social legislation passed in Britain at the end of the last century was often circumvented by Jewish entrepreneurs because their workshops were – or could be made to appear like – family establishments. One could exploit a relative as much as anyone else – and exploited they were – but they were glad to have work at all. They saved a few dollars, borrowed a few, and soon they were in business for themselves and exploiting the new influx of cousins. Generally, they prospered together: families became partnerships, and many a clan has remained together because to break up would be equal to going into voluntary liquidation. The family strengthened the links of commerce, and commerce the links of the family.

11 Family Fare

'Better a meal of herbs and love therewith than a stalled ox and hate therewith' is a passage in Proverbs, to which many Jews might add: but better still a stalled ox and love therewith. Jewish counsel has always been towards moderation; Jewish tendencies have been towards excess. Maimonides urged that one should always leave the table still hungry, that if enough was as good as a feast, less than enough was better:

Eat that ye may live and ban excess. Do not imagine that abundance of food and drink strengthens the body and expands the mind as though you were dealing with a sack which is filled by what is put therein. Overeating is in fact the cause of many maladies . . . do not incessantly nibble like mice; take your meals at fixed times in your homes.

Such precepts were more lauded than followed. The word '*nosh*', which has lately insinuated its way into the English language, is Yiddish for a mouth-watering morsel, a nibble, a titbit, something you eat when you're not hungry. Jewish culinary tradition is based on the belief that if a little of what you fancy does you good, a lot does you better. But even in times of plenty Jewish banquets stopped well short of Roman proportions; no meal was allowed to degenerate into an orgy. One was always conscious of restraints: partly arising from the dietary laws; partly from the feeling to which every minority is prone, that it is being watched by curious and not always friendly eyes; and, above all, by the restraints of poverty.

The dietary laws arising out of Mosaic Law are in themselves not too restrictive:

And every beast that parteth the hoof, that cleaveth the cleft into two claws, and cheweth the cud among the beasts, that ye shall eat. Nevertheless these ye shall not eat of them that chew the cud, of them that divide the cloven hoof; as the camel and the hare and the coney: for they chew the

The first steps towards a feast: bringing poultry home from market, by Issachar Ryback (1897–1935)

cud, but divide not the hoof . . . And the swine, because it divideth the hoof, but cheweth not the cud . . . These shall ye eat of all that are in the waters; all that have fins and scales shall ye eat. And whatsoever hath no fins and scales ye may not eat . . . (Leviticus 11:3–12).

This meant that the Jewish diet had to exclude pork and shell-fish (and, according to some authorities, turbot) – all minor prohibitions that added little to the burden of keeping house. The major prohibition stems from an obscure verse in Deuteronomy: 'Thou shalt not seethe a kid in its mother's milk' (14:21), the exposition of which fills twenty-eight pages in the Talmud and eleven sections and sixty-two sub-sections of the *Shulchan Aruch*. As a result, many, perhaps most, Jewish homes have two sets of cutlery and crockery: one for meat dishes and the other for milk. Many have two distinct kitchen sinks, and kosher catering establishments have to double up on everything – even two kitchens. As one is also required to use distinct dishes for Passover, this means that anyone setting up a traditional Jewish home will often have four sets of cutlery and crockery, besides the space to store them. This, of course, adds immensely to the cost of keeping home but, if one has the money, is not in itself a restraint. The main restraints come from the Jewish method of preparing meat, derived from two verses in Leviticus:

Moreover ye shall eat no manner of blood, whether it be of fowl or of beast in any of your dwellings. Whatsoever soul it be that eateth any manner of blood, even that soul shall be cut off from his people (7:26–7).

The Rabbis, accordingly, derived a method of slaughter and preparation to drain the meat of blood, and meat prepared in any other way – in effect, meat bought from any but a kosher butcher or prepared in any but an Orthodox home – is regarded as non-kosher. As meat or meat particles can find their way into almost any dish, the dietary laws have made it difficult, in fact almost impossible, for the observant Jew to eat in a non-Jewish home, or in Jewish homes that no longer observe *kashrut*. Indeed that is part of their purpose. Some authorities have gone further to say that one may not drink wine made, or even touched, by a non-Jew. Their reason is quite explicit – *mishum chatanot*, because of marriages: begin with a cup in hand and end with a wife in hand.

Every family has its own level of observance. A great many ignore the laws altogether, but even they will hesitate before scooping an oyster out of its shell or digging their fork into a pork-chop; many

A decorative wall tablet inscribed with the blessing of *eruv tavshilin*, which is recited to permit food to be prepared for the Sabbath when Friday is likewise a festival (Germany, 1806)

will avoid pork or shell-fish, but eat non-kosher mutton or beef. In England, many families have adopted the curious compromise of keeping kosher homes but eating non-kosher out. Orthodox Jews will hesitate to eat out, and when they do will be careful to choose fish, egg or vegetarian dishes. (When the Chief Rabbi of Britain is invited to lunch at Buckingham Palace, he is generally served a bowl of fruit and vegetables.) The ultra-Orthodox do not eat out, except in other ultra-Orthodox homes, and some will regard even that as hazardous. Reform Jews who have more or less jettisoned the entire corpus of dietary laws have tended to argue that what goes into the mouth is less important than what comes out of it, but obviously if one has to take constant care over what one eats it does have a certain chastening effect on a lusty appetite. The purpose of the laws, many mystics have argued, is refinement, to bring man nearer to his Maker; to ignore them is to recede from Him. 'Anything which gives the body too much independence,' wrote a nineteenth-century Rabbi, 'or makes it too active in a carnal direction, brings it nearer to the animal sphere.' Maimonides argued that the dietary laws 'train us in the mastery of our appetites. They accustom us to restrain both the growth of desire and the disposition to consider the pleasures of eating as the end of man's existence.' To the restraints of what one could eat were added preliminaries to eating. The devout Jew is expected to wash his hands before he breaks bread, make a blessing when drying his hands, another over the bread and conclude his meal with yet another.

On Sabbath and festivals there are three statutory meals, each of which is rich in ceremony and ritual. Each course is followed by the singing of table-hymns, and in some households, even a learned discourse. A stranger to such a table is sometimes left wondering whether he has been invited to a meal or holy communion. Every time a Jew bends forward to enjoy some palpable pleasure, there is always something to remind him that it is all directed to a higher purpose. All of which may lead one to believe that Jewish food is compounded of incense and *gefilte* fish and that Jewish mealtimes are a penance. But the contrary is true. It is possibly a sub-conscious awareness of all the 'mustn'ts' that makes the Jew enjoy those things he may with such gusto.

A great deal of Jewish tradition may be felt on the tongue. What are known as traditional Jewish dishes vary with each place of Jewish sojourn, and a comprehensive history of Jewish cooking would require a map of the Jewish dispersion. But many of the

Gefilte fish, the best known of Jewish foods, is a classic example of the talent to make a little go a long way

better-known Jewish dishes are but a means to making a little go a long way, and the best known of all, *gefilte* fish, almost symbolizes this aptitude. Fish, in the land-locked Central and East European areas that formed the main centres of Jewish life, was a luxury, something to be savoured only on Sabbath and festivals. One Polish rabbi visiting England in the nineteenth century, wrote back in wonder: 'No eye has seen, no mind can imagine the wealth of this land. They eat fish here on Sabbath *and* on weekdays. Has the world heard such a thing?' In Poland, they skimped on meals for the rest of the week, subsisting mainly on salt herring and black bread in order to have fish and white bread – *challot* – on the Sabbath. But even then, as their budgets were small and families were large, they concocted a dish that could reduce the role of the fish to a mere flavouring, hence *gefilte* fish – literally, stuffed fish. The proportion of the various ingredients varied from household to household, but bread – often stale bread left over from the daily meals – was as basic an element as the fish. The bread is allowed to soak (in modern homes they tend to prefer *matzo* meal) and then chopped together with onions, spices and, of course, fish – carp, bream or pike. Usually it was simply boiled and then left to cool until a jelly formed over it; sometimes it was shaped into balls or cakes and fried to look like meat rissoles. Fried fish was especially favoured among English-speaking Jews; the batter was prepared with eggs, bread-crumbs and *matzo* meal and had a dry crispy flavour all its own. As the whole operation is rather time-consuming, and as Fridays, especially in winter, are never long enough for the demands of the Sabbath, Thursday night was the frying night – at which time the Jewish areas of London, Manchester and Leeds were half lost in a mist of frying oil.

Meat and fowl were also considered luxuries in Eastern Europe and were reserved for the Sabbath, festivals and ill-health. If a man took to his bed, he was served boiled chicken, chicken soup and white bread. If that failed, one called a doctor. If fish, meat and fowl were beyond most pockets, what was left? The answer is herring, which one found in a variety of guises – salt, pickled, baked, soused, fried, grilled, chopped, in brine, tomato sauce, sour cream – but always with a plentiful accompaniment of onions and never less than piquant. It was so ubiquitous at Jewish tables that it almost became the heraldic fish of Judea, and although no longer cheap, it is still much favoured, even when glazed in aspic and served on *canapés*. The Jewish love of herrings is the source of the Jewish penchant for smoked salmon (as it is known in England) or lox (as

A festive holiday meal as depicted by the French artist and engraver, Bernard Picart

it is known in America). The herring became too identified as a symbol of poverty, and as Jews prospered, they sought out an animal with much of the piquancy of herring but without any of its harsh associations. Thus they alighted on smoked salmon, which was, moreover, fuller in body and rather more magnificent and festive in appearance; but smoked salmon was neither more nor less than a rich man's herring. The herring itself has risen so far in price that lately it can look the salmon in the face, and it has become a titbit instead of a staple, a *nosh* instead of a meal.

Another staple food was, of course, bread – usually enriched with caraway seeds within and poppy seeds without. It was at once nutritious and tasty (the black bread went particularly well with salt herring). But on Sabbath and festivals, something more delicate was desired, so one baked *challes*, or *challot*, which were light, white, made with plenty of eggs and glazed on the outside with egg yolk. The dough for the Sabbath *challot* was intricately plaited and elon-

The various forms of *challot*,
each symbolizing a different
occasion

gated in shape; on festivals they had a rounded shape; on the New
Year they were shaped like a ladder (to symbolize the higher hopes
and aspirations with which one was expected to approach the season).
The *challot* are said to symbolize both the priestly bread prepared
for the Temple and the manna that sustained the Israelites in the
wilderness; as they received a double portion of manna on Friday
to carry them over the Sabbath, it is usual to have two *challot* on
the table for each of the two main Sabbath meals, Friday evening
and Saturday afternoon.

The *challot* have a close relative called the bagel; it is a sort of
crisp doughnut, glazed on the outside with a dry, rather than a
sweet, flavour. The traditional bagel has assumed a different form

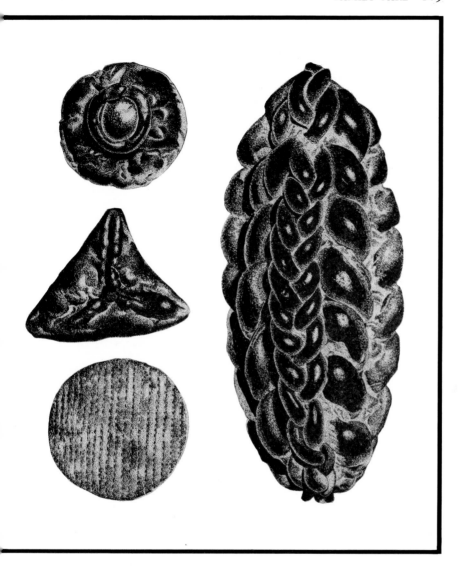

in America: it has lost its crispness and dryness, and its hole is reduced considerably. By way of compensation, it is sometimes liberally sprinkled with poppy seeds and is now the familiar companion of lox.

Cholent, which is still little known among non-Jews (one may not have to be Jewish to like it, but one does have to be Jewish to survive it) derived both from the needs of economy and the imperatives of Sabbath observance. One is not allowed to cook on the Sabbath, and any hot meal consumed on that day is prepared on Friday. The *cholent* was designed both to survive the long stay in the oven in an edible form and to make an expensive commodity – meat – go a long way. Its composition varies from land to land, but the classical, or what might be called the Queen's *cholent*, was composed of fat brisket of beef, haricot and butter beans with small quantities of onions, prunes and syrup. The beans were left to soak overnight and then placed at the bottom of a large casserole, with the brisket on top, a layer of potatoes together with some chopped onions, and on top of that the prunes and syrup. To crown it all was a covering of *kugel*, a dumpling composed of flour, grated potatoes, parsely, grated onion and raw chicken-fat. The *cholent* with *kugel* was then put in a low oven and allowed to bake for the next eighteen to twenty hours, but it sent forth its aroma as a foretaste of things to come long before it was ready for the table. One was already aware of it as one came home from the synagogue on Friday night. The spirit of it thickened as the evening wore on, until it was almost palpable. By the time the Sabbath candles had burned out and one was ready for bed, the rich, heavy soul of the *cholent* dominated the household. When finally presented at the table, it was a rich, moist, golden brown. The *kugel* formed a crust on top, and when it was removed, a cloud of steam hissed up from the *cholent* like incense over a Temple offering. It was at once meal, central-heating and soporific. Once eaten, one was unfit for anything but sleep. In some families, the *cholent*, though made for the Sabbath, was heated and re-heated (the oven was always on during the long Russian winter) and served up as the main meal for the rest of the week. The drawback to the *cholent* is that it is a slow poison (to which wags would retort, 'Who's in a hurry?'). Jewish women anxious to keep their persons within neat limits (though not always succeeding) took small portions. The men felt under no such obligation, took large portions and succumbed to dyspepsia and sundry other chronic complaints. The traditional Jewish home needs good plumbing!

The need for economy meant that there was hardly a part of the animal that was not put to good use. One man's offal is another man's delicacy. The Jews of Yemen, for example, work wonders with the bull's penis, and in Eastern Europe they concocted dishes even out of less promising organs, such as the *pupick* or hen's stomach. There is a particularly delectable dish, variously known as *putcha*, *fishnoga*, *pilsa* or *cholodnye*; it is made of such improbable materials as calves' foot, bone-marrow, onions and hard-boiled eggs and allowed to set into a jelly. Liver, usually chopped together with onions and chicken-fat and topped with a sprinkling of hard-boiled eggs, has been a consistent favourite. Which brings us to the most basic ingredient in Jewish cooking – *schmaltz*. The Jew could not

A pestle and mortar of
brass from Morocco (19th-
century) for grinding spices

use butter in his meat dishes, vegetable cooking-fats were not yet
generally available, and therefore he resorted to *schmaltz* – rendered
down goose-fat or chicken-fat. One found it in everything – soups,
stews, roasts, puddings. There was hardly a conceivable meat
dish without it, and it could be spread on bread and eaten as a food in
its own right. Yeshurun waxed fat on fat.

The baking of *matzo*, the traditional staple for Passover that has of late become the weight-watcher's staff of life

If Sabbath had its special dishes, so did almost every other occasion in the Jewish calendar. On Rosh Hashanah it is usual to eat honey-cake, symbolic of the hope for a sweet new year. Some oriental communities serve up sheeps' heads, as symbolic of the hope that Israel will be the head among nations. In Germany, *tzimmes* – sliced carrots glazed with honey – symbolized the hope of a golden year. On Succot and Simchat Torah, one ate *chaluptzes*, made of cabbage leaves stuffed with minced meat and rice and cooked with raisins and lemon. One prepared enough on the first day to last for the entire week of the festival, and it improved with each re-heating; by the end of the week, it looked like a burnt offering, but it was a dish fit for the gods. On Chanukah one eats hot *latkes* – ground potatoes fried in *schmaltz*. They are said in some ways to symbolize the miraculous cruse of oil which burned for eight days and are universally found in all Jewish communities, but whatever their origin they are an excellent dish on a cold winter's night. On Purim there are the large triangular cakes filled with poppy seed, variously known as *homan tashen* (Haman's pockets) or *oznei haman* (Haman's ears). And on the festive meal towards the close of the day, one eats *kreplach*, small triangles of dough stuffed with minced meat and baked in a slow oven. On Passover there was, of course, *matzo*, and a host of dishes derived from *matzo* meal. The most popular are *kneidlach* or *chremzelach*, dumplings, which may or may not be stuffed with meat, and baked in *schmaltz*. Pentecost is traditionally a time for dairy dishes – curds, whey, cream cheese, cheese-cake and cheese *blintzes*, pancakes filled with sour cream, as distinct from *knishes*, which are pancakes filled with minced meat. Many of the dishes have become too popular to be confined to any particular festival, and *latkes*, *blintzes* and *chaluptzes* are eaten all the year round, while *matzo* has gone beyond mere Jewish use to become the weight-watcher's staff of life.

Jews rarely become intoxicated from drink – partly because they are so often intoxicated on food. The Jew was traditionally brought up to eat bread with everything (sometimes even with bread-pudding). Nowadays he may have cake instead, but he is rarely able to have even as much as a cup of tea by itself, and drinks in Jewish company are generally served with something to nibble or nosh. The Jewish child is almost weaned on wine, usually on the thick, syrupy sacramental variety, which sometimes serves to cure one of drink for life. He will have a small cup with the *kiddush* that precedes the Friday-night meal, another at lunchtime on

A Sephardi family around the table for a modest Saturday morning *kiddush*

Sabbath, a third with the *havdalah* ceremony at the end of the day. He will have the same on most of the festivals, and at the *seder* table on Passover, he imbibes four full cups of wine. Among ultra-Orthodox Jews and Chassidim, spirits, or schnaps, are consumed in considerable quantities, but with surprisingly little drunkenness. The favourite in Eastern Europe was vodka, or even spirits, which is as close to alcohol absolutum as is potable.

The drinking time for the traditional Jew is Sabbath and festivals between the completion of the morning service and lunch. It is known as *kiddush*, or sanctification, for it is preceded by a blessing over wine. It is followed by a light meal of *hors-d'oeuvres*, including chopped herring, fried fish-balls, smoked salmon, salted nuts, olives, pickled gherkins, pickled herring, chopped liver and schnaps. During the Feast of Tabernacles there is a continuous round of *kiddushim*, and one can stagger from *succah* to *succah* drinking to the health of one's friends. These occasions are generally attended *en famille*, in place of afternoon tea (though in summer, when the days are long, one goes out to afternoon tea as well), and if the men usually take spirits, the wives, as a rule, are content with tomato juice, the children with Coca Cola, and the grandmothers with cherry-brandy and advocaat, little blobs of red among sizable blotches of yellow that is said to taste less revolting than it looks. Among the ultra-Orthodox, a *kiddush* is an all-male affair and is enjoyed with even greater gusto: it is all done in the name of Heaven and what might otherwise be considered a mere booze-up is elevated to something approaching a religious experience.

The many exhortations in Jewish writing against drink suggest that Jews once drank more heavily than they do now. 'Who hath woe?' asked Proverbs. 'Who hath sorrow? Who hath contentions? Who hath babbling? Who hath wounds without cause? Who hath redness of the eyes?' Who indeed?

They that tarry long at the wine; they that go to seek mixed wine. Look not thou upon the wine when it is red, when it giveth his colour in the cup, when it moveth itself aright. At the last it biteth like a serpent, and stingeth like an adder (23:30).

Against this formidable indictment one could set the line from Psalms that wine 'maketh glad the heart', which a great many people did, to the considerable annoyance of the thirteenth-century philosopher Brachya who felt compelled to refute the matter:

Those who praise wine forget its evils; for it dries up the brain . . . man's senses become destroyed, and his knowledge changes . . . his limbs

The *kiddush* cup is used whenever the occasion demands a blessing over wine. In most cases it is made of silver, as is this turn-of-the-century version from Iraq

The Hebrew text visible in the illustration includes: בריך, לחיים, and on the table: אני הצעיר צבי דוד אייזער מטאַ

This 19th-century folk calendar of East European origin dwells on the month of Adar and carries the inscription 'When the month of Adar begins, merriment multiplies.' Wine plays no small part in that merriment

become weak, his hands and feet tremble, the heat of his blood increases and fever ensues, blotches, pimples and boils develop in the body, his digestive system is dragged to ruin, and diseases of the liver take hold . . .

He did, however, allow that one could drink diluted wine. Later Rabbis felt that Jewish asceticism as far as drink was concerned had possibly been carried too far, and a famous Chassidic figure, the Kotzker Rebbe declared: 'He who is a total abstainer is rarely possessed of wisdom,' which perhaps best sums up the Jewish attitude. The Jewish faith does not dwell excessively on the hereafter and, on the whole, Jews have been inclined to look after this world and let the next one look after itself. The self-denying ascetic has been an uncommon figure in Jewish society and contrary to the mainstream of Jewish tradition. There has never been any shame in enjoying a good repast, as long as one kept *Hamepharnes* – the Provider – in mind.

In a sense, the Jewish concern for food arises out of a concern for health, though it could be argued that the latter is a by-product of the former. It was only among Jews that one closed a conversation with the words, *zei gezunt* – be well. Until comparatively recent times it was generally believed that good health could be measured in bulk and that a full body was a healthy one. Indeed, in certain communities, at least among males, it was something of a status symbol. The man of substance was expected to look substantial, and he carried his body before him as proof of divine approbation. 'Withold from thy belly and put it on thy back', Ibn Gibbon, a Jewish physician,once counselled his sons, but it was not the sort of advice that was generally followed. If one was short of money, one skimped on other things, but one went to great lengths to get the right foods in the right quantity, especially for the Sabbath. Eating was a form of folk medicine and plenty of it was regarded as a panacea; at a time when many diseases were due to some deficiency, there was some wisdom in the belief. The tendency to feed the over-fed was thus a lingering reaction from the lean years, but now this has all but died out, and the Jewish neurosis about being underweight has given way to a neurosis about being overweight. Wherever Jews gather for a meal, the talk is all of calories, and young men at coffee reach for their little boxes of sweeteners much as they might have reached for their snuffbox in an earlier age. Jewish mothers have even been heard to caution their children: 'Don't eat!'

The fact that the Jewish meal was traditionally accompanied by small religious rituals, like washing of hands and blessings, has meant that there was a certain formality to the occasion, and it generally required the whole family at the table. To the middle-class family, mealtimes were always a formal occasion, and although the Jews, in the main, were in the working class, in this respect they had middle-class habits. This, too, helped keep the family together.

Many of the dietary laws are observed only by a few, but the faith seems to linger in the stomach long after it has vanished from the soul, and there has developed among American and English Jews a type of religion that has been dubbed by its critics as '*gefilte-fish Judaism*'. And, to be sure, food is a link of sorts: a glass of whiskey and chopped herring to anyone brought up in a Jewish home has the distinct flavour of Sabbath morning; *cholent* conjures up memories of distant lunchtimes; and *matzo*, nibbled even for the sake of one's diet, can bring the taste of Pássover to one's lips. The appeal, in fact, is less to the stomach than to one's sense of the past; they are snatches of childhood felt on the tongue.

The ritual practice of washing one's hands before a meal adds a certain formality to the thrice-daily occasion

12 The Seasons

There is hardly a month in the Jewish calendar without its feast or fast. Some of these are of a purely religious nature, but most commemorate some event in Jewish history – and there is much to commemorate.

On most weeks of the year most synagogues in the Western world are half empty, and some have rarely more than a quorum. But when the High Holy Days (as the New Year and Yom Kippur are generally referred to) approach, they are not numerous enough, nor, with all their extensions, large enough to accommodate everyone clamouring for a place, and every year church-halls, cinemas, public rooms and concert halls are drafted into use as auxiliary synagogues for what are known as 'overflow services'.

Rosh Hashanah, the New Year, is also known as the Day of Remembrance and the Day of Judgement, and the shrill, almost unearthly sound of the *shofar* (ram's horn) can rouse even the most dormant souls to the significance of the occasion. It is a time of intense introspection and contrition, culminating in the fast of Yom Kippur, at which time one recalls one's failings during the past year and resolves to improve in the year ahead. The confessional is said, with bowed head and hand on the heart:

We have trespassed, we have dealt treacherously, we have robbed, we have slandered, we have acted perversely and we have wrought wickedness, we have acted presumptuously, we have done violence, we have framed lies, we have counselled evil, we have spoken falsely, we have scoffed, we have revolted, we have provoked, we have rebelled, we have committed iniquity, we have transgressed, we have oppressed, we have been stiff-necked, we have acted wickedly, we have corrupted, we have committed abomination, we have gone astray, we have led others astray.

It is all couched in the plural, for every Jew is meant to feel guilty

The blowing of the *shofar*, associated with Rosh Hashanah, signifies the call to a period of introspection and contrition. This event was photographed at the Western Wall in Jerusalem

for the faults of the other, as if he, personally, had had some share in the wrong-doing. The prayers, which begin on the eve of Yom Kippur, continue, almost without a break, throughout the day, and the unfamiliar sight of a packed synagogue and the sound of a thousand voices raised in supplication induce a particular sense of awe. Even the prayers that are part of the daily liturgy assume a special significance when uttered at this time:

> Sovereign of all the worlds, not because of our righteousness do we submit our supplications to Thee, but for Thy great mercies. What are we? What is our life? What our piety? What our acts of righteousness? What our salvation? What our strength? What shall we say before Thee, O Lord our God, and God of our fathers? Are not the mighty as naught before Thee, and men of fame as though they were not, and the wise as if they were unknowing, and the understanding as if they were void of discretion? For much of their work is empty, and the days of their life are vanity before Thee; and the dominion of man over beast is naught; for all is vanity.

Each prayer has its own tune, some of which are sung by the *chazan*, some by the congregation. It is difficult to say whether one part of the liturgy is more important than another, but some assume a special significance, as the *U'Nettaneh Tokef*, for example, because of the history attached to it. It is said on Rosh Hashanah and Yom Kippur and forms what is perhaps the high point of the service, both for the depth of its feelings and because it evokes the whole dark history of Jewish martyrdom. It is associated with a tenth-century Jewish merchant, Amnon of Mainz, whom the Bishop of Mainz sought to convert to Christianity. When Amnon refused, his hands and feet were amputated and salt rubbed into his wounds. When the New Year came, he asked to brought to the synagogue, and in his final agonies he recited the *U'Nettaneh Tokef* and then died at the foot of the ark. Three days later, according to legend, he appeared in a dream to Rabbi Meshullam ben Kalonymos of Mainz, who recorded the prayer for posterity:

> We will celebrate the mighty holiness of this day for it is one of awe and terror. Thereon is Thy dominion exalted and Thy throne established in mercy, and Thou sittest thereon in truth. Verily it is Thou alone who art judge and arbiter, who knowest and art witness; Thou writest down and settest the seal, Thou recordest and tellest; yes, Thou rememberest the things forgotten. Thou unfoldest the records, and the deeds therein described proclaim themselves; for lo! the seal of every man's hand is set thereto.

The great trumpet is sounded; the still small voice is heard; the angels are dismayed; fear and trembling seize hold of them as they proclaim: Behold the Day of Judgement.

Even the less than devout are affected by the solemnity surrounding Rosh Hashanah and Yom Kippur and the religious fervour that they bring out in others. If one is part of a sincerely devout congregation, an inability to follow the prayers does not insulate one to their meaning. One is enveloped in spirituality almost in spite of oneself – if one's own faith is deficient, one is pulled in by childhood memories and by the faith of one's fathers – and one has to make a conscious effort to feel untouched by the advent of the High Holy Days.

In the old days, Jewish merchants were often away from home for long periods at a time, sometimes extending over months, but whatever the demands of business, they endeavoured to be back with their families for the main festivals, and especially for the High Holy Days and Passover. Today, journeys are shorter and

A pewter Passover plate from Holland with the various ritual foods that play a role in the *seder* inscribed around the rim

less hazardous, but people – especially young people – are more scattered and mobile, yet they still feel the tug of the family when the New Year and Passover approach. These two occasions are bi-annual roll-calls: to be away from synagogue on the High Holy Days is to have fallen away from one's faith; to be away from the *seder* is to have fallen away from one's people.

The other occasion that the vast majority of Jews take seriously – though it is not, as a rule, celebrated in the synagogue – is Passover, or rather the Passover *seder*, the ceremonial meal celebrated on the first two nights of the festival. While other events are overlooked or forgotten, the *seder* has traditionally served, and continues to serve, as a family reunion. Anyone missing from the *seder* is deeply felt. The dead seem to crowd in among the living, for once the formal part of the proceedings are over, the meal has been eaten, the wine drunk, the songs sung, and the youngest children are in bed, there comes an exchange of family gossip, and voices fall away as they touch on some figure who was there before, but is no more.

Passover, in essence, celebrates the genesis of the Jewish people. Before the Exodus from Egypt, the Israelites were but a loose as-sociation of tribesmen. Their common experiences of bondage and of subsequent liberation, their wanderings in the wilderness and the granting of the Torah on Mount Sinai transformed them into a nation. Today, Passover is celebrated by many Jews who have long since jettisoned any religious belief, and the celebrations take the form of recreating something of their ancestral experience. Bread is banished from observant Jewish households and *matzo* (unleavened bread) is eaten instead:

And they baked unleavened bread of the dough which they brought forth, out of Egypt, for it was not leavened; because they were thrust out of Egypt, and could not tarry, neither had they prepared for themselves any victual (Exodus 12:39).

No crumb of leaven is allowed to remain in the household and as Passover approaches, housewives with sleeves rolled up and hair clamped down brace themselves for their annual battle with the house, in which everything is pulled inside out and upside down – books dusted, shelves cleared and rearranged, furniture shifted – not so much a spring-cleaning as a catharsis. It is like the pre-Sabbath cleaning operation, but more thorough and extended over weeks, sometimes even a month, with everything progressing at an ac-celerated pace, and the housewife becoming a whirling fury lost in a haze of sweat and dust, as the eve of the festival draws nearer.

And then, on the morning before the festival, it is all over. Any leaven of the house (which has been searched by candle-light the night before) is ceremoniously burned. The cutlery and crockery in use all year round is stacked away, and the special vessels used only for Passover are brought down from the loft. The whole house seems different.

Passover is not Passover without guests, and they begin to assemble in the early afternoon – sons down from university or working away from home, married daughters with their children, maiden-aunts, stray cousins. They may not all be accommodated in the house (though in more spacious times they were), but they will all have a place at the festive table, the *seder*. *Seder* means order, for there is a set procedure to the festive meal held on the first (and in some homes on the second) night of Passover. It is, in fact, part banquet, part prayer-meeting, part holy communion replete with its own liturgy – the *Hagadah* – and it is rich in history and symbolism. The first *seder* was celebrated by the Israelites after the Exodus

After the house is throughly cleansed and all the leavened foods disposed of, it is traditional to burn the leaven ceremoniously

וּבְיָד חֲזָקָה וּבִזְרֹעַ נְטוּיָה ❖

בְדוֹלִים בְכֹל אֲשֶׁר עָשָׂה

יְיָ אֱלֹהֵיכֶם בְּמִצְרַיִם לְעֵינֶיךָ ׃

וּבְאֹתוֹת זֶה הַמַּטֶּה כְּמָה שֶׁנֶּאֱמַר

וְאֶת הַמַּטֶּה הַזֶּה תִּקַּח בְּיָדְךָ

אֲשֶׁר תַּעֲשֶׂה בּוֹ אֶת הָאֹתֹת ❖

וּבְמֹפְתִים זֶה הַדָּם כְּמָה שֶׁנֶּאֱמַר

וְנָתַתִּי מוֹפְתִים בְּשָׁמַיִם

וּבָאָרֶץ ׃ דָּם וָאֵשׁ וְתִמְרוֹת עָשָׁן

דָּבָר אַחֵר בְּיָד חֲזָקָה שְׁתַּיִם וּבִזְרֹעַ נ

נְטוּיָה שְׁתַּיִם ׃ וּבְמֹרָא גָּדֹל שְׁתַּיִם ׃ וּבְאֹתוֹת

שְׁתַּיִם ׃ וּבְמֹפְתִים שְׁתַּיִם

אֵלּוּ עֶשֶׂר מַכּוֹת שֶׁהֵבִיא הַקָּדוֹשׁ בָּרוּךְ

הוּא עַל הַמִּצְרִים בְּמִצְרַיִם

דָּם צְפַרְדֵּעַ

כִּנִּים עָרוֹב

דֶּבֶר שְׁחִין

בָּרָד אַרְבֶּה

חֹשֶׁךְ מַכַּת בְּכוֹרוֹת

These pages from this *Hagadah* written out by the hand of Abraham Tang (England, 1768) deal with the Ten Plagues brought down on Egypt as 'encouragement' to free the enslaved Hebrews

from Egypt and in some oriental communities the participants take packs on their backs and re-enact some of the scenes from the Exodus. In Roman times, it was celebrated in great style with all the male members of the household reclining on couches like emperors, and to this day the head of the household, who conducts the *seder*, is required to sit on a specially prepared chair, bolstered up with cushions and pillows to look like a throne. On Passover, every Jew is 'king for a night', though his table is full of remembrances from sadder times: the horse-radish and the bitter herbs recall the bitterness of bondage, the *charoset* (made of apples, nuts, spices and wine) recalls how the Israelites were forced to make bricks without straw. In contrast, the damask table-cloth, the gleaming silver goblets, the bottles of wine – of which each celebrant is expected to imbibe at least four cups – and the elegantly dressed company effuse a holiday atmosphere. The *seder* begins with the usual blessing over wine and then, at an early stage of the proceedings, the head of the household raises the *matzo* and makes a formal invocation:

This is the bread of affliction which our forefathers ate in the land of Egypt. Let all who are hungry come in and eat; let all who are needy enter and celebrate the Passover. This year we are here, next year we shall be in the land of Israel. This year we are slaves, next year we shall be free men.

No man should be left without means to celebrate the Passover and none should be left on his own. The *seder* calls for company and one is either a guest or has guests.

Next comes the *pièce de résistance* of the *seder*, the 'four questions', which are asked by the youngest member of the company:

Why is this night different from all other nights?
On all other nights we may eat leavened or unleavened bread,
on this night we only eat *matzo*.
On all other nights we eat all kinds of herbs,
on this night we eat mainly bitter herbs.
On all other nights we do not dip even once,
on this night we dip twice.
On all other nights we may eat either sitting or leaning,
on this night we all sit leaning.

In answer one turns at once to the *Hagadah*:

We were slaves unto Pharaoh in Egypt, and the Lord our God brought us forth from there with a strong hand and an outstretched arm . . .

This *seder* in progress is an illustration from a *Hagadah* whose commentary is in Spanish written in Hebrew characters

The questions are an invitation to go on to an outline of the history of the Children of Israel from the time of Abraham to the Exodus, ending the record in thanksgiving with Psalm 114:

> When Israel went out of Egypt,
> the House of Jacob from a people of strange language;
> Judah was his sanctuary, and Israel his dominion.
> The sea saw it and fled,
> the Jordan was driven back
> The mountains skipped like rams
> and the hills like lambs.
> What ailed thee, O thou sea, that thou fleddest?
> thou Jordan that thou went back?
> Ye mountains that ye skipped like rams,
> ye hills like lambs?
> Tremble thou earth at the presence of the Lord,
> at the presence of the God of Jacob;
> which turned the rock into standing waters,
> the flint into a fountain.

The Psalm is generally sung, as are the four questions, and the purpose is not only to introduce life and colour into the proceedings but to give the children – especially through the four questions – an immediate feeling of participation. A properly conducted *seder* can last four, five or even six hours, and ancient ploys are used to keep the children interested and awake. There are Pesach songs – as familiar to the average Jewish child as Christmas carols to a Christian child – that are saved for the very end. They are, in fact, popular nursery rhymes set to catchy tunes, some of them taken from the pop songs of their time. The most beloved of all is perhaps *Chad Gadya*:

> This is the kid that father bought for two zuzim,
> poor little kid, one little kid.
> And this is the cat that ate the kid . . .
> And this is the dog that bit the cat . . .
> And this is the stick that beat the dog . . .

This goes on and on until the Angel of Death triumphs over all, and the Almighty appears to triumph even over him.

After the meal is over, but before the songs begin, there is yet another diversion. Three *matzot* are used on the *seder* plate, and at an early stage of the proceedings, the father splits the middle *matzo* and distributes half of it round the table; he hides the other half

Echoes of the celebration of Passover as a spring festival are embedded in the traditional *Chad Gadya* rhyme

for the close of the meal, at which time the child who finds it is entitled to a gift. Children are, in fact, central to the celebration of the *seder*, and a childless *seder* can be a very melancholy affair. It can be melancholy, too, if one is surrounded only by grown up sons and daughters; there comes a stage when one looks to a grandchild to ask the four questions and enliven the proceedings. The whole *seder* is part of the stuff of childhood – the concourse of relatives, the new faces, the festive table, the wine, the sense of occasion, the ancient tunes – all form the climax of the long, long year. If it is still observed religiously by even the irreligious, it is, in part, out of a desire to snatch something of times past, to recapture a whiff of childhood. Nostalgia is in many cases the final remnant of faith.

Passover is also a spring festival and the Song of Songs is read in the synagogues:

> For lo, the winter is past,
> the rain is over and gone;
> The flowers appear on the earth;
> the time of the singing of the birds is come,
> and the voice of the turtle is heard in the land (2:11–12).

The season colours the memory. The New Year and the festivals which crowd beyond it, on the other hand, are celebrated amidst the gathering mists of autumn. In Temple days, devout Jews from all over Judea, and beyond, went on a pilgrimage to Jerusalem on Passover, Pentecost and the Feast of Tabernacles; together they came to be known as the *Shalosh Regalim*, the three pilgrimage festivals. All three are deeply rooted in the land of Israel and all are agricultural festivals: the first saw the cutting of the first barley crop, the second marked the picking of the first fruits and the third was the great ingathering festival; the pilgrimage, therefore, was partly an occasion of thanksgiving. All three are also connected with the Exodus: Passover, of course, commemorates the Exodus itself; Pentecost, the giving of the Torah; and the Feast of Tabernacles (Succot), the way of life in the wilderness, the temporary structures in which the Israelites rested:

> Ye shall dwell in booths seven days; all that are Israelites born shall dwell in booths. That your generations may know that I made the Children of Israel to dwell in booths, when I brought them out of the land of Egypt: I am the Lord your God (Leviticus 23:42–3).

Northern climates make it impractical to actually dwell in booths,

opposite The highlight of the Passover celebration is the *seder*, with as many generations as possible arranged around the traditional table
overleaf This masked ball of the Sephardi community in Amsterdam was part of their celebration of the feast of Purim (1780)

but many Orthodox families build temporary wooden huts in their backyards (in parts of Jerusalem they rise from every balcony), with roofs of pine and laurel, in which they have their meals throughout the seven days of the festival. They are decorated with fruit, paper chains and baubles, and children tend to regard them as play rooms and can hardly be drawn out of them.

There is another ordinance connected with the festival, which adds further colour and gaiety to it:

And ye shall take you on the first day the boughs of goodly trees, branches of palm trees, and the bough of thick trees, and the willows of the brook; and you shall rejoice before the Lord your God seven days (Leviticus 23:40).

A palm frond entwined with willow and myrtle branches is taken in one hand and a citrus in the other (they are known collectively as the *arba minim*, the 'four types') and they are paraded ceremoniously in the synagogue – an Orthodox synagogue resembles a moving forest. It is a mellow, happy time of the year, full of glad associations, but the gladness is not allowed to get out of hand. On each of the three pilgrimage festivals one reads a passage from the Bible appropriate to the season: on Passover, as we have noted, the Song of Songs; on Pentecost, the Book of Ruth, with its evocation of pastoral life and distant summers; on Succot, one reads Ecclesiastes:

Vanity of vanities, saith the Preacher, vanity of vanities; all is vanity. What profit hath a man of all his labour which he taketh under the sun? One generation passeth away, and another generation cometh; but the earth abideth for ever. The sun also ariseth, and the sun goeth down, and hasteth to his place where he arose (1:2–5).

The cycle of festivals that begins the Jewish year closes with Simchat Torah, which celebrates the completion and resumption of the reading of the Torah. Again, children are at the centre of the celebration. All the Scrolls of the Law are taken from the ark and paraded seven times round the synagogue. Children join the parade with flags and miniature scrolls, which they carry aloft above their heads, and are showered with sweets and chocolates from the crowded ladies' galleries. The seventeenth-century diarist Samuel Pepys happened to wander into a synagogue during one such celebration and was appalled at what he saw:

. . . the disorder, laughing, sporting and no attention, but confusion in all their service, more like brutes than people knowing the true God, would make a man forswear ever seeing them more: and indeed I never

A profusion of Chanukah lamps from all over the Jewish world (from left to right):
top A 19th-century stone lamp from Morocco
upper row A 17th-century brass lamp from Italy; a 14th-15th-century brass lamp believed to have originated in Spain; an Italian brass lamp of the 16th century showing Judith with the head of Holofernes
lower row An 18th-century silver lamp from Germany; a 19th-century silver lamp from Russia
bottom An 18th-century brass lamp from Italy

did see so much, or could have imagined that there had been any religion in the whole world so absurdly performed as this.

The Orthodox Jews spend so much time in the synagogue that they could not possibly behave with the decorum usual in a church. God, moreover, is so familiar a part of their universe that they exist on more-or-less informal terms with Him, and they feel free to be fairly relaxed with their friends, gesticulate to their wives or daughters in the ladies' gallery, go out for a chat in the vestibule – all within limits – in His house. On Simchat Torah, however, the synagogue is given over to almost unbridled merrymaking. There is singing and dancing with the scrolls in hand, and if the children have sweets, the adults retire for something more substantial. Every year, two leading congregants are honoured with the title 'Bridegroom of the Law'. In England, they dress like virtual bridegrooms, in top hats and striped trousers, and generally pay for the honour by providing a plentiful flow of whisky and herring. Very rarely does anyone drink to the point of getting drunk, but many a worshipper is sufficiently merry to earn stern glances from his womenfolk in the gallery (which may be another reason why decorum in an Orthodox synagogue is rather less complete than in church: the husbands are separated from their wives).

There is one other occasion in the Jewish year when drink flows fairly freely, even abundantly, and that is Purim. Purim, like Chanukah, is a comparatively minor festival. It is not sanctioned in the Pentateuch like the other occasions we have described, but arose out of a much later event in Jewish history. The whole story is told in the Book of Esther: how a wicked vizier, Haman, sought to destroy the Jews of Persia and how his plans were foiled through the intervention of the beautiful Jewish Queen Esther and Mordechai, a court Jew. The entire book is read out in the synagogue on the eve of the festival and on the following morning. In the evening, especially, the synagogue is crowded with children who whistle, clatter, stamp their feet and bang their pews every time the name of Haman is mentioned – with the result that many a child grows up with the belief that Haman is the hero of the story. He is to the Jewish child what Guy Fawkes is to the English one, so popular a villain as to be regarded almost with affection. Purim (the name means 'lots', for Haman cast lots to see on which day he should carry out his plan) generally falls at the end of winter when spring is already in the air; it is the nearest thing in Jewish life to the pre-Lenten carnivals and is enjoyed with something of the

opposite An illustration from a work entitled '*Seder Kreiei Mo'ed*' (Vienna, 1811) showing the ceremonial parade of the *arba minim* on Succot
overleaf This illustration from the 1 April 1865 edition of *Frank Leslie's Illustrated Newspaper* recaptures the spirit of an American Purim ball of the times

same abandon. It is the one occasion on which there actually is encouragement from tradition to drink and get drunk 'until one doesn't know Mordechai from Haman'. There are fancy dress-parades and masquerades for children, and at one time in Israel there was an annual carnival procession.

There were sometimes fears that the celebrations might get out of hand, especially at Purim masquerades where men dressed as women and women as men. 'Woe, woe,' said a medieval Rabbi, 'lest your behaviour on Purim should be the cause of another Tisha B'Av.' But in spite of such admonitions, Purim has remained true to itself – a day off from restraints, a moment free of inhibitions. Special poppy-seed cakes, known as *homan tashen*, are baked for the occasion, and the day closes with a festive meal.

Chanukah, another minor festival, lasts eight days and also celebrates a post-biblical event: a successful revolt of Jewish nationalists against their Greek overlords. The victory was a miracle in itself, but what proved even more miraculous – and what has given to Chanukah the name of 'Festival of Lights' – was the fact that a cruse of Temple oil sufficient to last one day continued to burn for eight. Most Jewish households have a small candelabrum, and the family will gather about it nightly lighting one candle on the first night, two on the second and so on until the final night of Chanukah. There are a number of songs traditional to the occasion, but the most popular is *Maoz Tzur*, which recounts the numerous occasions that the Israelites were saved from calamity through the intervention of the Almighty. There is also a special dish for Chanukah (as we have seen, there is hardly a Jewish occasion without one) called *latkes*, a potato batter fried in oil, which should be eaten crisp and hot. In Israel, the traditional dish is hot doughnuts filled with jam.

Chanukah is often taken to symbolize the continuing clash between Judaism and alien cultures, but it could be argued that Chanukah itself has, to an extent, been sustained in the Western world by the fact that it often coincides with Christmas. The attractions of Christmas – the lights, the Christmas trees, the carols, the presents, the aura of goodwill – are known to every child brought up in the Western world, and Chanukah is a useful counter-attraction that has been fostered as such by the Reform synagogues. It, too, has lights and songs, and the practice of giving Chanukah *gelt* ('Chanukah money') to one's children has, in some circles, been enlarged to a full-scale, Christmas-style exchange of gifts, replete with festive wrappers, among the entire family.

This 18th-century French Purim plate of faience, used to serve up the sweets enjoyed on this festival, depicts Mordechai's humiliation of Haman

There has, as a result, evolved – though only in America – something called 'Chrisnukah'. One can see it in action on and around Fifth Avenue in New York from the day 'Santa comes to town', and the eight-branched Chanukah candelabrum looms behind, or beside, the Christmas wreath. It is a way of pulling Jews into the seasonal shopping spree without making them feel that they are intruding on an alien event. 'Chrisnukah' has not been formally adopted as such by either Christians or Jews, and must be abhorrent to traditionalists among both, but it is cheerfully accepted by Jews who want the best of both worlds. American Jews can celebrate Thanksgiving with a whole heart, for it is an entirely secular occasion whose family character commends itself richly to Jewish tradition. In a sense, some argue, so does the Christmas dinner, so much so that it has been adopted by many Jews on the plea that it is purely a social occasion, rather like New Year, which has lost its Christian character and is as open to Jews as to anyone else. Others go further and have Christmas trees, asserting (where

they feel the need to apologize) that such trees hark back to a pre-Christian era. Others, while not being traditionally minded themselves, have sufficient respect for the traditions of their Christian friends not to intrude upon them. The festive mood of the season is, however, infectious, and they find an outlet in the celebration of Chanukah.

There are three fast days that are still widely observed among Jews (apart from Yom Kippur, which is almost universally observed), and they commemorate a black year in Jewish history, 586 BC, when the Babylonians began the siege of Jerusalem (Tenth of Tevet), broke into the Holy City (Seventeenth of Tammuz) and destroyed the Temple (Ninth of Av). This last date commemorates a double calamity, for on the same day some 600 years later, the Romans destroyed the Second Temple. The Seventeenth of Tammuz falls out three weeks before the Ninth of Av, and among ultra-Orthodox Jews, the whole period is treated as one of mourning: men will not shave or cut their hair; no new clothes will be

Chanukah is actually a festival commemorating an heroic age in Jewish history, but over the ages it has come to be thought of as a children's festival *par excellence*, and the custom of giving Chanukah *gelt* has expanded in gross proportions

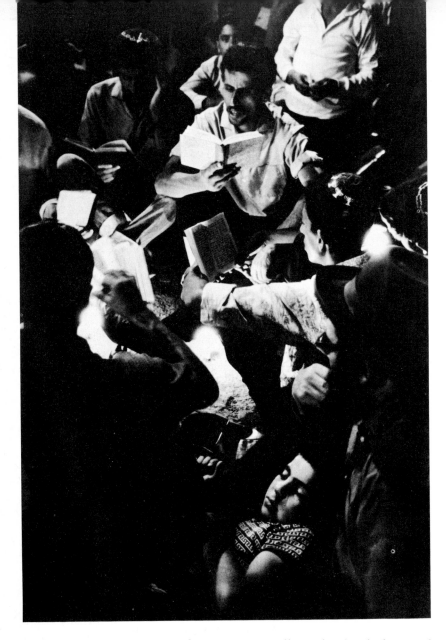

bought or worn; no sort of merriment is allowed. The dark mood heightens as the Ninth of Av draws near, and one experiences a sense of bereavement, as if the Temple fell only yesterday and the smell of smoke is still in the air. The fast begins at nightfall. The congregations assemble in the synagogues, sit on low chairs, as they might at a family bereavement, and read in low voices from Jeremiah's Lamentations, in which the prophet forewarned the events they are now mourning:

> How doth the city sit solitary,
> that was full of people!
> How is she become a widow!

She that was great among the nations,
and princess among provinces,
how is she become tributary!
She weepeth sore in the night,
and her tears are on her cheeks;
among all her lovers she hath none to comfort her;
all her friends have dealt treacherously with her,
they are become her enemies (1 : 1–2).

On the Ninth of Av, one mourns not only the fall of a city and
Temple, but the end of Israel as a nation and the beginning of the
long night of exile. Jewish nationhood has since been restored and
so has Jerusalem (though not the Temple), but the Tenth of Tevet,
the Seventeenth of Tammuz and especially the Ninth of Av still
continue to be observed as fast days, and the Lamentations of
Jeremiah are still read in low voices, on low stools. The habits
ingrained for over 2,000 years are not easily discarded.

In Israel, the anniversary of the declaration of Independence on
the fifth of Iyar is celebrated as a national holiday, and it has
spread among Diaspora Jews as something of a festival. But ultra-
Orthodox communities have remained cut off from it, for if distant events seem near to Jews, near events can sometimes seem
distant.

The various occasions of the Jewish year, whether solemn or
joyous, cannot be easily celebrated in isolation. Indeed, for those
living alone, they are bound to bring their loneliness home to them.
That is one of the reasons why tradition is so insistent that no one
be left on his own, that no festival is complete without a guest at
table. Among the very Orthodox, moreover, no one remains
alone for long. If he is single he will – unless he moves very quickly –
be found a wife and if for any reason he cannot marry, he will
become a *ben bayit*, a member of the household, an honorary
member of the family. But such hospitality is less common than it
used to be, and it becomes less common still as one moves further
away from Orthodoxy. Among assimilated English-speaking Jews
the hospitality tradition has been tempered by the English penchant
for privacy, and if one is invited as a guest to their homes, one
remains a guest – unfamiliar with their gossip, a stranger to their
jokes, alone in their crowd. For those living alone, the feasts can
be too many, too frequent and too burdensome, and the Sabbath
can be a weekly taste of desolation. Jewish tradition presumes a
family.

A 19th-century silver
charity box that belonged
to the Jewish community
(synagogue) of Petrikov,
Poland, as attested by the
inscription

13 Honour Thy Father

If bringing forth children is a supreme duty, rearing them is not always a supreme reward. There was hardly a biblical father who was not troubled by a wayward son – or a wayward daughter. 'A daughter,' wrote Ben Sira, 'is a false treasure to her father. Because of his anxiety for her he does not sleep at night.' The older she grew, the more she was a source of concern, and the Talmud advised: 'If your daughter is adult (and still single) free your slave and give him to her.' Marriage was not only necessary to the fulfilment of her role in life; it was essential to the peace of mind of her parents. The Talmud debated whether a father was obliged to ransom a daughter taken in captivity but left the matter unresolved. And it is significant that of all Shakespeare's plays the one that has been performed most often in Yiddish and Hebrew is *King Lear*.

The Fifth Commandment, 'Honour thy father and thy mother,' is the only one to promise remuneration in this world – 'that thy days on earth may be lengthened' – possibly because the sort of child who might be inclined to dishonour his parents is not interested in the world to come. To hit, or even curse, a parent was a capital offence:

If a man have a stubborn and rebellious son, which will not obey the voice of his father, or the voice of his mother, and that when they have chastened him, will not hearken unto them: then shall his father and mother lay hold on him, and bring him out unto the elders of the city, and unto the gate of his place. And they shall say unto the elders of his city. This our son is stubborn and rebellious, he will not obey our voice; he is a glutton and a drunkard. And all the men of his city shall stone him with stones, that he die; so shalt thou put evil away from among you; and all Israel shall hear and fear (Deuteronomy 21:18–21).

The Rabbis hedged these laws with so many conditions that they

'Jews in the Synagogue' (1925) by the Polish painter Arthur Marcowicz never were – and never could be – put into effect. But they were frequently quoted to show how imperative it was for a son to obey his father and how necessary it was for a father to chastise his son, a point frequently reiterated in Proverbs:

> He that spareth his rod hateth his son:
> but he that loveth him chasteneth him betimes (13:24).
> Train up the child in the way he should go;
> and when he is old he will not depart from it (22:6).
> Correct thy son and he shall give thee rest;
> yea, he shall give delight unto thy soul (29:17).
> Chasten thy son while there is hope (19:18).

For the last there was also a Yiddish version: Hit your son before he is big enough to hit you back!

There is no injunction to love one's child, for that is a natural disposition. The injunctions to chastise arose out of a Jewish tendency to carry the natural disposition to unnatural lengths, to let love outweigh every other consideration and blind parents to the faults of their children. This is well illustrated in the story of Isaac and his sons, Esau and Jacob. Jacob was the more obedient son, yet Esau was the favourite; impulsive, lusty, a wild, roistering creature, a hunter, 'a man of the field' who lived for his appetites, Esau is regarded in Rabbinic writing as the embodiment of everything that Jacob was not. The two brothers passed into the language of Jewish rhetoric as synonyms for sinner and saint. 'And it came to pass, that when Isaac was old, and his eyes were dim' (Genesis 27:1) was interpreted figuratively to show that Isaac was blinded by love to his son's transgressions, and countless cautionary tales were derived to show that one must temper affection with reproof. Some argued that a little distance on the part of the parents was also beneficial: 'Children will be healthy and well-bred,' said Nahman of Bratslav, 'if parents do not play with them too much and do not indulge them too generously.' Alexander Suesskind, who lived at about the same time, took the matter a step further: 'I never kissed my children, nor took them in my arms, so as not to accustom them to silly talk such as people are in the habit of addressing to the young.'

With all the love that Jews had for their children, there was an impatience to see them mature and get on with the serious business of life – the most serious of which was study. For example, literature addressed to children is usually of a serious, didactic nature. Solomon Schechter, Reader in Rabbinics at Cambridge in the early years of

this century and the foremost Jewish folklorist of his age, could in all his researches discover only one Jewish lullaby – and that of relatively recent origin – and it, too, carried its little message:

Education, the serious business of life, began at a tender age, as depicted in 'A Visit to the Rabbi' by the Hungarian artist Izidor Kaufmann (1853–1921)

> O, hush thee my darling, sleep soundly my son,
> Sleep soundly and sweetly till day has begun;
> For under the bed of good children at night,
> There lies till the morning, a kid snowy white.
> We'll send it to market to buy *sechora* [supplies],

> While my little lad goes to study Torah.
> Sleep soundly at night, learn Torah by day,
> Then thou'll be a Rabbi 'ere I've gone grey.
> But I'll give thee tomorrow ripe nuts and a toy,
> If thou'll sleep as I bid thee, my own little boy.

Jewish mothers often sang German or Russian lullabys to their children, a matter which occasionally earned them the reproof of the Rabbis, though some of the songs in the Passover *Hagadah*, like *Chad Gadya*, are in fact of German origin.

The eagerness of the father to get his son to the *Beth Midrash*, the house of study, arose not merely because study was regarded as an end in itself, but because it was seen as the panacea for all – or almost all – ills. The basic cause of Jacob's piety, according to tradition, was that he spent his days in study, that of Esau's iniquity was that he did not. But impatience also arose from the fact that infant mortality was high and life expectancy was low, and a father felt the need to equip his son with the essentials of life while there was still time. There is a Hebrew expression, *tzar gidul banim*, 'the pain of bringing up children', and the pains took many forms – sickness, death, insubordination. The Talmudic sage Rav Meir had thirteen sons, all of whom died in infancy – two on the same day. It was easier, said one Rabbi, to plant a whole forest than to rear one child. And yet the general feeling, expressed in a multitude of Jewish sayings, was that in children and children's children lay all the true joys of life. Brachya asked himself if this was in fact so:

> For I say, what advantage is there in them, when they are in want of bread, and in want of a home; and what is the good of them when they possess neither knowledge nor understanding, or when the father fondles them, being half-witted, thus adding to his trouble and labour, for you cannot buy honour and respect for your children when they possess no good qualities. Then, think of the pangs of conception and childbirth, and its attendant danger, often proving fatal to the mother ... And whence arise all the labour and toil of the father, but from the desire to supply his children with bread? And how great the trouble of rearing them, bearing with their illnesses and adopting measures for their recovery. And when they thrive physically and grow to manhood, and are exemplary in doing what they should do, how great a responsibility even then. As regards the males, it is enough to drive sleep from the eyes, as it is said, 'He that spoileth his father and chaseth away his mother' (Proberbs 19:26). And as regards the females, they make the heart palpitate with fear ... But if, on the other hand, the children grow up, and run wild, then they bring grief upon the family hearth; the injury which they cause increases as

the expectations from them decrease, as it is said: 'There is a generation that curseth their father, and doth not bless their mother' (Proverbs 30:11).

A cradle from a Jewish home in Bokhara

This was perhaps written in an hour of disenchantment. Most of the details we have of Jewish life at this date, and in later centuries, suggest a more attractive picture of children walking diligently in the ways of their fathers: on their way to and from synagogue, carrying their prayer-books, standing with bowed heads on Friday nights awaiting their parents' blessing, poring over the small print of the Talmud. And when they began their studies, they began in earnest: in small, stuffy, dimly lit rooms called the *cheder*, poring over their dog-eared pages of the *siddur* and *chumash* (prayer-book and Pentateuch). The scene is evoked in the most beloved of all Yiddish songs:

above The child walking diligently in the way of his father was the typical picture of the relations between generations throughout the centuries, as portrayed in this drawing by the Austrian illustrator Ephraim Moses Lilien (1874–1925)

left The same theme continues to be played out on the streets of certain quarters of Jerusalem today

אבבגדהוז
חט בבךל
מםנ זסעפף
וץקרששתת

The *melamed* teaching his charges the *aleph-bet* in a contemporary *cheder* that bears much resemblance to its European predecessors

In the hearth a fire crackles,
and the room is hot,
and the Rabbi with his charges small,
are learning *aleph-bet*.

The *cheder* was a small, cramped schoolroom with cracked windows, walls bare of everything save moisture, long benches and scarred desks. More scarred than the desks was the *melamed*, the teacher, a harassed, broken figure, book in one hand, stick in the other, trying to induce both Torah and order and, as a rule, inducing nothing but chaos. Almost everyone in the Jewish community was presumed to have some learning. The *melamed* had less than most, but he turned to teaching because he was useless at everything else. He was a licensed unfortunate and usually combined his calling with that of *shammes*, synagogue beadle and general

The *cheder*, of course, was not restricted to Eastern Europe. This was a village *cheder* in Tissint, Morocco, forty years ago

factotum of the burial society, laying out the dead and, when the deceased had no immediate relatives, saying memorial prayers for them. Teaching was by rote; it was believed that words said in chorus helped to embed them in the memory and that a whack across the ear aided the process further. Corporal punishment was anything but frowned upon, and some *melamdim* literally ruled their classes with an *eizerne rot*, 'a rod of iron'. The boys with high spirits and low cunning conspired to make their life a misery, and they retorted in kind. It is one of the miracles of Jewish life that in spite of the *cheder* most boys emerged with their love of learning intact. Their main teachers were, in fact, their parents: the mother while the children were young, the father as they grew older. Sometimes he would study with his children on weekday evenings, but if not then, religiously on the Sabbath. The usual subject of study while the children were young was the *chumash* (the Pentateuch) – not only the stories, which had their own en-

The *melamed* who ruled his class with 'a rod of iron', as depicted by the artist Saul Raskin

chantment, but the commentaries and the homilies surrounding them. Every line, every word, carried some lesson with immediate bearing on family life: Cain and Abel taught the dangers of fratricidal strife; Joseph, the need for brotherly love; Korach, the dangers of rebellion. If the clear meaning of the text did not convey the intended message, the words could be bent a little; but all study, all knowledge, all his limited experience, predisposed the child to regard all the wisdom as wise.

Nor, as he grew older, did one discern any widespread rebelliousness. Rebellion called for a spaciousness that did not exist, options that were not available. The Jew, crammed into the narrow *Judengasse*, was unaware of any pattern of existence beyond that of his faith. In addition to the natural family loyalty that derived from love was the loyalty that arose out of common needs and common dangers; it was the happiness that the Jew found among his wife and children that enabled him to survive the harassments

The *Judengasse* of Vilna, Poland, in 1929 was the epitome of being hemmed in, physically and culturally

of the outside world. Only when the outside world became less menacing did the Jew find increasing discomfiture in his own. One could not, perhaps, have one without the other, for the very forces which eased the atmosphere outside the family occasioned frictions within it. The *sorrer v'morrer*, the rebellious son encountered in Deuteronomy, was a mere lout, but the age of enlightenment brought forth a new type of rebel, one who questioned the whole creed on which his father's life was based – the doctrinal rebel. Hitherto, children grew up in much the same world as their parents, and if circumstances differed, their basic outlook did not. But that changed. There were new hopes, new opportunities, great mo-bility – even for the Jew. One grew up in one world, while one's children matured in another. The generation gap was here. (Not every gap, one must hasten to add, represented a domestic tragedy. Parents, wittingly or unwittingly, sometimes worked hard to create it.) Every father strove to put his children a step ahead of himself, not always with the happiest results, as one can see from this reproachful letter written by Judah Ibn Tibbon, a twelfth-century Jewish physician and scholar, to his son. Ibn Tibbon lived in Moorish Spain where the Jews enjoyed a spaciousness that they would not experience elsewhere in Europe until the eighteenth century:

> Thou knowest, my son, how I swaddled thee and brought thee up, how I led thee in the paths of wisdom and virtue. I fed and clothed thee; I spent myself in educating and protecting thee, I sacrificed my sleep to make thee wise beyond thy fellows, and to raise thee to the highest degree of science and morals. These twelve years I have denied myself the usual pleasures and relaxations of men for thy sake, and I still toil for thine inheritance.
>
> I have assisted thee by providing an extensive library for thy use . . . I journeyed to the ends of the earth and fetched for thee a teacher in secular sciences. I neither heeded the expense or the dangers of the ways. Untold evils might have befallen me and thee on these travels had not the Lord been with us.
>
> But thou, my son, didst deceive my hopes . . .

But even if sons fulfilled the hopes of their fathers, conflicts still could arise between the generations that neither love nor respect could bridge. Love, if anything, made them all the more painful. The nature of such conflicts is well illustrated in the life of Montagu Samuel, a Liverpool merchant of German-Jewish stock, who prospered, changed his name to Samuel Montagu, moved south to London, set up as a banker, married into a prosperous Anglo-Jewish clan, entered Parliament, was raised to the peerage as Lord Swaythling and became patriarch of the Orthodox community. He was defender of the faith, an example to the faithful, living proof that in England one could rise to the highest levels of society without sacrificing an iota of one's faith. He had a large family, however, and not all his children shared his outlook. One of his daughters, Lilly, a woman of deep religious belief and intense piety, became one of the leaders of a break-away movement in the community, the Liberal Jewish Synagogue. When her father could do nothing to restrain her, he disinherited her. Lilly, who later became the first woman preacher in England, was distressed by the drawing-room gossip that these conflicts had occasioned:

Samuel Montagu as portrayed in a cartoon from *Vanity Fair*

Of course they could not tell beneath the strain occasioned by the different point of view between father and daughter there was essential sympathy and deep understanding love. The daughter felt so much reverence for her father's principles that she could never discuss them with him; the father felt such tender sympathy and yearning sorrow for the, to him, mistaken views of his daughter that he could not articulate any remonstrance, nor certainly any kind of vituperation. There was just a pained silence beneath which hearts ached to commune.

Lilly Montagu, at least, never moved completely away from the type of Jewish environment that she had found in her father's house, for often children ceased to find satisfaction or happiness in their parents' world. This feeling was excellently described by the literary critic David Daiches (whose father was rabbi of the Edinburgh Jewish community) in an autobiographical volume appropriately called *Two Worlds*:

Lilly Montagu, Samuel's daughter, who became one of the leaders of the breakaway Liberal Jewish Synagogue and the first woman preacher in England

My father in his innocence took much for granted. Most of all he took for granted that the deep unmentioned roots of his own faith would spread automatically down the generations. He was an orthodox Jewish rabbi and a student of Hume and Kant, had finally solved the relation between Judaism and modern secular culture and showed how one could be a free and equal citizen of a Western democracy while keeping up all orthodox Jewish observances: there was nothing for me to do but to follow in his footsteps.

And for a long time he did, for affection led where reasoning did not, but towards the end of his university studies, Dr Daiches met a Scottish girl whom he wanted to marry. After pondering over the matter for several years, he decided that there would have to be a show-down, but discovered that this was not always possible. He was too stifled by affection, too anxious to avoid the pain of giving pain, and the show-down never took place. Instead, much against his will, he left Britain to start a new life in America. For the sake of his parents' feelings, he converted his wife to Judaism, even though, as he readily confessed, he was an agnostic. Gradually, over the years, the wounds healed and father was reconciled to son.

In the case of Daiches, if father and son occupied different worlds, they at least spoke approximately the same language: one was a scholar of the old school and the other of the new, and there was the common bond of scholarship. But in many families of that generation, a father's struggle to earn a livelihood left him with neither a Jewish nor a secular education, only with a sufficient belief in learning to assure that his sons would not be so deprived. So he borrowed and skimped and scraped to send them to grammar school and university, but when they finally emerged, tassled and gowned with diplomas in hand, they no longer spoke the same language. 'My son the doctor' was thus both a source of pride and despair, for he had different friends, different interests, different beliefs (supposing he had any at all). Such a son, to paraphrase the words of Ben Sira, was 'a false treasure' to his mother and because of her anxiety for him, she does not sleep at night. For who could tell whether during his internship he might not be trapped into marriage by some scheming, immoral, *shiksah* nurse?

Immigrant fathers did not really expect their graduate sons to follow in their ways, for, apart from anything else, they themselves had departed from the ways of *their* fathers. They could also forgive their sons' lack of religious observance, for there was a tacit belief that a good education was a form of absolution, that a B.A. was as good as a penance, and a Ph.D. assured one a place in the world to come. Many fathers had themselves ceased to be Orthodox and were only nominally observant, but they still expected a minimal commitment on the part of their sons, and a minimal commitment to them was to marry in the faith. Often they did not get even that, and if a father was consequently distant from his son, he was sometimes totally estranged from his grandsons.

But family life was not without its storms even when children were fully committed to Judaism (sometimes they were too fully committed, which could in itself lead to storms). The one thing that a Jewish parent wants of his children is, to use a Yiddish expression much heard in the Jewish home, *naches* – a mixture of gratification, pride, joy, thankfulness, a sense of beatitude, the feeling that God is smiling down assentingly. It is something to be had only from children. One does not look for *naches* in business or the professions, for example; there one merely hopes for success. But if one's child succeeds in either, then his parents will have *naches* – as will his grandparents (if they are still about). If a parent says reproachfully, 'I only want you to be happy,' he means all I want from you is *naches*, and *naches* is best gained if the child does what his parent would have done had he been in the child's place. When children are small, they give *naches* merely by being there (which may be one of the reasons why parents sometimes try to prolong childhood for as long as possible), but as they mature, trouble begins. Children grow up not only without their parents' hindsight (which is a deficiency common to every generation)

The young Golda Meir, who stood her ground and pursued the career of her choice as a school teacher and ultimately reached the pinnacle of power in the Jewish world

but, for the past two or three generations, without any knowledge of the circumstances that formed their parents' *Weltanschauung*. This is well illustrated in an autobiographical fragment by Mrs Golda Meir: when she left school, she wanted to go on to college to be a teacher, but this caused some unhappiness, for her parents feared that if she became a teacher, she might remain a spinster, and they urged her to take a secretarial course instead. They were Russian immigrants recently settled in Milwaukee, and for them there was but one career for a daughter – marriage. It is difficult, or it was then, for the Jewish parent to think of his child as a distinct entity with a life of his own, a will of his own and, indeed, a destiny of his own. Most Jews with a traditional upbringing, and not a few without, have a sub-conscious belief that if they have children, and their children have children, they are immortal. They think of themselves as an updated version of their fathers, their children as an updated version of themselves and are confounded when their children find happiness in situations that would have given them grief. They genuinely do want their children to be happy, but in situations that would have made them happy too. Thus, the defection of a child nearly brought their world to an end.

Since then, the defectors have likewise experienced defections. The generation that recalled the bitterness and strife that the differences between their parents and themselves occasioned was determined that there should be none between their children and themselves. They, too, only wanted their children to be happy, but (enjoying the benefits of their own hindsight) without any attempt to impose their beliefs or attitudes on them. All this while the pace of change, which had been continuing at a trot, accelerated to a gallop. The family became fragmented, generation from generation, kith from kin, and, not infrequently, husband from wife. It was difficult for the broken family to control its children – and not all that easy for the unbroken family to do so. Controls and restraints of any sort were in disfavour among parents, and every child was able to do what was right in his own eyes. People changed their jobs, homes and their whole life with increasing frequency. Grandfathers, always an important influence on a young child, were distant figures who sent birthday presents. Children disappeared for two or three months in summer camp; as they grew older, for three or four years in university; and on completing university, they disappeared altogether. All of which was not always a condition of parental *angst* (worry). In the past, parents lived for and through their children, but once it became clear that

An 18th-century enamel-painted ceremonial beaker of the Holy Burial Society of Prague (see chapter 15)

children preferred to live for themselves, parents also decided to live for themselves and limited their family to that end. As a result, the conditions necessary for the transmission of mores, the closeness, the continuity, the stability, the mutual respect and, indeed, the compulsion to transmit ceased to exist. Today there is less a sense of family and more a sense of self; mutual involvement has given way to mutual exclusion. In most cases, all that has remained is a vague, undefined, aching affection. One no longer even looks for *naches* in a child; one only hopes he will not be a cause of *tzores* (vexation).

The new situation has not brought much joy to either parents or children, and as a result one can see that a gradual re-evaluation of old attitudes, a reconsideration of modern beliefs and a rediscovery of old life-styles is beginning. External events have, of course, played their part in all this: the Holocaust and the dramas surrounding the emergence and existence of the State of Israel have both given rise to a new Jewish awareness. In times of bewildering change, everything old has something to commend it – whether it be an article of furniture, a home, a country or a way of life – and many a child has retraced for himself the pathways neglected by his father. The age of reason, moreover, has brought the world to such straits that there is an increasing resort to unreason. The supernatural is enjoying a new vogue, and many of the young people who are finding their way back to Judaism have not sought a place among their Reform, Conservative or even Orthodox brethren, but among ultra-Orthodox Chassidim. In a sense, they are responding to their age in much the same way that the founders of Chassidism responded to theirs. Chassidism was a reaction against the dry scholasticism that dominated Jewish life and thought in eighteenth-century Poland. These Jews wanted emotion, colour, zest to their faith, and they found it.

One does not have to suspend one's rational faculties to revert to traditional Judaism (though some would say it helps). At first sight it does not strike one as eminently reasonable – this attitude is unwholesome, or that precept illogical – but, taken as a whole, it has worked in the past and could be made to work in the present, and even with all its imperfections, it has more to commend it than any known alternative. Some have reached this conclusion empirically, some from the example of their friends, some through a leap in faith, but the trends evident in earlier decades are being reversed: old ways are being revived because new ones have been found wanting.

As people often came from afar and different directions to pay their respects to the dead, they left a small rock on the gravestone as testimony to other members of the memorial party that they had already come and gone. Over the years, however, pragmatism developed into custom, and the rocks were interpreted as an effort to keep the soul of the deceased in his grave, lest it return to haunt the living (see chapter 15)

valiter Ruth manipulos suos excutit
qortum ide redacti socrui sue ostentum g
narrat ei omnem Booz erga se humanitate

14 Nor His Daughter

Neither shalt thou make marriages with them; thy daughter thou shalt not give unto his son, nor his daughter shalt thou take unto thy son. For they will turn away thy son from following me, that they may serve other gods; so will the anger of the Lord be kindled against them (Deuteronomy 7:3-4).

This warning to Moses on Sinai was against marriage with Canaanites. But there were strong feelings against such marriages long before the Torah was given. When Esau took two Hittite wives 'they were a bitterness of spirit unto Isaac and Rebekah,' and Rebekah spent anxious hours in the fear that Jacob might do the same: 'I am weary of my life because of the daughters of Heth; if Jacob take a wife of the daughters of Heth, such as those are of the daughters of the land, what good shall my life do me?' (Genesis 27:46). It is a feeling with which many a mother of a later generation has sympathized. Rebekah's fear was unwarranted; the anxieties of later generations of Jewish mothers were not.

There is a constant tension between the group that, for reasons of its own self-preservation, resents the outsider, and the individual who welcomes him – or more frequently her. In Deuteronomy we find a modification of the original injunction:

When thou goest forth to war against thine enemies, and the Lord thy God hath delivered them into thine hands, and thou hast taken them captive. And seest among the captives a beautiful woman, and hast a desire unto her, that thou wouldst have her as a wife. Then thou shalt bring her home to thine house; and she shall shave her head and pare her nails. And she shall put off the raiment of her captivity from off her, and shall remain in thine house, and bewail her father and mother a full month: and after that thou shalt go in unto her, and be her husband, and she shall be thy wife (22:10-13).

Naomi and her daughter-in-law Ruth, the most famous convert to Judaism and the model for generations to come, from a 13th-century French illuminated manuscript of the Bible

But even this modified injunction was not completely observed. It is obvious from the reading of the Bible that intermarriage in Judea and Samaria was not uncommon. The tendency is well illustrated in the story of Samson and the woman of Timnah: 'Get her for me,' he told his parents, as if it were the most natural request in the world. His parents demurred in terms that have become painfully familiar: 'Is there never a woman among the daughters of thy brethren, or among all my people, that thou goest to take a wife amongst the uncircumcised Philistines?' (Judges 14:3). But they complied with his wish all the same.

Samson was a prince in Israel, and other princes, including David and, of course, Solomon, took foreign wives. But lest it be thought that the people at large were more attentive to the Mosaic injunctions, Judges makes clear that this was not so:

And the children of Israel dwelt among the Canaanites, Hittites and Amorites, and Perizzites and Hivites and Jebusites: And they took their daughters to be their wives, and gave their daughters to their sons' sons, and served their gods (Judges 3:5–6).

And that, as the Prophet warned, was the cause of their downfall. Only much later, under Babylonian, and then Persian, dominion, when the Jews no longer comprised an independent entity, did the group instinct for survival assert itself. A reaction against intermarriage set in and has continued until the present day. When the Return to Zion came under Ezra and Nehemia in the fifth century BC, Ezra ordered the dissolution of all mixed marriages:

And Ezra the priest stood up and said unto them. Ye have transgressed and taken strange wives to increase the trespass of Israel. Now, therefore, make confession unto the Lord God of your fathers, and do his pleasure: and separate yourselves from the people of the land and from the strange wives. And all the congregation answered and said with a loud voice: As thou hast said, so must we do (Ezra 10:10–12).

But later congregations were rather less compliant, and as the Persians gave way to the Greeks, the problem reappeared: the Greeks were proselytizers in a way that the Persians and Babylonians were not, and Greek culture – Hellenism – proved attractive in a way that other cultures had not. Hellenism, indeed, came to symbolize all the allure of the outside world that the Rabbis feared, even to the point of proscribing the study of Greek. The events celebrated on Chanukah were a victory in the continuing struggle between Hellenism and Judaism, although at other times this

struggle took the form of civil war, for many Jews saw in Hellenism a higher life and a better life to which Judaism should aspire. They also saw in it great material advantages and, through the acquisition of Greek language and culture, they were able to prosper not only at home, but in the various provinces of the Greek empire. The rise of Rome in some ways expedited this process, and the Jewish Diaspora began to outnumber the Jews living in their own homeland. But the more Jews were accepted in the outside world, the more the defenders of the faith – the zealots – pulled back into their own. The end of Roman tolerance and the rise of Christianity, however, changed all that, and for a while Judaism ceased to feel threatened. Great dangers were still to be faced, but they were physical rather than cultural.

Jewish and Christian society were mutually exclusive, and one could move from one to the other only through a definite act of apostasy. This was also largely true of Jews under Moslem rule in Spain and North Africa. And the situation remained more or less constant throughout the succeeding centuries. In the sixteenth century, however, there was a revival of Greek ideas and a new

Hellenism proved attractive to the Jews in a way that other cultures had not. The mythological Pan was one of the more prominent symbols of that culture

Moses Mendelssohn
(1729–1786), the 'father of
the Jewish enlightenment',
whose descendants were
lost to the faith after a
generation or two

'enlightenment' spread across Europe. This new wave took longer
to touch the Jewish community, and evidence of it appeared only
towards the end of the eighteenth century. But when it did arrive,
its impact was immediate and startling and is symbolized best in
the experience of Moses Mendelssohn, the father of Jewish enlightenment, whose descendants, after a generation or two, were all lost
to Judaism. The process was much hastened by the French Revolution, which pulled down the ghetto walls, although nearly another
century was to pass before even the Jews of Western Europe could
claim to be fully emancipated. Many families had made their own
accommodation with the times by discarding a Judaism that they
could no longer accept for a Christianity in which they did not
believe but that afforded many advantages. Jews crowded into the
universities, the professions, the arts; they prospered in commerce,
and where they moved freely among non-Jews, they intermarried
in droves.

The mass of Jewry, however, lived in Eastern Europe, mainly

under Russian rule, and they were hardly affected by the cultural revolution in the West. Any contact with the non-Jew, beyond mere business dealings, required a certain amount of daring, and anyone who went so far as to marry outside the faith knew that he thereby cut himself off from his people. Just as Tevye's daughter, in Sholem Aleichem's story, had to leave Anatevka, one who intermarried was forced to leave the village and hide in the big city, or, more commonly, to leave Russia altogether.

Then came the great exodus. Between 1881 and 1914 some 2,500,000 Jews from Eastern Europe established new homes in the Western world, over 2,000,000 of them in the United States alone. They found themselves in a different universe, with new possibilities, new hopes and new prospects. Secular education was not merely available, it became compulsory, and in the majority of cases, the religious beliefs and traditions of the Old World did not survive for long. The kosher home, for example, was nearly universal among recent immigrants, but less common among

New York's Lower East Side, where a good proportion of the Jews who emigrated from Eastern Europe to America made their first homes

Lord George Gordon (1757–1793), leader of the 1780 Gordon riots and undoubtedly Britain's most infamous convert to Judaism

their sons and rare among their grandsons. This, except where Jewish communities were small and isolated, did not lead to any high incidence of exogamy, for if there were no longer any religious restraints to keep one within the fold, there were any number of social and psychological ones. If the American gentile was not the roistering Russian peasant, he was still a *goy*, still one of *them*. No matter what one's personal experience with gentiles, the general attitude was affected by the tales of parents and grandparents, and if no longer kept distant, the Jew still kept his distance. The 'pursuit of happiness', though a legitimate and, in America, a sanctified goal, was not something one sought without regard to how it might affect one's family. The feeling that 'it's my life and I shall live it as I want' is a recent phenomenon and among Jews is far from universal even now. One is still very much aware of the family, and one's happiness is still affected by the happiness or unhappiness of those around him. What happened is, as generation gave way to generation, the attitudes of the elders changed. The first young people to marry out of the faith caused unspeakable distress to their families – they often sat *shiva* and mourned them as dead – but as others followed their example, it became less of a calamity, and if a calamity, the best was made of the situation. Instead of reconciling themselves to the loss of a son, many families found that they could gain a daughter just by approaching their rabbi to have their prospective daughter-in-law converted to Judaism.

Now this was an entirely new experience for most Orthodox rabbis. There was a period when Judaism was a proselytizing faith, and converts to Judaism were fairly numerous during the time of the Second Temple, but in later times the attitude tended to be ambivalent. The Talmud itself does not speak with one voice on the matter. 'Do not have faith in the proselyte until twenty-four generations have passed,' said one Rabbi. 'Proselytes are beloved of the Lord,' said another, and it was recalled that some of the greatest of all the Talmudic sages – Akiva, Meir, Shammai and Avtalyon – were all descendants of proselytes. In fact, the royal House of David, from which the Messiah himself would in due course stem, was descended from Boaz and Ruth, a proselyte. In later centuries, after the rise of Christianity, converts were so few – the plight of the Jew was so dire that one had to have a positive taste for martyrdom to embrace his faith – that the whole issue became academic. Even after the eighteenth century, when Jews could enjoy a fairly tolerable existence, the traffic was almost entirely one way – Jews converting to Christianity. If the occasional individual did present himself for conversion, the Rabbis did their best to dissuade him – a formal dissuasion is, in fact, part of the conversion ritual. If he persisted, then he was advised to undergo a course of study, at the end of which he was further examined, and if the Rabbis were persuaded of his sincerity, he was circumcised, immersed himself in the *miqvah* and was accepted as a full member of the House of Israel. If the convert was a female, she merely had to undergo a ritual immersion, after which she too was fully accepted. But this was the sort of phenomenon that a rabbi might expect to encounter twice or thrice in a lifetime. It only became fairly common after the Second World War. The upper classes have always been fairly exogamous and, although to a lesser extent, so have the elements at the base of society. But in the post-war years, the middle class, even the English middle class, which was the most closed of all, also began to open up to newcomers, and the problem assumed a scale of such proportions that it could no longer be dealt with on an *ad hoc* basis; rabbis had to come together to formulate a common policy.

To the Reform synagogue, the matter was not so much a problem as a source of gratification, and every avenue is open for the convert who wants to be accepted into their congregations. They prescribe a basic course of study in Jewish history and religion and a declaration of faith, but they make no ritualistic requirements. Some Reform rabbis are even prepared to marry Jewish congregants to non-Jews and accept the non-Jewish partner into their congregation provided their children are brought up as Jews. The Conservative synagogues' attitude is also positive, but requires acceptance of the would-be convert by a *Beth Din* of at least three rabbis, a prolonged and testing course in Jewish studies, circumcision (if the convert is male) and ritual immersion. The attitude of Orthodoxy is divided. In Israel, where a convert would find himself in a Jewish society, there is less fear that he would be a weakening influence or that he would relapse into the gentile society from which he stemmed. Moreover, many immigrants from Communist countries have arrived in Israel with non-Jewish spouses, and their rapid conversion was a necessary means of easing what could have become a major social problem. In the Diaspora, however, the average Orthodox rabbi finds it difficult to believe in the sincerity of the prospective convert, and his scepticism is not entirely misplaced. Technically, the convert is presumed to want to embrace Judaism for its own sake; there must be no

ulterior motive, but, of course, in most cases there is. The great majority of conversions arise out of romantic attachments and the rabbis find it difficult to see how an applicant for conversion can be sincere, or the effects of the conversion lasting, when the religious loyalties of even the Jewish partner are shaky or non-existent; the motivating force is not so much the desire of a believing Jew to have his beloved share his faith, as his eagerness to spare the feelings of his parents.

The initial contact for conversion will usually be made through a local rabbi, who will then refer the applicant to the *Beth Din*, who,

Immersion in the *miqvah* is an integral part of the conversion ceremony for both men and women. This non-traditional portrayal of the ritual bath is by Marc Chagall

in turn, will in the first instance – as it is formally bound to do – say no. If the applicant tries again, he shows the necessary quality of persistence and will be brought before the *Beth Din* and questioned on his motives. If he – or more commonly, she – admits that it is because she wants to marry a Jew, then that's the end of the matter, and her application is rejected. But usually she has been instructed what to say, and she will then be asked why she seeks a place in Judaism, with all its burdens and travails, when as a Christian she is only required to observe the seven Noachide laws to be assured a place in the kingdom of Heaven. As a Jewess she would be required to keep the laws of Sabbath, *kashrut*, *niddah* and many other observances, and the breach of any one of them could lay her open to serious penalties in this world and the next. If she should nevertheless wish to proceed, she is required to move in with an Orthodox Jewish family and undergo a prolonged and detailed course of instruction in Hebrew and the Jewish religion. The course usually takes about two years (in Israel the whole procedure is completed within twelve months) and can take three or four. At the same time the *Beth Din* summons her Jewish partner to satisfy itself that he is living a satisfactory Jewish life, that he eats kosher and observes the Sabbath. If not, he is given an opportunity to mend his ways. If he feels he cannot, then that too ends the matter, for the *Beth Din* feels that if the Jewish partner has no interest in keeping a Jewish home and leading a Jewish life, the conversion can be neither sincere nor lasting. If he can, the conversion is allowed to proceed. The girl is tested on her knowledge, undergoes a ritual immersion in a *miqvah* and emerges fully Jewish. She cannot marry a descendant of the priesthood – for in Jewish law it is presumed that any non-Jewish woman must be a non-virgin – but otherwise she is subject to the same laws, the same restraints and the same privileges as all other Jews. Jewish society is perhaps not always as liberal as Jewish law in this respect, and there are individuals who tend to regard converts as not quite kosher. But converts are, in fact, often more observant than the community they have entered, and many a young man who had a casual, easy-going attitude to his faith, on marrying a convert found what the full rigours of Judaism entailed.

There may come a time – if it is not already here – when rabbis will look back on the years when young men actually begged to have their wives accepted into Judaism as a golden age, for an increasing number of Jews are content to take gentile wives without any endeavour to bring them into the faith or bring up their children as Jews. Statistical surveys show that Jews are less likely to marry out of their faith than Protestants or Catholics, but that when they do, they are less likely to bring up their children within it. Under Jewish law, the child of a Jewish mother is considered to be Jewish whatever the faith of the father. But if the father is Jewish and the mother is not, he cannot – as far as the Orthodox community is concerned – bring up his children within the Jewish faith, even if he wants to, unless he leaves his wife and converts the children to Judaism.

Given definite religious beliefs and the acceptance that exogamy is against Jewish law, a community will maintain a low rate of intermarriage no matter how small or isolated it is. There are for example, two Jewish communities, one on each side of the river Tyne in north-east England: the one, Newcastle, has about 3,000 Jews; the other, Gateshead, about 350. But Gateshead, which is basically built around the local *yeshiva* of that name, is ultra-Orthodox, and exogamy is hardly known, whereas in Newcastle, which maintains the general level of Orthodoxy or non-Orthodoxy common to Anglo-Jewry, it is fairly widespread. Given the decline in religious belief, one is left with group cohesion. The larger the group, the greater the sense of cohesion and the lower the incidence of contact with outsiders. The smaller the community, the larger the periphery of contact compared to the internal mass, and the rate of exogamy can almost be anticipated in geometric terms. In the state of Indiana, for example, between 1960 and 1963, the rate of exogamy in the state's five large cities was 38.6 per cent, while in the smaller towns with only minute Jewish communities the rate was 63.5 per cent. All this has had a marked effect on the distribution of Jewish populations. A half century ago there were viable Jewish communities scattered along the Welsh valleys, for example, each with its own synagogues, schools and ministering clergy, but as the rate of intermarriage grew, the more Orthodox parents feared for the future of their children and moved from the small town to a larger one. Since then there has been a move from the large towns into still larger ones, and today British Jewry is largely concentrated in and around the London area. In America, there are the same concentrations around the great conurbations, and this has helped to keep the exogamy rate on the whole down to about 7 per cent.

In Israel the rate of intermarriage is generally minute, and one cannot, in fact, undergo a mixed marriage ceremony within Israel itself, as the Rabbinate has sole jurisdiction over marriage and divorce. Couples may occasionally fly to Cyprus and have a civil ceremony or, more usually, they may simply cohabit. In the Diaspora, it is the greater or lesser degree of observance that establishes one's claims to Jewishness; in Israel there is no need to establish any such claim. But there are circles to whom the whole code of Jewish law is of no consequence, and among them exogamy, where it does occur, is a matter of no concern. Even if they move abroad – there are 200,000 Israelis in the New York area alone – they do not suffer from the usual Jewish compulsion to settle in a Jewish area, join a synagogue, or even a Jewish burial society, and although there are no statistics available on the matter, it is an observable fact that exogamy among them is high.

The upward exogamous trend is not necessarily irreversible. In Australia, where the pre-war exogamy rate was fast obliterating the community, the rate has been drastically lowered by the influx of newcomers from Europe after the Second World War who offered both a wider choice of partners and who, on the whole, tended to be Orthodox. But as a rule exogamy is low among newcomers and grows higher with each successive generation. In the greater Washington, D.C. area, for example, a recent survey showed that exogamy increased from 1.4 per cent among new arrivals to 10.2 per cent in the second generation and 17.9 per cent in the third. The overall statistics were kept relatively low as a result of the continuing influx of newcomers from Europe. Once this ceased, the rise has been inexorable.

Ruth Blau, a heroine of the French Resistance, who converted to Judaism and became the wife of the leader of the ultra-Orthodox Neturei Karta sect in Jerusalem

The man with the non-Jewish wife is now such a familiar fact of Jewish life that there is hardly a family without one. But even where both the man and his wife are fully accepted into the family, it is difficult to think of the wife's parents as being accepted – or wanting to be accepted – as *machatonim*. The Jewish family *en masse* is not something to be encountered without some sort of fore-warning and training; those used to the thin air of normal family life could find the sudden enrichment of atmosphere that comes with being part of the Jewish family – the *mishpoche* – suffocating. Newcomers will usually be received with every courtesy and politeness, but it is this very politeness that acts as an insulator, for the essence of being part of a *mishpoche* is ease; the minute one introduces strangers into the *mishpoche*, one has to be on one's good behaviour. The *mishpoche* is, in a sense, a club of like-minded, like-blooded people, and a stranger suddenly thrown into its midst can spoil it for everyone. Within a *mishpoche* one talks; introduce a stranger, and one has to make conversation. And *mishpoche* talk is largely talk of the *mishpoche*; who is going with whom, who is marrying whom, who is about to bring forth, who has brought forth, who hasn't and why haven't they. And one *does* have to be Jewish to enjoy all this; one has to be Jewish even to tolerate it, to find it sufferable, to survive it! A new intake of *machatonim* usually means whole new worlds for gossip – but not gentile *machatonim*. They live their own enclosed, private lives and lend little or nothing to the common fund of gossip.

It is quite possible that some cases of exogamy may be due to a craving for that very privacy, to live a life of one's own, to end the link with Abraham, Isaac and Co. and to start out in life on one's own account. Not everyone finds the pressures of the wider family entirely to his taste. One does not, of course, have to marry out of the faith to escape – but it helps. The great mobility of life is, in many ways, a threat to the Jewish family. Yet, even if families are more scattered than they once were, it is also easier to get together than it once was. But the *mishpoche* does not always depend on physical presence; it is based on a mutual awareness, on telepathy. The introduction of a foreign element disturbs the lines of communication. The *mishpoche* thus abhors exogamy because it is a threat to its own continuity. It does impose a burden on the family's powers of assimilation, but the more assimilation, the greater tolerance to newcomers, and in this greater tolerance lie the greatest threats. For the next stage is to find exogamy acceptable and, beyond that, positively welcome. And once that happens the Jewish family, as it has been known, dependant not only on marriage within the faith, but within the right group within the faith, is finished. One is urged in the *Shulchan Aruch* to marry one's niece, which is an ideal not always attainable, and which, indeed, not everyone would wish to attain; but the further one moves from one's immediate group, the less the *mishpoche* likes it, and exogamy thus represents not so much a move, as flight.

Exogamy, in fact, used to be regarded as a quick and final way out of Judaism. In the inter-war years, when the American Jewish exogamy rate was between 2 and 3 per cent, the rate for Jews in countries in Central and Western Europe (Austria, Hungary, Germany, Holland) was between 20 and 30 per cent. Jews were going through harsh times, anti-Semitism was rife, and many a young man saw the best hope for himself in vanishing in a gentile crowd. There are no longer any serious handicaps to being a Jew; some in America might argue that there are actually positive advantages to that status, and the wish to escape can no longer be regarded as a serious cause of exogamy. Yet something of the stigma remains. There is still a feeling that to marry 'out' is a form of apostasy, even though one undergoes a civil marriage, and the gentile partner is no more committed to Christianity than the Jewish one is to Judaism.

But exogamy is not basically a matter on which reason plays so much as it is a part of folk experience. 'The whole idea that one should marry within his group was deeply ingrained in them,' one young man who had taken a non-Jewish wife told a recent social survey. 'They just believed it all their lives. It is the same as asking us: why do you feel it's wrong to rob banks?' Another said: 'My parents feel that all gentiles hated Jews. This was the result of their whole education. They never got over that.' But other responses showed that the feelings of the Jewish parents on this matter were not entirely misplaced. A non-Jewish girl told an interviewer:

My mother said, 'You have an old family and a fine one. You should marry someone of equally good family – don't taint the blood.'

A Jewish daughter-in-law: 'My in-laws objected because they hated Jews. They were real anti-Semites from way back.'

A Catholic daughter: 'My parents said, "If he didn't look so Jewish, it wouldn't be so bad! What will our friends and neighbours think?"'

And another: 'My mother was horrified at his being Jewish. The children would not have the advantages I had . . . She felt they might be born with Jewish features or revert back to their Jewish ancestry.'

The fact that a man's parents do not get on with his wife, or that he himself may be disliked by his in-laws would be a serious barrier to *shalom bayit* in an extended family of the old type – with brothers, sisters, uncles and cousins living near, with, or, indeed, on top of each other. But the extended family has broken up into small components, and today it is enough that a wife can get on with her husband. Moreover, the barrier of mutual antipathy between Jew and non-Jew, which is still evident in some places, is easing. Inner cohesion is vanishing and so is outer exclusion. Among young people the exogamy rate is kept down less by conscious choice than random chance, and given present trends, one can foretell the extinction of the Jewish family within the next three or four generations. But there is no natural law that says present trends must continue, and one can sense evidence where, in fact, these trends are being reversed.

15 The House of Life

The traditional Jewish family called for many children and different generations all in amity under one roof, but the facts of contemporary life make that difficult, if not impossible. For a start, roofs are no longer as big as they were, and people live longer than they did. *Die alte bobbe*, the old Jewish grandmother who figures so richly in Jewish lore, may have looked ancient, with her white hair and black skirts, but was rarely beyond her seventies. The great longevity enjoyed by the Patriarchs and other biblical figures did not prove hereditary, and the Talmud regards anyone over sixty as old. The traditional Yiddish wish – *bist hunderd und tzwantzig* – that one should live to 120 was not something that one wished on himself. Old age might have been revered, but it was not welcomed, for as the Talmud acknowledged, 'a man of one hundred is as good as dead,' and perhaps even worse, for he was a burden both to himself and his fellows. *Die alte bobbe* and, to a lesser extent, *der alter zeide* (the old grandfather) were very much alive and useful members of the household – the latter as teacher to the children, the former as supernumerary mother, who cooked, baked, washed, scrubbed and sewed. Their presence enriched the whole life of the family. Today, there are few *alte bobbes* about, for if a grandmother still enjoys full use of her faculties, she will prefer to live her own life and does not like to be regarded – and certainly does not regard herself – as an adjunct to the life of her children. She will, of course, be on hand in case of emergency – when there is a child due or during illness – but the independence that the young demand of the old is a two-way process, and where the former have chosen to go their own way without restraint, so too have the latter gone their own way.

It is only when the old have outlived their faculties that they become dependent on their children, and by then the children

The tomb of Rabbi Judah Loew, the creator of the Golem, in the old Jewish cemetery of Prague

are not always in a position to help them. *Al tashlicheni be'et ziknoh*, 'cast me not off in old age', go the words of an old Jewish prayer, but by the time a parent needs help, his children are themselves often grandparents, and they may not have the physical or financial stamina to do so; hence the growth of old-age homes. These were initially intended for the lonely and destitute, those who had been cut off from their families by the upheavals of Jewish life or were single or childless, but over the years their clientele has moved up the social and economic scale and includes men and women from fairly prosperous homes. The accommodations have not been sufficient to cope with the demand, and many old people are deposited in private hotels or bleak little colonies that are really commercial old-age homes. The community establishments are usually better staffed and better appointed, but the old, thrown exclusively among themselves, even in palatial surroundings, form a melancholy sight. Now garrulous, now quarrelsome, now silent and morose, groaning from this ailment or that pain, they gather together in cheerless packs, each a burden on the spirit of the other, and fade out of life removed from children and grandchildren. It is said that a mother can bring up ten children, yet ten children cannot support but one mother.

Maimonides argued that Judaism was based on thirteen principles, the last of which is:

I believe with perfect faith that there will be resurrection of the dead at the time when it shall please the Creator, blessed be His name, and exalted be the remembrance of Him for ever and ever.

This is intoned by many Jews every morning, but, in the main, Jews are content to live their lives as if this were the only existence that they are ever likely to know. Except in time of grave calamity, they are disinclined to leave for the next world compensation for everything they have missed in this one. The Jewish Kingdom, for most Jews, is of this world, and the sense of loss on a bereavement is therefore absolute. 'The Lord giveth and the Lord taketh away,' goes an old prayer, but there is no consolation in the thought. The feeling of pain is intense, and it draws together all the scattered members of a family as no other experience can. It is the occasion that, more than any other, evokes one's filial sense of duty, and a father anxious to correct an erring son need only drop dead to get his way. Judah Ibn Tibbon, our twelfth-century scholar, was aware of this, and in his will he exhorted his son: 'Though thou didst not follow me when I was near, obey me when I am far from

thee . . .' and we may be fairly certain that his son did. If one drops into almost any synagogue on a week-day evening, one will hear at the close of the service almost everyone present joining in an incoherent chorus. It is the *kaddish*, the memorial prayer said for the departed during the eleven months after their death and on every anniversary (*yohrtzeit*, as it is called in Yiddish) thereafter. Few synagogues would remain open on weekdays – and some not even on the Sabbath – if not for *kaddish*-sayers. Wherever a Jewish community takes root the first institution it forms is the *chevra kadisha*, the burial society, and its first investment – even before it acquires a permanent synagogue – is in a cemetery or, as it is known in Hebrew, a *beth chayim*, a house of life. (Another name is *beth olam*, the house of eternity.)

There is a death-bed confession, but it is not often read among Jews, for few Jews, or their relatives, will allow themselves to believe that death is near while they have still enough breath left in their body to utter a prayer. It is not so much a formal confession as a final request:

I acknowledge unto thee, O Lord my God and God of my fathers, that

This scene of elderly Jews left to one another's company – in Warsaw Gardens before the Holocaust destroyed the Polish Jewish community – is now more often played out on the well-tended grounds of old age homes

both my cure and my death are in thy hands. May it be thy will to send me a perfect healing. Yet, if my death be fully determined by thee, I will in love accept it at thy hand. O may my death be an atonement for all the sins, iniquities and transgressions of which I have been guilty against thee. Bestow upon me the abounding happiness that is stored up for the righteous. Make known to me the path of life: in thy presence is fulness of joy; at thy right hand, bliss everlasting.

Thou who art the father of the fatherless and judge of the widow, protect my beloved kindred with whose soul my own is knit. Into thy hands I commend my spirit; thou hast redeemed me, O Lord God of truth. Amen.

He then utters a formula heard at the end of the Yom Kippur service:

The Lord reigneth; the Lord hath reigned; the Lord shall reign for ever and ever.

Blessed be His name, whose glorious kingdom is forever and ever. The Lord He is God.

And then, in his final breath:

Hear O Israel: the Lord is our God, the Lord is One.

There is, at the source of it all, a sense of resignation that later permeates the entire funeral service. The presence of a rabbi is not essential to the confession, though many rabbis will try to be at the bed of a dying congregant. The concept of hell does exist in Jewish teaching, but it has never been so crystallized as to give it a firm place in the sub-conscious. One may regret leaving this world, but for most Jews the next one holds no terrors.

When death is established, the mouth and eyes are closed by the eldest son or nearest relative, and the arms and hands are placed by the side of the body, which is then lowered onto the floor and wound up in a sheet with feet towards the door. A lighted candle is placed at the head, and mirrors are covered up so that they should not be witnesses to misfortune. A corpse should never be left on its own until interment and either close relatives or members of the *chevra kadisha* remain by the body reading Psalms. It is the *chevra kadisha* that carries out the *tahara* (purification) ceremony: the body is raised to an upright position and washed, its hair is combed, the finger-nails and toe-nails pared, and it is then wrapped in a shroud.

The *chevra kadisha* was originally an honorary society to which only the most respected members of a community could be elected. In some areas – especially among the ultra-Orthodox – it still functions in this same way, but in most places it has been replaced by a

professional funeral staff who may be employed either by the congregation or by a commercial undertaker. Among the English Sephardim, however, there still exists a society known as The Institution for Preparing for Internment the Deceased Members of the Spanish and Portuguese Jewish Congregation, London, which dates back to the earliest days of the community. Membership in the society is a prized privilege to which only the most respected congregants aspire. Sir Moses Montefiore, for one, was a member for seventy-one years.

Burial follows death as shortly as is practically possible. This is out of deference for the dead, for in hot countries, where the customs first took root, decomposition was rapid. But some critics have argued that the dead are sometimes buried with indecent haste. This may have been the private feeling of Ezekiel Katzenelenbogen, an eighteenth-century German rabbi, who left clear instructions that his coffin should have seven large holes in the lid. Solomon Heine, a German banker and philanthropist (and uncle of Heinrich

An 18th-century painting of a Jewish funeral in Italy

For Jews, the tearing of garments, rather than dressing in black, is the traditional sign of mourning

Heine, the poet) went even further and ordered that under no circumstances should his funeral take place until seventy-two hours after his death. There have, in fact, been instances where the corpse stirred to life while it was being douched with cold water during the *tahara* ceremony, or even of a frantic stirring inside the coffin while it was being lowered into the grave. In 1879, a young boy died after a short illness in a Polish hamlet. As there was no local cemetery, his body was taken to the next village; there, while being prepared for burial, he sat up and asked for a drink. In a few days he was well enough to return home. But for the fact that there was no Jewish cemetery in his own village, he would almost certainly have been buried alive.

Before the funeral, the immediate family tear their garments, usually through an incision in their lapels, and there is a brief service in the home before the body is taken out to the waiting hearse. Psalms 23 and 130 are read ('The Lord is my shepherd . . .', 'Out of the depths I have cried to thee, O Lord . . .'), and then a prayer special to the occasion is added:

As for man his days are as grass; as the flowers of the field, so he flourisheth. For the wind passeth over it, and it is gone; and the place thereof shall know it no more. But the loving kindness of the Lord is forever and ever . . .

It is an acknowledgement of the vanity of human wishes and ends with the lines:

Who may ascend the mountain of the Lord? And who may stand in his holy place? He that hath clean hands and a pure heart; hath not set his desire upon vanity, and hath not sworn deceitfully. For the end of it all is this: Fear God and keep his commandments, for that is the whole purpose of man. The day is short, and the work is great, and the labourers are sluggish, and the reward is much, and the master of the house is urgent. It is not thy duty to complete the work, but neither art thou free to desist from it. Faithful is thy master to pay thee the reward of thy labour; and know ye that the reward of the righteous is in the time to come.

There is a deep tradition of reverence for the dead. Among the ultra-Orthodox, the entire community will stop work to attend a funeral, no matter how insignificant the deceased, for death is in itself a form of distinction. There will be a large attendance in the house, and a long line of cars will follow the *cortège* to the cemetery. Attendance at funerals is considered to be the minimum duty that one Jew can perform for another.

Psalm 23 is usually also read at the burial service itself (it is the most frequently read and widely known of all the Psalms) and is often followed by Psalm 16:

> Guard me, O God,
> for in thee I take refuge.
> I say unto the Lord, Thou art my Lord;
> I have no good beyond thee . . .
> I have set the Lord before me always;
> because He is at my right hand I shall not be moved.
> Therefore, my heart is glad and my glory rejoiceth:
> my flesh also shall rest in hope.
> For Thou wilt not abandon my soul to the pit,
> nor suffer thy loving one to see corruption.
> Thou wilt show me the path of life;
> in thy presence is fulness of joy;
> at thy right hand, eternal bliss.

The pallbearers pause three times as they recite the Psalm, and the body is then slowly lowered into the grave to the words: 'May he come to his place in peace.'

Some individuals went to considerable lengths to prescribe exactly how they should be buried. Don Judah, a fifteenth-century Spanish Jew, asked: 'Do not bury me upright, or lying down, but a strong chair shall be placed in the grave and my body must be seated thereon facing the east towards the rising sun.' Ben Yehuda Loeb, a mystic who lived some centuries later, had a more morbid request. He was obsessed with a sense of his own iniquity and asked that his body be strangled and stoned posthumously by way of atonement. He added a touching footnote:

Poverty was a common fact of Jewish life, and it also affected the mode of Jewish death. In the absence of burial societies, the community often buried its poor members out of funds collected by charitable means. This is a 17th-century bronze charity cup of Italian origin

All my life I lived in narrow and straitened circumstances; deal not so with my death. Inter me not in a narrow grave but enlarge the place of my eternal rest.

In most Jewish families women remain at home and do not go to the cemetery. It is to the home that the male mourners now return. In some communities it was customary to hire professional women mourners who clapped their hands and sang dirges and lamentations, but there was a sufficient sense of grief without them, and the custom has not survived into modern times. There is a period of seven days of mourning – *shiva* – during which the immediate family, that is, widow or widower, parents if any, brothers and sisters and children, will remain at home for a week, to be visited and comforted. They sit on low stools as a sign of mourning, the menfolk remain unshaven, the women do not use make-up.

It was customary for relatives and friends to bring food for the household in bereavement so that they should not have to exert themselves to prepare their own meals, but now the position seems to have been reversed. Many of the visitors travel a considerable distance – some cross oceans – to attend the funeral and comfort the mourners, and hospitable instincts have prevailed against custom and in many a house of mourning caterers are brought in to look after the guests. The place gets crowded. People see familiar faces they have not encountered in years, and many a visitor who comes to comfort the mourners is left to wonder whether he has not intruded upon some family celebration. Mourning is always suspended for the Sabbath and festivals, on much the same grounds that a hearse must always give way to a wedding carriage: the glad occasions have priority over the sad ones. Perhaps law and tradition alone do not sufficiently explain the great pains taken by Jews to attend a house of mourning. A death not only excites immediate compassion, but it also stirs memories – what one might call the 'Alas poor Yorick' syndrome. At one and the same time, it brings intimations of one's own mortality and vivid recollections of distant events. Acquaintances are milestones and whenever one falls away the epoch he represents immediately comes to mind. When the *shiva* is not for some anticipated event like the death of an aged parent, but, say, a young child, one becomes painfully aware of how much one's own family means to him, and with that awareness comes a deep sense of involvement with the bereaved. Each one also has private memories of grief and recollections of how much a visit from even a casual visitor helped to ease the day. One is not allowed to study during the *shiva*, and one's reading matter should be confined to the literature of grief, like the Book of Job. Company is therefore a desperately necessary diversion. A *shiva* is more tolerable and can even be positively helpful when one is part of a community that conforms to all the traditions of mourning and whose members will make every effort to spend some time with the bereaved. In such company, among friends and sympathizers, a man may talk of his loss, break down and cry, or merely sit silent and sigh, but his sorrow is eased, something of his burden of grief is purged. But when one is alone, especially an observant, traditional Jew among people who are not, one can become a prisoner in one's own home throughout much of the *shiva*, with no one to see and nothing to do except to watch the flickering memorial candle and contemplate one's own misfortune. In such a situation, far from being helped by the mourning customs, one can be driven

overleaf The Hall of Remembrance at Yad Vashem, the permanent memorial to the victims of the Holocaust, in Jerusalem. Few are the Jews of this generation who have not lost a relative in one of the death camps recorded here

mad by them. As a result, the *shiva* is now less commonly observed than it used to be, not merely because people are busier than they were (though that is part of the reason) but because most people find the best antidote for grief is work. Thus many Jews will only keep one day's mourning, although a great many will go to immense inconvenience to say the *kaddish*.

The *kaddish* is a curious prayer: it contains no mention of death or the dead; it is written in Aramaic, the lingua franca of Babylonian Jewry, and not in Hebrew; and it is from beginning to end a hymn of praise to the Almighty:

Magnified and sanctified be His great name in the world which He has created according to His will. May He establish His kingdom during your life and during your days, and during the life of all the House of Israel, even speedily and at a near time, and say ye, Amen.

Let His name be blessed for ever and to all eternity. Blessed, praised and glorified, exalted, extolled and honoured, magnified and lauded be the name of the Holy One, blessed be He; though He be on high above all the blessings and hymns, praises and consolations, which are uttered in the world; and say ye, Amen . . .

It is, in origin, a plea for charity and forgiveness to the deceased so that he might be allowed to enter and remain in the divine presence, or at least be spared divine wrath. (According to the Zohar, a father is humiliated in the after-life by his son's iniquities and honoured by his virtues.) One does not know how many Jews who say *kaddish* religiously actually believe this, but one's own beliefs enter into it less than those of the deceased. A death in the family brings out guilt feelings in everyone, and after the death of a parent, one tries to make amends for one's filial shortcomings during his lifetime. And thus if one cannot attend synagogue three times a day, one will at least make an effort to be in synagogue on the Sabbath and on the *yohrtzeit*, the anniversary of the death. In some Jewish households the occasion is also marked with an evening of study, and in nearly all a *yohrtzeit* candle will be lit. A candle is also lit on Yom Kippur.

The *shiva* is not the complete period of mourning. One continues to be an *avel*, a mourner, for an entire year, and during that time many Orthodox Jews will not attend any place of entertainment nor family celebrations, such as weddings. Many do not shave for a month after their bereavement. The *kaddish*, however, is only said for the first eleven months, for to say it for a full year would reflect on the all-forgiving character of the Almighty. There are also four times in the year, corresponding to the three pilgrimage

festivals (Passover, Pentecost and the Feast of Tabernacles) and Yom Kippur, when a special memorial prayer is said for the dead. This is known as *yiskor*, remembrance, and the prayers have a touching simplicity:

Lord what is man, that thou regardest him? Or the son of man that thou takest account of him? Man is like vanity; his days are as a shadow that passeth away. In the morning he bloometh and sprouteth afresh; in the evening he is cut down and withereth. So teach us to number our days that we may get us a heart of wisdom . . .

Congregations are much augmented during *yiskor* and not a few tears are shed, especially in the ladies' gallery. The *yiskor* is a sort of communal roll-call. The actual prayers are intended mainly for one's parents, but in the mood of recollection one becomes acutely aware of others who are no more – brothers, sisters, uncles, cousins, friends, the close ones who peopled one's immediate universe and who have since fallen away. The synagogue was the place where one saw them *en masse* in their festive best; their faces are now gone from the throng, their places taken by younger figures from another generation. A prayer is added in most synagogues for the victims of the Holocaust, and as there are few Jews of the present generation who have not lost a relative in the death camps, the names of the camps, as they are read out: Auschwitz, Bergen-Belsen, Buchenwald . . . stab one like a knife, for they represent a tragedy more acute than the bereavements of normal life. *Yiskor*, 'Remember O God, the souls of my grandfathers and grandmothers, my uncles and aunts, my brothers and sisters . . .', and the congregations remember them, and others beyond them: the crowd being marched out of the Warsaw Ghetto, the city aflame behind them; a cattle wagon with its human cargo on the Auschwitz sidings; the gas ovens . . .

The *yiskor* has, to an extent, reverted to its original function, for it evolved as a memorial to the many Jews massacred during the Crusades. Each community had its own role of martyrs that was read out in the course of the service, and it was only later that it came to be adapted to the memory of one's parents. There is a superstition current in some congregations that anyone with both parents living should not be in the synagogue during *yiskor*, and the decorum that the occasion demands is often spoiled by the wholesale exodus of youthful worshippers. Children in particular have always regarded the *yiskor* as a licensed interval from the rigours of prayer.

As we have seen, the Hebrew name for a cemetery is *beth chayim* (house of life), or *beth olam* (house of eternity) and it indicates the traditional attitude to death as life-everlasting, to which one's sojourn on earth is but a brief prelude. A paragraph in the burial service sums up this philosophy:

> If man live a year or a thousand years, what profiteth it him? He shall be as though he had not been. Blessed be the true Judge who causeth death and reviveth . . . The Lord giveth and the Lord taketh away; blessed be the name of the Lord.

The Rabbis discouraged excessive grief or lamentation. It suggested a lack of confidence in the ways of the Almighty, a disbelief in the world to come. The words of Jeremiah are often quoted in this context: 'Weep ye not for the dead, neither bemoan him' (22:10). Brachya saw little to commend in a long life if it meant a mere prolongation of old age:

> . . . the more a man's years increase, the more do his sighs, and sorrows and distresses increase, the more is there added to his sins and transgressions . . . for they are renewed day by day. He despises everything that is pleasant and is weary of what is nice and he becomes as one who lives against his will.

In such a situation, he suggested, death was almost welcome. Chassidism has discouraged undue contemplation on this point. 'Be not too eager to inquire into first things and last,' said a mystic, 'for both life and death are fulfilment. What is the destiny of the plant that springs from the soil? To grow and to wither. It is the law and the will of God. And therewith man must likewise rest content, without inquiry into the whys and the wherefores. Let him rejoice at being called into life, and return to the fountainhead of his being when the call to him goes forth.' Maimonides saw it all in more pragmatic terms and regarded death as a benign and necessary means of 'perpetuating existence and the continuity of individual beings through the emergence of one after the withdrawal of the other'. In other words, the world was too small a place for immortality. The life-everlasting, said Maimonides, was in the world to come.

Biblical references to the hereafter are vague; those in the Talmud are more explicit. Hell, or *Gehinnom*, as it is called, was a place of 'the wicked one whose tongue hangs out to lap the water of the river, but is unable to reach it', which is clearly reminiscent of Homer's account of the travails of Tantalus. Josephus, on the other hand, speaks of *Gehinnom* as a cold and dark cave. All versions

agree that it was a thoroughly unpleasant place. There were also different versions of paradise, but the most common one, as described in the Talmud, was a sort of eternal house of study, a world where 'there is no eating or drinking, no begetting children, no commerce, envy, hatred or competition, but only this: that the righteous sit with crowns on their heads and delight in God's presence.' To which one Lithuanian cynic is said to have remarked: 'If that is the best that the next world can offer, please, O God, prolong my stay in this one.'

According to Jewish legend, those who die young are ushered into the presence of the Almighty, who teaches them Torah to make up for the education they forfeited on earth, and it was generally believed that one could look to a reunion with one's loved ones

The cemetery on the Mount of Olives, Jerusalem, the most coveted burial ground for Jews because of the belief that those interred on the Mount of Olives will be the first to be resurrected with the coming of the Messiah

Jewish tombstones tend to be simple today, but in antiquity, especially during the Second Temple period, it was not unusual for the wealthy to erect great edifices to preserve their memory. This structure, known as Absalom's Pillar, is one of a number of mausoleums of antiquity in the Kidron Valley, Jerusalem

after death, but even so one had to strive to stay alive. The following will, written by an eighteenth-century Polish rabbi, illustrates something of the general attitude to life and death (and is, incidentally, a touching indication of the affection which reigned in many a Jewish household):

My beloved Esther, once from our great love we clasped our hands and mutually promised that when either of us two died, the other would pray to die soon afterwards, that we might quit the world together. But that wish was not right, and you have my pardon if you live to be a hundred. I altogether undo our compact. But if you die first, which God forbid, you must do the same. I ask you not to marry again, though I know I need not say it, but I add the words out of my overwhelming love for you.

It was also somehow believed – and to an extent it still is – that if one were buried near one's loved ones, one had a greater assurance of their company in the world to come. One can see something of this belief in the following will and testament written in the fifteenth century:

I beg of you . . . that no funeral oration be spoken in my honour. Do not carry my body on a bier, but in a coach. Wash me clean, comb my hair, trim my nails, as I was wont to do in my life-time, so that I may go clean to my eternal rest, as I went clean to synagogue every Sabbath day . . . At a distance of thirty cubits from my grave, thou shalt set my coffin on the ground and drag me to the grave by a rope attached to the coffin. Every four cubits thou shalt stand and wait a while, doing so seven times, so that I might find atonement for my sins.

And as the author's final wish:

Put me in the ground at the right hand of my father, and if the space be narrow, I am sure that he loves me well enough to make room for me by his side.

And yet, with it all there is a certain undefined longing for immortality on earth. Eternity may be all right in the world to come, but one wants some touch of it in this world – or at least some assurance that one will not be forgotten. The burial service is, in part, a plea to be remembered: 'Just art Thou O Lord, in causing death and reviving, in whose hand is the charge of all spirits: far be it from Thee to blot out our remembrance.' The darkest curse in the Hebrew language is *yemach shemo vezichro*, 'may his name and remembrance be blotted out'. Hence, the *kaddish*, the anniversary candles and the anniversary prayers. 'Remembrancing' has, in fact, developed into something of an industry among Jews. Many *yeshivot* (Talmudic colleges) derive a considerable income from burning candles and saying prayers in memory of their benefactors, although benefactors tend to prefer something more concrete nowadays. If, for example, one visits a Jewish hospital, one will find every ward, every bed and almost every article of furniture bearing a plaque to perpetuate the name of the donors, both living and dead. At the Hebrew University in Jerusalem, every building, every patch of garden, almost every wall, carries the name of a benefactor. Only two people have colleges named after them in both Oxford and Cambridge and both of them are Jews: one is Jesus Christ, the other is the Jewish philanthropist Sir Isaac Wolfson. The practice derives only in part from a forgivable desire to have one's generosity recognized; it is mainly a craving for immortality. The levirate law was in part an answer to this craving, but it has been discontinued and so must be given an outlet in some other way.

The memorial stones in Jewish cemeteries tend to be rather simple, austere affairs without winged angels or weeping goddesses. In Greek times it was not unusual to erect great edifices of stone to mark the resting places of the wealthy or the renowned, but this practice incurred the wrath of Rabban Simeon ben Gamaliel: 'One does not erect monuments to the righteous. Their works are their memorial.' In some Orthodox cemeteries only small stones of uniform size and fairly uniform inscriptions are allowed.

Many Reform Jews opt to be cremated, but the very idea of cremation is anathema to most Orthodox Jews, who regard mortal remains as sacred. Some have gone so far as to riot in Israel over the right assumed by some hospitals to carry out autopsies. Ultra-Orthodox Jews who may have an organ or limb removed in the course of an operation will bury it or preserve it for burial until the day of death. The idea behind this is that a person's body is not his property in the first place, and that the least he can do is to return it in as sound a condition as possible to the original owner.

One does not send wreaths to a Jewish funeral, nor tend graves with flowers, but it is usual among Orthodox families to visit the graves at least once a year, normally in the weeks before the New Year. The old are perhaps more scrupulous about such acts of remembrance than the young, but the young are a memorial in themselves, for it is in them and their children that the Jew sees his true hope of immortality. One generation passeth away, and another generation cometh, but the family abideth forever.

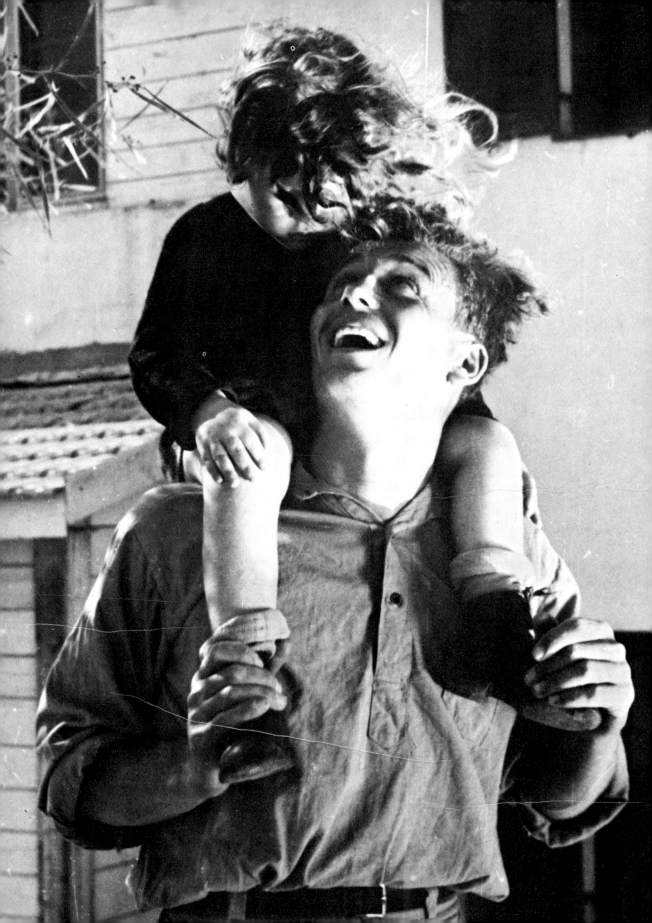

16 A New Life

When the kibbutz was first established, the family came low on its list of priorities. Indeed, there were prolonged debates on whether families should be raised at all. But such debates were purely academic; kibbutzim, even at their most ascetic, were never monasteries. Men and women worked together and lived together, and children came forth. As their numbers multiplied, priorities and ideologies changed, and today a stranger to kibbutz society might easily think that it was specifically designed for the benefit of mother and child.

Childbirth may be almost painless nowadays, but child-rearing, as we have seen, is not. Indeed, it would seem that the less painful the one, the more painful the other. In the kibbutz, however, the young mother is relieved of every burden short of the foetus. Once the infant is conceived, the mother is confined to light work and encouraged to take a nap every day, and if the pregnancy should prove difficult, she is relieved of work altogether. Deliveries generally take place in a hospital, and when the mother returns, the baby is taken into the charge of a trained nurse in the baby-house. The mother is relieved of all work for six weeks and goes to the baby-house as often as she needs to feed the child, but all the accompanying drudgery – the washing, the changing and coping with small ailments – are left to the baby-house staff. When the six weeks are over the mother returns to part-time work, but if the baby is breast-fed she remains off work until it is weaned. The infant remains in the baby-house until he can walk and talk and is then moved, with five or six others of his age group, into a children's house in the charge of a *metapelet*. The literal translation of *metapelet* is one who copes, and, in fact, she combines the functions of governess, nanny and a touch of the mother-in-law, for if she feels that the mother's approach to the child is wrong, she

Placing one's child above oneself is one aspect of Jewish family life inherited from the past by the radical social experiment of the kibbutz

will not hesitate to put her right. She has, or should have, more experience with children than the parents, and, like the Edwardian governess, she sees more of them than either the father or mother. Parents suffer no disturbed nights nor disturbed mealtimes and can join in the rich social and cultural life of the kibbutz without worry about baby-sitters; nor need they trundle children along if they should want to steal away for a quiet week-end together. Kibbutz holidays are short and rarely extend to more than a fortnight, but if parents need to go abroad for some reason, they can quite easily leave their children at home.

But that is not the full extent of the benefits enjoyed by the kibbutz family. In Israel there is free compulsory education till the age of fourteen. In the kibbutz, children remain at school till eighteen, and many then go on to university and training colleges. In town, classes are large, there is a high turnover of staff, and facilities are frequently poor; in the kibbutz, classes are usually small, facilities are generally good, and the level of teaching is often superb, for the teachers themselves are members of the kibbutz and, in a sense, the pupils are their children. They watched them grow up and are

Although the question of raising families was seriously debated in the earliest days of the kibbutz, by 1926 nature had firmly taken over from ideology, as this photo of a children's house at the time shows

A *metapelet* with her charges today

familiar with their needs, their aptitudes, their problems. Nothing is spared to advance the child. If he shows any talent or skill, be it in music or painting, he will receive lessons in that field. As children grow older, they are expected to take an increasing part in the work of the kibbutz, especially during the harvest seasons (and there is nearly always something to be picked or plucked in Israel), but if, for example, they are good athletes and need time for training, they will get time off and a first-class coach to supervise them. They are taken on picnics and educational tours from one end of the country to the other, accompanied by their *metapelot* if small, by teachers and *madrichim* (guides) as they grow older. The swimming pool has high priority in most kibbutzim, and mainly because of the children. The parents rarely have time to enjoy it, but they will be seen together, by the side of the pool, *en famille* on a Sabbath morning. Were it not for the fact that the transistors crackle news instead of music, the blue skies, the blue water, the waving palm trees and the relaxed postures would strike one as improbably Californian.

All this might lead one to the conclusion that kibbutzim are veritable child factories where mothers bring forth year after year; in fact, with the possible exception of Kibbutz Hadati (the religious kibbutz movement), which has some scruples about birth control, nothing is more rigorously planned on the kibbutz than the size of a family. Numbers are limited during the straitened years and relaxed during the prosperous ones, and one can tell the lean years from the fat by a glance at the age groups. Kibbutzim have always been determined that their children should get the best of everything, which usually involved a strict limit on the size of families. One sometimes heard complaints that *chaverim* (members) were extending themselves too much for the sake of the children. Yitzhak Tabenkin, a veteran of the kibbutz movement, speaking at a kibbutz conference in 1923, suggested that such self-sacrifice was good neither for the old generation nor the new:

> At times the large gap between the material supplies for the children and those for the parents are absurd. The children must also learn to be aware of the actual economic conditions of their parents . . . Instead of spoiling the children, we should restrain and encourage them to accommodate themselves to a simple and modest life; we should develop in our children a love of artisanship, which is in short supply . . .

Such counsel fell on deaf ears, and *chaverim* continued their efforts to maintain their children in a rarefied universe. In this they were not merely perpetuating the old Jewish habit of affording their

This children's house may not appear to be evidence of the best of everything, but it was the most comfortable residence on the kibbutz fifty years ago

children all the advantages they were denied themselves, they were anxious to create a new type of society and a new sort of child – a new sort of Jew. To an extent they succeeded, for the kibbutz child did look and act differently: he was healthier, taller, brawnier, more self-assured; his very pigmentation seemed different, and it was a source of pride to some parents that their children didn't even look Jewish.

Some students of the kibbutz movement, including Dr Bruno Bettelheim, have suggested that kibbutz children are a little too cosseted, too carefully reared, too closely indoctrinated and, as a result, they tend to be somewhat conformist in their outlook, lacking in initiative and unventuresome. But this view has been challenged, and certainly those children of the kibbutz who formed a sizable part of Israel's officer corps in three wars have shown themselves to be deficient in neither initiative, daring, nor any of the other necessary qualities of leadership. It could be argued that the kibbutzim may never bring forth a Beethoven, a Picasso or a Joyce, but all the available evidence suggests that few children can hope to have a happier, healthier or more wholesome upbringing than that offered by the kibbutz.

In light of these facts, it comes as something of a surprise to dis-

right Some students of the kibbutz maintain that kibbutz children are too pampered. Nonetheless, they are integrated into the responsibilities of adulthood, such as contributing to the economy of their kibbutz, much earlier than their contemporaries in the cities

cover that the entire kibbutz movement has a population of under 100,000, and although it may form an influential and prestigious section of the community, it only comprises 3 per cent of Israel's Jewish population. Why are the numbers so limited when it offers so much to the child? One reason may be that it demands too much from the adult. The Jew has never been particularly attracted to agricultural life, and he is an individualist; he likes to be master of his own fate. He is venturesome and will take great risks for great rewards; in the kibbutz, he resigns his will to that of the group, there is no risk, and the reward is the same whatever the effort. The oriental immigrants who poured into Israel after 1948 regarded the kibbutznik who worked long hours under strenuous conditions and without pay as eccentric, if not downright crazy.

One of the reasons that children were kept separate from their parents in their own dormitories was that it gave the group a more complete share in their destiny. Children reared in common helped to intensify the sense of family, and, as in a family, they helped to keep together people who might otherwise have been disposed to move apart. It was the group that deliberated jointly on the upbringing of the children, on the form and content of their education, on what they should do after school; it gave the single and childless a share in them as well and helped to make the kibbutz a throbbing, organic entity. But there was another reason for the separation of children from parents – the liberation of the mother. It was decided early on that the *chalutzah* (woman pioneer) would not be the mere helpmate of the *chalutz*, she would be his equal and partner. And there were strenuous attempts to make her so. One can see in the publications of the 1920s and 1930s pictures of girls on guard-duty with rifles on their shoulders, girls on horseback, girls knee-deep in water working on drainage, girls on tractors. A book published in 1932 called *The Plough Woman* was also designed to give the same impression of virile womanhood assuming the burdens of what was a man's world, but it represented aspirations rather than fact. Guard-duty remained largely a male preserve; most of the routine agricultural tasks were thought to be too strenuous for most women; few women took it upon themselves to prove otherwise, and by the time mechanization eased the work, most women had made a furtive retreat back into the kitchen and the wash-house. Nor were women to be seen in any number in the administrative jobs in the kibbutz secretariat; few aspired to such office, and few were elected.

In the 1920s and 1930s, it was not uncommon to find women serving on guard duty, and the woman's desire to reach full equality often required that she be 'liberated' from the restrictions of traditional role of motherhood

A parent coming to claim
his child at the appointed
hour

It was difficult, in the early years of the kibbutz, for the woman
to appear womanly, and any attempt to do so would have been
regarded as frivolous. If few women took men's jobs, most of
them dressed like men, in boots, dungarees or shorts, with hair
kept short and clamped down under *kova tembels*, and their com-
plexions becoming parched and wrinkled in the fierce sun. What
began from need hardened into ideology, and even after working
hours, the *chalutzah* was rarely transformed into a temptress.
Cosmetics were taboo, and even the use of perfumed soap would
have been regarded as a form of self-indulgence and, worse, an
unseemly reversion to *bourgeois* ways; the liberated woman smelt
of carbolic. But feminism gradually reasserted itself, and the more
the *chalutzah* became a woman, the more she hankered to be a
mother, not only as one who brings forth children, but to have
her children about her.

The kibbutz mother was not cut off from any meaningful contact with her children, but the contact was confined to certain
licensed hours, usually from five to seven. In the kibbutz these are

called the sacred or golden hours, and the whole ritual is vaguely reminiscent of the practice of nannies bringing the children downstairs from the nursery to have tea with papa and mamma. Here too they descend at tea time. The children may, in fact, have fruit juice or Coca Cola with biscuits and sweets, rather than the English ceremonial tea, but the mood is tea-timish, with nursery rhymes and stories and games. There is a Jewish saying that one has *tzores* (pain) from one's children and *naches* from one's grandchildren, to which one precocious lad once retorted that one has *tzores* from one's parents and *naches* from one's grandparents. In the kibbutz one's parents become a species of grandparents or Dutch uncles – smiling, indulgent, generous. Discipline, instruction and chastisement are received elsewhere; the sacred hours are for love and affection, for fun and games, for being spoiled. And indeed every home will have its games' cupboard for the occasion, as well as a store of sweets and biscuits and an endless supply of drinks. The parents are entirely at the disposal of their children; all work, meetings, debates and social activities cease at these hours, and it is a social *faux pas* of the gravest order for one *chaver* to call on another while the children are at home. And the time passes all too quickly for most of the parents, if not for all of the children, many of whom are anxious to be out and among their friends. The homeward parade from the children's houses in the late afternoon is one of the most characteristic, and in some ways one of most touching, sights of kibbutz life. The intense heat of the day has passed, the air is stirred by the evening breeze, and trees sway lazily. The sun is beginning to set and the surrounding hills are bathed in pink. It is as if the very forces of nature conspire to make this the gladdest hour of day. The mother pushes a pram, the father may have a small child round his neck and another by the hand, and their relaxed pace almost brings the sound of Wagner's 'Siegfried Idyll' to the ears. All the discomforts of agricultural life, the harsh toil, the long hours, the weariness of soul are forgotten. These two hours together are a daily Sabbath.

It is at this time in particular that the single feel their singleness, the childless their childlessness. All *chaverim* may have an equal say in the upbringing of the children, but not all derive an equal pleasure from them, and if traditional Jewish society has no recognized place for the bachelor or spinster, the revolutionary society represented by the kibbutz does not accommodate them too cheerfully either. There are many single people in the younger kibbutzim, but they generally pair off as the years go by. Those who do not

opposite Seated near the kibbutz watchtower, the children have an informal lesson on the history of their settlement
overleaf A family relaxing together during 'visiting hours'

gradually tend to drop out, for much of the budget and effort goes on the children, much of the talk is about them, and the whole kibbutz revolves around them. They are at the centre of all the festivals – some of them traditional, like Chanukah, Purim, and the Festival of the First Fruit, some of them developed by the kibbutzim themselves, like the sheep-shearing festival. The kibbutz, in this respect, is very much like a middle-class Jewish suburb, and a middle-class Jewish suburb is not the sort of place in which most single people would care to make their home.

Young people in the older kibbutzim, which is to say, the second or third generation of prospective *chaverim*, often complain of being bored – a familiar refrain in suburban homes – and some of the more prosperous kibbutzim have provided discotheques for them. No curfew tolls at seven, but every parent is aware of the hour without even looking at his watch, and the children return to their houses briskly, with the protesting cries of small infants echoing through the darkness. Seven o'clock is seven o'clock, not five past, ten past, and certainly not half past. To return a child late is to assume a liberty not permitted to others. The occasional offender will get only a dark look (and no parent cares to collect too many from a *metapelet*), but the persistent offender is brought before the *mazkirut*, the secretariat. The realities of communal living make it necessary to abide by rules, and the greater the commune, the more numerous the rules. If it should be the will of the *chevrah* to extend the sacred hours to ten past seven or half past, or, indeed, to midnight, then that is fine, but if it decides on seven, then every member is expected to abide by the decision. Such decisions, however democratically arrived at, can be irksome and resented, especially by young mothers enjoying their first child. 'It's a little like taking a book out of the lending library,' said one mother. 'They don't actually stamp the hour it should be returned, but you feel that perhaps they should.' Some parents got into the habit of smuggling their children into their rooms – much as Oxford undergraduates used to smuggle their girl-friends into theirs – and there often comes a point when a mother asks herself: whose child is it anyway, mine or theirs? This very question was raised at a conference of Kibbutz Hadati, which in many ways has been most hesitant to depart from the traditional ways of bringing up children, and the conclusion reached was that children 'were the property of their respective kibbutzim', in other words, if the actual parents were the legal guardians, the kibbutz was the moral guardian. This was not a

In contrast to its radical break with the traditional view of the family, the kibbutz does maintain successive generations under the same (albeit collective) roof, a mode of family living that goes back as far as the Patriarchs. These grandparents continue to contribute to the collective economy by working in the kibbutz book bindery

principle that was easily accepted by all kibbutz mothers. Golda Meir, who was a member of Kibbutz Merhavia for a time, once described the agonies of separation:

Everything seems alright. But one look of reproach from the little one when the mother goes away and leaves it with a stranger is enough to throw down the whole structure of vindication. That look, that plea to the mother to stay, can be withstood only by a superhuman effort of will.

What happened at first was that the mother, and sometimes the father, stayed; instead of leaving the child tearful in the charge of the *metapelet*, they undressed her, washed her, put her to bed, told her a story, carefully tucked her in for the night and tip-toed out. All this was feasible if a family only had one child (or rather, it was imperfectly feasible, for there were three or four other sets of parents putting their children to bed at the same time in the same room and one had to converse *sotto voce*), but if there were four, five or even six children in different age groups – which meant in different children's houses – one could spend half the night hurrying from one to the other. And even then there might be parting pains, and four or five other children might be kept awake by the sixth. But inconvenience apart, the women preferred their children home under their own roof at night. The kibbutz, in a sense, had given woman the worst of all possible worlds: it had not liberated her from domestic drudgery, but intensified it, for instead of the variety of small tasks which she has around the house – cleaning, washing, cooking, seeing to the children, mending their clothes, making their beds – she was confined to one dreary task all day long, either among the steaming vats in the kitchen, bent over the iron in the laundry, or perpetually sewing on patches in the *machsan*, the clothing store. If the kibbutz had light industry she could be a factory hand, hardly a liberating experience. She wanted to be a *baalat bayit*, a housewife, for at least part of the time. As a result, an increasing number of kibbutzim decided, not without misgiving, to restore the children to their parents, first those of school age and then the pre-school group. Technical obstacles remained. Children had been given the first priority in everything. Parents in the newer kibbutzim, or even during their first years in the older ones, slept in one-roomed shacks or a concrete hut that contained a bed, a wardrobe and precious little else, whereas children's houses were equipped with every comfort and involved an investment of many thousands of pounds. To return the children meant a massive new building programme, larger houses, more rooms, but gradually, as the kibbutzim became more prosperous, the new building was undertaken. The children's dormitories were adapted to new uses and renovated houses with red roofs, front porches and small gardens sprang up, with the approaches littered with bicycles, scooters, broken toys, deflated balls, and all the cheerful paraphernalia of childhood. The whole atmosphere of the houses changed. They became less orderly and more boisterous. Even when the children are asleep, one can sense the difference in atmosphere; their mere presence under the roof affects the nature of the house. It has ceased to be a place where one came to sleep or rest; the *shikun*, the dwelling place, has become a home.

The common rearing of children was the ultimate resignation to the group; it enriched the group relationship. *Chaverim* were trained to regard all the children of the new generation as their children, and the relationship between the older generation and the new was of an intensity not normally experienced outside an immediate family. Whenever there was fighting between Jew and Arab, kibbutz members were in the front line of action and bore the heaviest casualties. The sense of bereavement that one *chaver* suffered on the death of another, even though a generation removed, was deep and personal; it was as if he had lost his own son. The use of the word family in this context was not merely metaphorical. Blood relationships were almost secondary to those forged by common experience and common dangers. To an extent the

Chaverim tend to look upon all members of the next generation as their own children and bear a responsibility in their upbringing and education towards accepting the kibbutz way of life

readiness to allow children to creep back to their parents has fulfilled some of the worst fears of the system's critics. All strove to get the best of everything for their children, but now not all could feel a sense of sharing in their destiny. The closer the child moved to the parent, the further he moved from the group.

And once the children's dormitories were closed it was feared that other institutions might be threatened. *Chaverim* began to fear for their *chadar ochel*, the communal dining-room. If the kibbutz thought of itself as a large family, the sense of family was best felt in the dining-room. Breakfasts and lunches were hurried and staggered, for *chaverim* often began their work at different hours. But in the evening, when they were washed and changed and rested, they could meet together over supper and talk over the events of the day. And on Friday night, even in the militantly anti-religious kibbutzim, the white tablecloth gradually insinuated its way over the scrubbed wooden table top (until in its turn it was replaced by polished formica), with a little jam jar of wild flowers, and perhaps even some lighted candles. The Sabbath crept into the dining-room, if not into the private houses, and once more it was welcomed. The communal dining-room was also the village hall. Here the general assemblies, the debates, the cultural evenings,

The young tending the young as part of their education for future responsibility

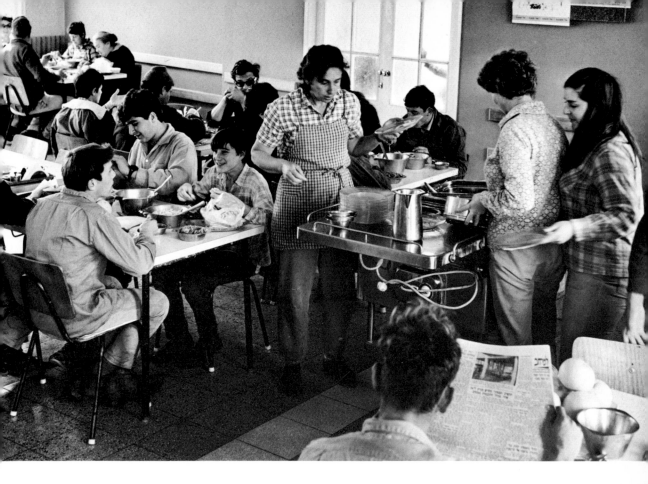

the amateur theatricals, the movie shows, the yearly celebrations of Chanukah and Purim were all held. As kibbutzim prospered, they build *heichalei hatarbut*, culture halls for the public occasions, but the dining-room remained the principal place of assembly, the focal point of kibbutz life. They were not always the most comfortable of places – squat, low-ceilinged, with concrete floors and the dark soul of spent meals perpetually hanging over them, they could be unbearably hot in summer, cold in winter and cheerless at almost any time – but they alone had enough space. Gradually the old dining-rooms were replaced by lofty, ornate, air-conditioned establishments with marble floors and panelled walls, but no sooner had the *chevrah* a place where they could relax over a meal in comfort than a growing number of *chaverim* opted to relax in their own homes. The evening parade of children from the children's houses has given way to the parade of foragers from the dining-room, homeward bound with their evening meal, some carrying it in a triple-tiered saucepan specially designed for the purpose, others, with larger families, pushing it home on a trolley. The dining-hall is half empty most evenings, but the houses are full, lights ablaze in every room, the clamour of

On a normal work day, young children are conspicuous in their absence from the communal dining room

children, the crying of babies, and the sound of harassed parents are heard from every window. The family is back in business.

But there is a better proof of this than the mere hue and cry of family life. Among the many things that the new, enlarged kibbutz family hoped to avoid was the selfishness and egotism of the small unit, the eagerness to advance one's children, certainly at one's own expense, but if need be at the expense of society, the relentless careerism of Jewish life, the eagerness always to be a step ahead of the next person. The kibbutz looked to a more benign universe and geared its entire teaching philosophy to that end. Its classes were classless. One rose from year to year according to age and not on the basis of examination. There was no grading, no tests, no spirit of competitiveness, and the brighter elements in the group were neglected for the sake of the duller ones. This was part of the higher egalitarianism that the kibbutz adopted. Education was intended to prepare a child not for a career – indeed it was careful to eschew careerism as one of the besetting sins of *bourgeois* society – but for the higher life, for the perpetuation of the society that give them birth. But the more the children reverted to their parents, the more the kibbutz family reverted to the ways of the Jewish family throughout the ages, and a speaker at a kibbutz conference in 1958 noted despairingly: '. . . many of the parents desire their children to continue their studies beyond the twelve grades of schooling. They argue that it is true that "I renounced my studies and my development, but my child must do otherwise."' The kibbutz is, in fact, a large family full of small families screaming to get out, and in recent years they have begun to get out.

The kibbutz was never designed as a social experiment, but its experience suggests that even if the traditional family, with its traditional ways, is not the most efficient – or even the most wholesome – social unit, it is the most natural one. Alternatives could be devised – and the kibbutz is one example – but, given time, there will always be a reversion to the type of family traditionally known. The family will out.

Bibliography

Abrahams, I., *Jewish Life in the Middle Ages*, London, 1932

———, *Hebrew Ethical Wills*, Philadelphia, 1926

———, *Jewish Life under Emancipation*, London, 1917

Ackerman, H. W., *Treating the Troubled Family*, New York, 1966

Aguilar, G., *Women of Israel*, London, 1889

Agus, A., *The Heroic Age of Franco-German Jewry*, New York, 1969

Baron, S., *A Social and Religious History of the Jews*, New York, 1952

Bein, A., *The Return to the Soil*, Jerusalem, 1952

Bettelheim, B., *Dialogues with Mothers*, New York, 1967

Birnbaum, N. and G. Lanzer, *Sociology and Religion*, New York, 1969

Box, G. H., *Apocrypha of Abraham*, London, 1918

British National Council of Social Work, *The Family*, London, 1953

Buber, M., *Hassidim and Modern Man*, New York, 1966

Buchler, S., *Cohen Comes First*, New York, 1933

Crow, D., *The Victorian Woman*, London, 1971

Daiches, D., *Two Worlds*, New York, 1954

Elman, P., *Jewish Marriage*, New York, 1967

Epstein, I., *The Jewish Way of Life*, London, 1946

Epstein, L. M., *Sex Laws and Customs in Judaism*, New York, 1948

———, *The Jewish Marriage Contract*, New York, 1927

Finklestein, L., *The Jews, Their History, Culture and Religion*, London, 1961

Fried, J., *Jews and Divorce*, New York, 1968

Ginzberg, L., *Legends of the Jews*, Philadelphia, 1926

Goldstein, S. E., *Meaning of Marriage*, New York, 1942

Gollancz, H., *The Ethical Treatises of Brachya*, London, 1902

Gordon, A. D., *Selected Essays*, New York, 1938

Goodman, P. and H. Goodman, *The Jewish Marriage Anthology*, Philadelphia, 1965

Harris, C. C., *The Family*, London, 1969

Hoch, P. and J. Zubin, *Psychopathology of Childhood*, New York, 1955

Hoenig, S. B., *Jewish Family Life*, New York, 1961

Holt, M., *The Patriarchs of Israel*, London, 1964

Jacobs, L., *Principles of the Jewish Faith*, London, 1968

Jakobovits, I., *Journal of a Rabbi*, New York, 1966

Katznelson-Rubashov, R., *The Plough Woman*, New York, 1932

Kaufmann, Y., *The Religion of Israel*, London, 1960

Kitov, E., *The Jew and His Home*, New York, 1963

Kobler, F., *A Treasury of Jewish Letters*, New York, 1956

Laing, R. and A. Easterson, *Sanity, Madness and the Family*, New York, 1964

Lazarus, H. M., *The Ways of Her Household*, London, 1923

Lenski, G., *The Religious Factor*, New York, 1961

Mace, D. R., *Hebrew Marriage*, New York, 1953

Maybaum, I., *The Jewish Home*, London, 1953

Mayer, J. E., *Jewish Gentile Courtship*, New York, 1962

Mead, M., *Family*, New York, 1965

Miller, D., *The Secret Life of the Jews*, Oakland, 1932

Moore, G. F., *Judaism*, Harvard, 1927

Neher, A., *Moses and the Vocation of the Jewish People*, London, 1959

Neufeld, E., *Ancient Hebrew Marriage Laws*, London, 1944

Patai, R., *Sex and the Family in the Middle East*, New York, 1959

Pearlman, M., *Adventure in the Sun*, London, 1949

Rabbinowitz, H., *A Guide to Hassidism*, New York, 1960

Rabin, A. I., *Growing Up in the Kibbutz*, New York, 1965

Reid Banks, L., *The Kibbutz*, London, 1972

Rosenthal, G. S., *The Jewish Family in a Changing World*, New York, 1970

Rotenstreich, N., *Jewish Philosophies in Modern Times*, New York, 1968

Roth, C., *Anglo-Jewish Letters*, London, 1938

———, *Jews in the Renaissance*, London, 1959

Roth, L., *God and Man in the Old Testament*, London, 1955

St John, R., *Shalom Means Peace*, New York, 1949

Samuel, M., *The World of Sholom Aleichem*, New York, 1943

Sarna, N., *Understanding Genesis*, New York, 1970

Schauss, H., *The Lifetime of a Jew*, Cincinnati, 1950

Schechter, S., *Studies in Judaism*, Philadelphia, 1903

Spiro, M. E., *Kibbutz: Venture in Utopia*, New York, 1963

———, *The Children of the Kibbutz*, New York, 1965

Solis-Cohen, E., *Women in Jewish Law*, New York, 1932

Soulson, A. B., *Marriage and Jewish Family Life*, New York, 1959

Syrkin, M., *Golda Meir Speaks Out*, London, 1973

Trachtenberg, J., *Jewish Magic and Superstition*, New York, 1961

Vainstein, Y., *The Cycle of the Jewish Year*, Jerusalem, 1953

Viteles, H., *A History of the Co-operative Movement in Israel*, London, 1967